Contracts in Counselling and Psychotherapy

The *Professional Skills for Counsellors* series, edited by Colin Feltham, covers the practical, technical and professional skills and knowledge which trainee and practising counsellors need to improve their competence in key areas of therapeutic practice.

Titles in the series include:

Counselling by Telephone
Maxine Rosenfield

Medical and Psychiatric Issues for Counsellors
Brian Daines, Linda Gask and Tim Usherwood

Time-Limited Counselling
Colin Feltham

Personal and Professional Development for Counsellors
Paul Wilkins

Client Assessment
edited by Stephen Palmer and Gladeana McMahon

Counselling, Psychotherapy and the Law
Peter Jenkins

Contracts in Counselling
edited by Charlotte Sills

Counselling Difficult Clients
Kingsley Norton and Gill McGauley

Learning and Writing in Counselling
Mhairi MacMillan and Dot Clark

Long-Term Counselling
Geraldine Shipton and Eileen Smith

Referral and Termination Issues for Counsellors
Anne Leigh

Counselling and Psychotherapy in Private Practice
Roger Thistle

The Management of Counselling and Psychotherapy Agencies
Colin Lago and Duncan Kitchin

Group Counselling
Keith Tudor

Understanding the Counselling Relationship
edited by Colin Feltham

Practitioner Research in Counselling
John McLeod

Anti-discriminatory Counselling Practice
edited by Colin Lago and Barbara Smith

Counselling Through the Life-Course
Léonie Sugarman

Contracts in Counselling and Psychotherapy

second edition

Professional Skills
for Counsellors

edited by
Charlotte Sills

Los Angeles | London | New Delhi
Singapore | Washington DC

First edition published 1997
Reprinted 2004, 2005
This second edition first published 2006

SAGE Publications Ltd
1 Oliver's Yard
55 City Road
London EC1Y 1SP

SAGE Publications Inc.
2455 Teller Road
Thousand Oaks, California 91320

SAGE Publications India Pvt Ltd
B-42, Panchsheel Enclave
Post Box 4109
New Delhi 110 017

SAGE Publications Asia-Pacific Pte Ltd
3 Church Street
#10-04 Samsung Hub
Singapore 049483

British Library Cataloguing in Publication data

A catalogue record for this book is available from the British Library

ISBN-10 1-4129-2065-5   ISBN-13 978-1-4129-2065-0
ISBN-10 1-4129-2066-3 (pbk)   ISBN-13 978-1-4129-2066-7 (pbk)

Library of Congress Control Number: 2005938707

Typeset by C&M Digitals (P) Ltd., Chennai, India
Printed in Great Britain by Ashford Colour Press Ltd, Gosport, Hants.

Contents

List of Contributors

Charlotte Sills is a counsellor and UKCP registered integrative psychotherapist in private practice. She is also Visiting Professor at Middlesex University and Head of the Transactional Analysis Department at Metanoia Institute, responsible for Diploma, MSc and BA courses in TA. For more than 20 years she has been working as a trainer, supervisor and consultant in a variety of settings, including the National Institute of Social Work and mental health organisations. Recently she is a co-designer and Director of Ashridge Consulting's Coaching for Consultants Course. She is the author or co-author of a number of books and articles in the field, including *Integration in Counselling and Psychotherapy* by Lapworth, Sills and Fish (Sage 2002) and *Transactional Analysis – A Relational Perspective* by Hargaden and Sills (Routledge 2001).

Jenifer Elton Wilson D.Psych. is a Chartered Counselling Psychologist, UKCP Registered Psychotherapist and BACP Accredited Supervisor, whose work as a practitioner has, until recently, focused upon the design, validation and implementation of a doctoral programme in psychotherapy by professional studies, delivered as a joint programme by Middlesex University and the Metanoia Institute. Jenifer has published widely in the professional field, particularly with regard to effective and time-conscious therapy. She is a member of the Membership and Professional Training Board of the British Psychological Society and is their representative on the Society-wide Ethics Committee. Having relinquished her recent role as Head of Department of the Middlesex/Metanoia Doctoral programme, Jenifer is in private practice as a therapist, a clinical supervisor, an academic and organisational consultant and free-lance trainer. She is currently engaged in co-writing a book on the objectives and outcomes of psychotherapy for the Open University Press.

Michael Jacobs is now retired, but was formerly Director of the Counselling and Psychotherapy programme at the University of Leicester. He is a Visiting Professor at Bournemouth University, a Fellow of BACP and a UKCP registered psychodynamic psychotherapist. Amongst his many publications, he is well known for *Psychodynamic Counselling in Action, third edition* (Sage 2004) and *The Presenting Past* (Open University Press). He has edited a number of series, including most recently an important international series *Core Concepts in Therapy* (Open University Press). He has a small independent practice and continues to contribute in a number of ways to the profession.

Peter Jenkins is a Senior Lecturer in Counselling at Salford University, a BACP Accredited Counsellor Trainer, and a member of the Professional Conduct Committee of the British Association for Counselling and Psychotherapy. He has extensive experience of training counselling practitioners and organisations on legal aspects of therapy such as confidentiality, and has published widely on this topic. His most recent publication on this topic is *Psychotherapy and the Law: Questions and Answers for Counsellors and Therapists* (Whurr 2004).

James Kepner is a psychologist and body-oriented psychotherapist. He serves as a trainer and in private practice. He is the author of *Body Process: A Gestalt Approach to Working with the Body in Therapy* (Gestalt Press 1987) and *Healing Tasks: Psychotherapy with Adult Survivors of Childhood Abuse* (Gestalt Press 1995).

Adrienne Lee is accredited by ITAA/EATA as a Teaching and Supervising Transactional Analyst and is a UKCP Registered Psychotherapist and a Master Practitioner in Neuro-Linguistic Programming. Adrienne has been a mother, a university teacher, and a psychotherapist for more than 30 years and specialises in facilitating people to integrate spirituality in their psychotherapy. She has been centrally involved in the development of TA in Britain from its very beginnings and is a Founder Member and past Chair of the UK's Institute of Transactional Analysis (ITA). She has been a Board Member of EATA, on the committees of the PTSC and COC and one of EATA's representatives on the Board of The European Association of Psychotherapy (EAP). Adrienne is now the President of EATA (July 2004–July 2007). Together with Ian Stewart, she has founded and is Co-Director of The Berne Institute in Nottingham. Her professional career is dedicated now to the professional training of TA psychotherapists and to the training and development of their trainers and supervisors.

Geoff Mothersole is a Consultant Counselling Psychologist and Head of Primary Care Mental Health for West Sussex Health and Social Care Trust. In this capacity he runs a Primary Care Counselling Service. His current interest is in using routine clinical audit to develop clinical work, and his doctoral research was on the use of the CORE system. He is current chair of the CORE Benchmarking Network, a practice research network interested in developing the links between practice and research in relation to the CORE system. He has written a number of articles and book chapters and is past Professional Development Officer of UKCP.

Brigid Proctor is a Fellow and Recognised Supervisor of BACP. She was first Chair of the Training and of the Standards and Ethics Committees. With Francesca Inskipp she has been responsible for developing Open Learning materials and training for supervisors. These now form the basis of the training work of CASCADE Associates. Formerly Director of SW London College Counselling Course Centre, she now works free-lance as a counsellor, supervisor, trainer, consultant and writer. Her current interest is developing and writing about creative group supervision. Her flexible working is grounded in her experience of the power of person-centred relating and the belief that that necessarily makes for varied and innovative practice.

Ian Stewart is Co-Director of The Berne Institute in Nottingham. He is accredited by ITAA/EATA as a Teaching and Supervising Transactional Analyst, and is a UKCP Registered Psychotherapist and a Master Practitioner in Neuro-Linguistic Programming. He is co-author (with Vann S. Joines) of *TA Today* (Lifespace 1987) and *Personality Adaptations* (Lifespace 2002), and author of *Transactional Analysis Counselling in Action* (Sage, 2nd edn 2000), *Eric Berne* (Sage 1992) and *Developing Transactional Analysis Counselling* (Sage 1996).

Keith Tudor has worked for nearly 30 years in the helping professions in a number of settings. He is a qualified and registered psychotherapist, group psychotherapist and facilitator, and has a private/independent practice in Sheffield offering therapy, supervision and consultancy where he is a Director of Temenos and its Postgraduate Diploma/MSc Course in Person-centred Psychotherapy and Counselling. He is a Teaching and Supervising Transactional Analyst, and an Honorary Fellow in the School of Health, Liverpool John Moores University. He is a widely published author in the field of psychotherapy and counselling, with over 60 papers and seven books to his name. He is on the editorial advisory board of three international journals and is the series editor of *Advancing Theory in Therapy* (published by Routledge).

Max Wide was until recently Lead Associate for Leadership and Cultural Change with the Society of Local Authority Chief Executives (SOLACE) Enterprises Ltd. He has now been appointed as Head of Strategy for BT Government. He is a graduate of Henley Management Centre. He no longer works in the world of counselling and pschotherapy but regards it as the best possible grounding for the work he now does in organisational development. He is a widely published author in his field, most recently *Transforming Your Authority* (Office for the Deputy Prime Minister 2005), *Leadership United: a Toolkit for Working in a Political Environment* (SOLACE Commission 2005) and *The Working Council* (TSO 2003). He lives in Somerset with his partner and their two sons.

Frank Wills was born in Birkenhead and is an avid supporter of Tranmere Rovers FC. He is an independent accredited counsellor and registered cognitive psychotherapist, practising in Bristol. He has co-authored several books on cognitive therapy, including, with Diana Sanders, *Cognitive Therapy: An Introduction* (Sage 2005). He has also recorded some video tapes demonstrating the skills of cognitive therapy, available from the School of Social Studies in the University of Wales Newport. He is currently working on a book describing the main skills of cognitive therapy.

Mike Worrall works as a counsellor and supervisor in Oxford. He studied English Literature and then worked for nine years in the Probation Service, before training in the person-centred approach at Metanoia. He is the author or co-author of a number of chapters and articles, co-editor of a collection of papers on person-centred supervision and co-author of two books on person-centred philosophy, theory and practice.

Foreword to the Second Edition

It has been a real treat to prepare this second edition; it has felt like being part of a whole new book. In this edition, there are two entirely new chapters, two that have been radically changed and two of the old chapters that have been either removed or amalgamated in light of the changing field of psychotherapy and counselling. The others have been revised and updated and it has been interesting and stimulating to read the revised chapters and to see how the authors have changed and developed their thinking over the years since the first edition. And not only the authors: so many developments in the field – in theoretical approach, in understanding about therapy and how it works – are reflected in the ideas in the book.

The previous edition of the book was called *Contracts in Counselling* as it was part of a series on *Professional Skills for Counsellors*. However, readers of the book regularly commented that this title seemed restrictive. The thoughts and ideas about contracts in this book apply as well to the practice of 'psychotherapy' as to 'counselling' and indeed to coaching, mentoring or statutory health work. As a result, we changed the title of the book and, in their revisions, the authors refer alternately to different traditions. Mostly we use the generic labels: practitioner, therapist or clinician throughout. If a specific form of psychological work is intended, this is made clear; otherwise the concepts are universal. Similarly we use gender pronouns randomly.

My thanks once again to friend and colleague, Keith Tudor, for his creative thinking about the design of the book and to Louise Wise and Rachel Burrows at Sage for their ongoing support.

PART I
An Overview

Introduction: The Therapy Contract – A Mutual Commitment

Charlotte Sills

A contract is an agreement made between two or more people concerning the type of activity or relationship they will have with each other. In counselling and psychotherapy, it is the agreement between practitioner and client about their work together; the mutual undertaking to enter into a therapeutic relationship. This book is concerned with the wide variety of contracts and contexts which are involved in the therapeutic process – from the initial contact and agreement for a first session, to the subtle negotiation of an ongoing and evolving counselling commitment.

Many therapists feel uncomfortable about using the word 'contract' in relation to their work, believing that it sounds overly constricting and sterile. However, therapists cannot *not* make contracts. Human society is founded on explicit and implicit agreements about how we can live in relationship with one another. They are one of the ways that we use to try to put order into a world that is essentially unpredictable and potentially dangerous. Despite much debate about whether it is effective or counterproductive, it remains the case that contracts are fundamental to any organised society. They are an essential and indispensable part of the functioning of any political, legal and social system.

Depending on their theoretical orientation, their personal preferences and their experience, therapists vary enormously in the amount and type of contracts that they make. At one extreme there can be a simple offer of a space and an opportunity to talk without any other expectations or agreements about time-frame or process. It may seem to some that it would be hard to be therapeutic in this relatively structureless context. Yet 'drop-in' centres, the Samaritans and the like operate successfully in just such an open situation. It is also interesting to reflect that when Carl Jung was asked by his grandson how people coped before there were analysts, Jung is said to have replied 'They had friends' (Nicholas Spicer, personal communication). In a similar vein, when Rollo May asked Karl Menninger for his comment on therapy, he replied 'People have been talking to each other for thousands of years. The question is, how did it become worth 60 dollars an hour?!' (May 1987). The implication is that people can be therapeutic with one another without making formal agreements about it.

Despite these reminders of the beneficial effect of simple human contact, most therapists would agree that further contracting is essential. Whether they work in private practice, the voluntary sector or the public sector, there will be, at least, a need for agreements about such administrative details as time, place, fees (if any) and duration. Indeed, the existence of such agreements is one of the defining features of formal counselling or psychotherapy, as opposed to the informal relationships described above (BACP 2000). In addition, there is normally some negotiation about goals. In complete contrast to this type of unstructured 'drop-in', some therapists and clients make a precise and detailed contract about a specific behavioural change to be achieved, how that change will be measured and the time-frame in which it will occur.

The importance of contracts in counselling and psychotherapy has become more and more apparent over the last 30 years. Although contracts were even used by the earliest psychoanalysts (see Jacobs, Chapter 2), they tended to be unilateral conditions imposed by the analyst on the patient about how the patient was supposed to behave. Other than this, the contract was largely confined, in the early days, to an agreement that the practitioner would give his or her services in return for a fee. It was only in the 1960s that the idea of mutual participation in a contracting process which specified the procedures and goals of the therapy was introduced into the counselling and therapy literature. Around that time, Berne (1966: 362) described 'an explicit bilateral commitment to a well defined course of action'. According to Goldberg (1977: 34), it was not until the late 1960s that the first psychoanalysts began to propose 'therapeutic work in terms of explicitly contractual and mutual participation of client and analyst'.

Research into psychotherapy outcome

Since the late 1960s a significant body of literature, including research, has been devoted to this area of the therapeutic relationship. Its conclusions are persuasive in convincing us that contracting is a vital feature of the therapeutic process. Much relevant research is reviewed by Goldberg (1977) who cites seven research outcomes that point to the same conclusion: the absence of appropriate contracting can lead to problems. The research clearly shows that failed or discontinued treatment is largely a result of difference in expectations between practitioner and client.

Other research sought to identify the facilitative factors in therapy. It demonstrates that successful outcome does not depend on the particular theory and methodology of the counsellor, but on the strength of the working alliance in the relationship between counsellor and client (Bergin and Lambert 1978; Luborsky et al. 1983; O'Malley et al. 1983; Hill 1989; Hubble et al. 1999). Research on the working alliance itself – what constitutes such an alliance, how it is formed and maintained – is considerable (e.g. Horvath and Luborsky 1993; Horvath and Greenberg 1994; and see Hubble et al. 1999). Broadly, it indicates that, from the client's point of view, an effective therapeutic relationship is one in which he or she feels understood and attended to and experiences mutual trust and respect. It is also one in which the client has a sense of 'common commitment and shared understanding' of the identified goal which will alleviate his or her distress (Bordin 1979, 1980, 1994). Bordin's work is of central importance here. He developed a model of the working alliance that incorporates *goals, tasks and bonds.* He describes the alliance as 'a mutual understanding and agreement about change goals and the necessary tasks to move towards these goals, along with the establishment of bonds to maintain the partner's work' (Bordin 1994: 13). This model has obvious implications for contracts.

Goldberg (1977: 38) also expresses eloquently this notion of a mutual commitment, speaking of giving the client the 'responsibility for collaborating in his own living experience'. He describes two types of therapeutic relationship. The first is the *status relationship* in which there is inequality of power and authority and there is reliance on the belief in the greater expertise and knowledge of the therapist. The second is the *contractual relationship* which is 'an arrangement between equals, that when explicitly formulated, rejects coercion and fosters personal freedom' (ibid.: 32). If therapists believe that their job is to assist in the empowerment of their clients, it is essential to invite them to be active in designing the counselling relationship, deciding on their goals and meaningfully pursuing them. Goldberg continues: 'When the practitioner appreciates the client's need for an equitable and predictable exchange in psychotherapy, the requirement for an explicitly contractual relationship becomes a necessity' (ibid.: 33).

In summary, many writers agree on the fundamental importance of the contract in therapy. However, as we come to understand the reasons for this importance, it becomes clear that contracting is a very subtle matter. This is discussed further in the rest of the book, but there is one significant factor which is a consistent influence on our contract-making, and needs to be mentioned here. This is the inevitable tension between order and chaos which is a vital part of creative therapeutic work.

Paradox

Earlier it was noted that humans have an essential tendency to attempt to impose order in a chaotic world. We have a strong need to make sense of the world, to provide it with structure and make it more predictable. It can be argued that the therapeutic relationship, with its inevitable power imbalance and its capacity to arouse very deep and disturbing issues, is in particular need of structure and order to contain it. The contract helps to provide this structure.

However, the process of therapy is intended to help the client achieve autonomous, creative solutions to problems and a new personal frame of reference. This sort of fundamental change seems to come not from order but from temporary therapeutic disorder. Storr (1996) describes how the greatest new ideas often emerge after a period of depression or confusion, and quotes the German philosopher Friedrich Nietzsche who said 'I tell you, one must have chaos in one, to give birth to a dancing star.'

Here lies the therapist's dilemma. On one hand she needs to promote the containment of structure through contracts. On the other hand this, in excess, leads to loss of spontaneity and of the possibility to expand boundaries. On one hand she desires freedom for the client – freedom to explore, to enter the unknown. On the other hand, without structure, this can lead to chaos which also causes anxiety and disintegration. In other words, the therapy situation is an invitation to clients to let go of many of their usual inhibitions and reserves, their fixed ways of being, their familiar belief systems. This can potentially be very unsettling, yet this very 'unsettledness' can be fertile ground for growth. The boundaries of the contract should offer a place of equilibrium within which this tension can be held.

There is a parallel, which therapists may find useful, in the experiences of organisational consultants who use complexity theory to understand the process of change (Stacey 1992; Waldrop 1992; Critchley 1997). They describe two types of dynamic in organisational systems – one based on order, structure and rules which produces stable equilibrium; the other characterised by lack of rules, boundaries and predictability which produces unstable equilibrium. The first state, in extreme, leads to repression and stagnation; the second to anxiety and chaos. They say that organisations fluctuate between periods of order and periods of disorder as they respond to the changing world. As they move from one to the other, they pass through a sort of border area known as 'bounded instability'. It is this 'edge of chaos' (Stacey 1992) which is the area of greatest creativity and from which fresh solutions and new paradigms emerge. The same is true of individuals and this has important implications for contract-making. In negotiating the work, therapists need to find the optimum balance which provides the most opportunity: the mid-point described in complexity theory as the place of most creativity within the 'stable system boundary' (Critchley 1997). This area of 'bounded instability' is reminiscent of Perls et al.'s (1989) concept of the 'safe emergency' where, again, the practitioner hopes to provide a space in which the client can feel contained enough to face the existential crisis or the avoided trauma, and then allow something new to emerge. It is interesting also to realise that the word 'analysis' comes from the Greek *analusis* meaning a loosening of bonds. Therapists usually aim to help the client achieve a 'loosening of bonds' which may allow for restructuring and change.

We have seen that the contract needs to accommodate the tension between the certainty of structure and the need for creative uncertainty. This creates a real *caveat* in relation to those contracts which identify specific goals for change. Watzlawick et al. (1970) describe first and second order change. First order change involves changes within the given frame of reference – the current paradigm with its assumptions and routines. It can only mean improvements to the present order, not revolutionary new ways of being. Sometimes changes which are carefully planned either do not come about or fail to achieve the desired outcome, causing disillusion and disappointment. A truly fundamental change involves a change in patterns of behaviour and feeling and also a real change in assumptions and ways of thinking. This second order change can only emerge from the area of bounded instability. Thus, there is a sense in which the change cannot be planned for, as any plan must by definition be formed in the current frame of reference. This points to the need for subtle flexibility in contracting and to the need for it to be an evolving process. This is discussed further in Chapter 1.

An introduction to the second edition

In conclusion, the making of contracts is both a necessity and a limitation. The skilled practitioner needs to find the appropriate middle ground in each unique situation. This book hopes to guide the reader through some of the complexities and subtleties of the process of contracting and help the therapist choose his or her own individual path. Chapter 1 considers a way of looking at the various types or levels of contracts based on Berne's (1966) model of *the administrative, the professional and the psychological contract* organised within the *contracting matrix*. Throughout the chapter, readers are invited to take the ideas as stimuli to their thinking rather than as prescriptions. Each practitioner needs to decide in each situation what is appropriate for him, given his own professional framework.

Subsequent chapters address different viewpoints on contracting. The very word 'contract' has different meanings and implications for different therapists. In Chapters 2–13, authors from a variety of different backgrounds discuss what 'contracting' means to them and what part it plays in their work. The writing and editing of the book also reflect a process of contracting and recontracting. In the first edition, contributors were asked to write on a particular focus and were then given an open brief to interpret the concept of 'contracts' as it was relevant to them. My contract with them for the second edition was to reflect on and update their chapters in the light of their changing or developing ideas about their topic as well as changes in the field. They were also asked to cross reference or comment on the other chapters in the book. It is fascinating to notice where and how their thinking has changed and where it has remained firm.

Part II reflects three different theoretical orientations. Michael Jacobs focuses on the significance of the contract in the conscious and unconscious process of psycho-dynamic therapy. Frank Wills, a cognitive therapist, focuses on goal setting, when therapist and client agree a rationale that a person's attitude and way of thinking can be both the cause of problems and their solution. From a humanistic perspective, Mike Worrall's chapter explores the contracts arising out of the establishment of the six conditions for an effective helping relationship as identified by the Person-centred Approach. In Part III, 'Types and Considerations', Ian Stewart describes a comprehensive method of making successful outcome-focused contracts and Adrienne Lee shows how moment-by-moment communication can be a method of contracting during the process of therapy. Geoff Mothersole looks at the assessment of risk and the controversial subject of 'no harm contracts'. Charlotte Sills and Max Wide explore ways in which the therapist can tailor the contracting process to the personality type of the client. Finally in this section there is a wholly new chapter – on contracts, ethics and the law, by Peter Jenkins. We felt that these litigious times called for a contribution in this area. In Part IV, 'Contracts and Contexts', two authors, Keith Tudor and Jenifer Elton Wilson, use the model offered in Chapter 1 to examine the various aspects of the topics they address. Tudor writes a new chapter on those situations which involve third parties, such as counselling in primary care, and examines the implications of this wider view of contracting, including the therapist's contract with society. Elton Wilson writes on time-limited and brief counselling, a context in which most practitioners are required to work. Brigid Proctor and Charlotte Sills, in another new chapter, examine the thorny issue of how to think about contracts with trainee practitioners whose personal therapy is a requirement of their training; and finally, Brigid Proctor looks at contracting in supervision and explores the additional considerations involved setting the safe space in which practitioners can develop.

References

BACP (British Association for Counselling and Psychotherapy) (2000) *Ethical Framework for Good Practice in Counselling and Psychotherapy*. Rugby: BACP.

Bergin, A.E. and Lambert, M.J. (1978) 'The evaluation of therapeutic outcomes', in S.L. Garfield and A.E. Bergin (eds) *Handbook of Psychotherapy and Behaviour Change*, 3rd edn. New York: Wiley.

Berne, E. (1966) *Principles of Group Treatment.* New York: Grove Press. (Republished 1994 by Shea Press, Menlo Park.)

Bordin, E.S. (1979) 'The generalizability of the psychoanalytic concept of the working alliance', *Psychotherapy Research and Practice,* 16: 252–60.

Bordin, E.S. (1980) 'Of human bonds that bind or free'. Presidential address to Tenth Annual Convention of the Society for Research on Psychotherapy, Pacific Grove, California.

Bordin, E.S. (1994) 'Theory and research on the therapeutic working alliance', in O. Horvath and S. Greenberg (eds) *The Working Alliance: Theory, Research and Practice.* New York: Wiley.

Critchley, B. (1997) 'A Gestalt approach to organisational consulting', in J.E. Neumann, K. Keller and A. Dawson-Shepherd (eds) *Developing Organisational Consultancy.* London: Routledge.

Goldberg, C. (1977) *Therapeutic Partnership: Ethical Concerns in Psychotherapy.* New York: Springer.

Hill, C.E. (1989) *Therapist Techniques and Client Outcomes.* Newbury Park, CA: Sage.

Horvath, O. and Greenberg, S. (eds) (1994) *The Working Alliance: Theory, Research and Practice.* New York: Wiley.

Horvath, O. and Luborsky, L. (1993) 'The role of the therapeutic alliance in psychotherapy', *Journal of Consulting and Clinical Psychology,* 61: 561–73.

Hubble, M.A., Duncan, B.L. and Miller, S.D. (1999) *The Heart and Soul of Change – What Works in Therapy.* Washington: APA.

Luborsky, L., Crits-Cristophe, R., Alexander, L., Margolis, M. and Cohen, M. (1983) 'Two helping alliance methods of predicting outcomes of psychotherapy', *Journal of Nervous and Mental Disease,* 171: 480–91.

May, R. (1987) 'Therapy in our day', in Jefferey K. Zeig (ed.) *The Evolution of Psychotherapy.* New York: Brunner/Mazel.

O'Malley, S.S., Suh, C.S. and Strupp, H.H. (1983) 'The Vanderbilt psychotherapy process scale: a report on the scale development and a process outcome study', *Journal of Consulting and Clinical Psychology,* 51: 581–6.

Perls, F., Hefferline, R.F. and Goodman, P. (1989) *Gestalt Therapy.* London: Souvenir Press. (First published 1951.)

Stacey, R. (1992) *Managing Chaos.* London: Kogan Page.

Storr, A. (1996) *Feet of Clay.* London: HarperCollins.

Waldrop, M.M. (1992) *Complexity: The New Science at the Edge of Order and Chaos.* London: Viking.

Watzlawick, P., Wheatland, J.H. and Fisch, R. (1970) *Change: Principles of Problem Formation and Problem Resolution.* New York: Norton.

Contracts and Contract Making

Charlotte Sills

The model in this chapter seeks to shed light on the different facets of the contract in therapy. It is based on the work of Berne (1966), originator of transactional analysis and one of the earliest therapists to write in detail about contracting. He defined a contract as: 'An explicit bilateral commitment to a well defined course of action' (1966: 362).

Berne identifies three forms of contract in the therapeutic world: the *administrative,* the *professional* and the *psychological contracts*. This chapter explores the model at the interpersonal level of the practitioner and the client. In Chapter 10, the same model is applied at the institutional and social levels.

The administrative contract

Sometimes also referred to as the business contract, this type of contract deals with all the practical arrangements such as time, place, duration, fees (if any), agreements with referring bodies or agencies, confidentiality and its limits. These are all apparently straightforward but it is surprising how often practitioners, with their eyes firmly fixed on the therapeutic work to come, can be unclear about them or overlook their importance. This importance is fundamental. Not only is clarity about administrative agreements an ethical (BACP 2000) and respectful necessity; the creation of this structure significantly contributes to the provision of the 'stable system boundary' (see Introduction) – the 'safe space' in Winnicott's (1960) terms or Lang's 'therapeutic frame' (see Jacobs in Chapter 2).

The administrative contract covers the following areas:

The venue, the time, the frequency of the therapy sessions

Some therapists offer as a matter of course and as a vital part of providing the containing structure, a regular unvarying time each week (or more than once per week), for example Smith (1991). There is no doubt that this structure does provide the sort of constant holding which allows people to feel safe to explore their deeper feelings. However, there are many other arrangements that can suit both parties. Sometimes a more flexible structure is appropriate. For example, Parkes, in his work with bereaved people, sets up an arrangement whereby sessions are organised for the following visit according to need, the space between the sessions being very variable (Parkes and Sills 1994). It is helpful if the counselling room remains unchanged, as this provides continuity and security, but this may not always be possible. The important factor is that whatever the arrangements, it is stated clearly and agreed at the start of counselling.

The duration of the commitment

Many counsellors work within a limited time-frame (Elton Wilson 1996, 2000 and see Chapter 11; Feltham 1997), either because of their work setting, or because of other considerations such as their particular approach or the needs of the client. Some (e.g. Talmon 1990) practise single-session therapy. Whatever the case, the contract needs to be clear, including arrangements for review and whether there is the possibility of extending the contract or referring on. If the practitioner offers an open-ended agreement, he or she may suggest a procedure for ending which may include a period of time for evaluation and closure.

Fees

The BACP *Ethical Framework for Good Practice in Counselling and Psychotherapy* (2000: 8) states that 'Practitioners are responsible for clarifying the terms on which their services are being offered in advance of the client incurring any financial obligation or other reasonably foreseeable costs or liabilities'. Any fee payment agreement must be made clear, including the possibility of fee increase over the course of a long counselling commitment; also what the policy is for cancellations, holidays and so on. Fees vary greatly between practitioners. It is quite common to charge more for short-term work (which protects the livelihood of the therapist), and also to take experience into account. Many practitioners operate a sliding scale which they negotiate with the individual client according to their circumstances. It is ethical practice to inform clients of the range of fees charged in the area and let them know if there are similar practitioners who may charge less. Often, counsellors who work for an agency which provides counselling at no cost make a point of acknowledging the commitment required from the client in terms of time, energy and, where relevant, the National Insurance contribution they make, in order to stress that the endeavour involves mutual engagement. For further discussion on the setting, changing and payment of fees see Tudor (1998) and Tudor and Worrall (2002).

Changes to the contract and how they will be negotiated

Either client or practitioner may at some time want to change the agreed contract. This may be unforeseen or it may be planned according to the needs of the client or the practitioner. Where possible changes in frequency, duration or fees can be predicted at the initial stage of counselling so that they are part of both people's expectations.

The involvement of other parties

Any involvement of an agency or other body is clearly agreed upon (see Tudor in Chapter 10). This may be relevant where the counsellor's fees are being paid by a third party, or where there is a procedure for accountability.

Confidentiality

The issue of confidentiality is so important and so sensitive that it takes a place in the *administrative contract* section, although arguably it is also part of the *professional contract*. Clients are being asked to come and share (usually unilaterally) their thoughts and feelings, their problematic behaviour, their perhaps embarrassing fears and sense of failure. They may sometimes need to give details of criminal or antisocial past or present behaviour. To provide a safe container it is important that they know they can do so in private and can trust their counsellor to respect their privacy. However, therapists may not feel able to commit themselves to total confidentiality. They may be required to liaise with other health professionals involved in the client's care or obliged by a contract with their employer to disclose certain information. They may wish to discuss the work with supervisors or to quote clients in written material (albeit with disguised identity). They may have ethical and moral principles relating to certain situations (such as the risk of harm to the client or another person, the mistreatment of children, the involvement of Class A drugs or other illegal activities) which cause them to consider breaking confidentiality. Practitioners should make any limits clear to clients from the start. This is not only ethical towards clients but self-protective with regard to the law (see Chapter 9). If an occasion arises during the course of the counselling which has not been predicted, the matter can be discussed and negotiated at the time, in order to obtain client consent where possible, taking into account that the client might agree in order to please a valued counsellor or through ignorance of the significance of what might be revealed in the counsellor's disclosure.

An interesting aspect of this area is that of *client* confidentiality. Is it reasonable for a practitioner to ask a client to respect any self-disclosure she may make? On the face of it, there would seem to be nothing against this. It could be said to fall into the area of mutual respect. Some therapists do suggest that their clients should not use the content of their sessions as the subject of social small talk, as this has the effect of diluting the power of the work. However, the practitioner needs to be careful in her approach. A blanket request for confidentiality might be experienced by the client as if he was being enjoined to secrecy, much in the same way as many abused children are urged 'not to tell'. Thus, what at first felt like a safe container might begin to feel like a hermetically sealed box.

Paradoxically, even in the area of therapist confidentiality, it could be argued that the issue of confidentiality can be overstressed. Emphasis on the boundaries of privacy could become confused with secrecy and might subtly give the client the impression that there is something shameful, abnormal and strange about their feelings or experiences – or indeed about their coming to therapy – and that it must at all costs be kept hidden. It may be valid to remember how a 'senior devil' coached his nephew Wormwood to torment people in C.S. Lewis' *The Screwtape*

Letters by urging them to keep their fears secret because 'shame does best in the dark' (Lewis 1942). Such issues may need to be addressed in therapy in order to avoid the reinforcement of shameful feelings.

Ethical code

Most counsellors and psychotherapists believe that it is necessary to make clear to the client the professional organisations to which they belong, and the ethical codes to which they adhere. Some advocate informing the client of the salient points of the code, for example that there can be no social or sexual contact, and so on. It is proper ethical practice to inform a client if the practitioner is a trainee, their stage of training and the training organisation to which the practitioner is accountable.

Written contracts

Some practitioners draw up written contracts which detail the agreements between them and their clients in order to ensure clarity. Appendix 1 and Appendix 2 contain two examples of such contracts, offered by Joanna Purdie and Graham Colbourne.

The professional contract

The professional contract defines the purpose and focus of the counselling/ psychotherapy and how it will proceed. Usually clients seek help because of some specific area of stress or discomfort. This may be expressed in behavioural terms, as in compulsive behaviour, or in affective terms, as with depression or anxiety. Client and therapist agree on what the problem is and what the focus of their work will be. Sometimes the client is not clear about what he wants and a preparatory contract to explore is agreed upon.

It is useful to take Bordin's (1979, 1994) model of *goals, tasks and bonds* to elucidate the professional contract. The *goal* is the shared articulation of the desired outcome of the therapy. The *tasks* are the 'specific activities that the partnership will engage in to investigate or facilitate change' (1979: 15) and the *bond* 'is likely to be expressed and felt in terms of liking, trusting, respect for each other and a sense of common commitment and a shared understanding in the activity' (1979: 16). Goals and tasks are both within the remit of the professional contract. Bonds are addressed under the *psychological contract*.

Setting the goal – the 'therapy contract'

Bordin (1994: 21) says 'Reaching an understood and mutually agreed-on change goal is the key process in building an initial, viable alliance.' Transactional analysts often make very specific change contracts in accordance with the spirit of Berne's (1961, 1966, 1982) idea of self-responsibility and equality in the relationship. Berne wanted to move away from the 'medical model' of therapist as expert and client as passive patient. He would ask his patients what they saw as the problem, what they wanted to change in their lives and what they wanted from him. He would explain to them how he worked and together they would decide if and how he could be helpful to them in achieving what they wanted for themselves. Then they would make an agreement – a mutual commitment not only concerning times, duration and so on but also about the specific goal of the therapeutic work. The philosophy behind this sort of contracting is that clients know and are able to say what they want to change in their lives. The client makes the therapy contract with him or herself as well as with the therapist, whose part in the contract is to offer skills and expertise to help the client to achieve the desired goal. What was then an innovative approach to therapy has since been validated by much outcome research. Berne's method of contract making is strikingly reminiscent of the client-directed approach proposed by Duncan and Miller (2000) whose ideas were built on powerful research evidence as well as experience.

Therapy contracts are traditionally defined as 'hard' or 'soft'. In a hard contract the goal is clearly defined in behavioural terms: for example, 'I will find myself a new job within six months', 'I will go somewhere away from my home once a day' or 'I will make three new friends by the end of the year'. Soft contracts are more subjective and less specific: for example, 'I will start enjoying my life', 'I want to reconcile my desire for closeness with my need for independence' or 'I want to get to know myself'. If, in the opinion of the therapist, any goal chosen by the client will involve other work that the client has not envisaged, then this too will be discussed. This process can be thought of in contrast to Goldberg's (1977) notion of the therapist meeting the 'present client' and gearing her work to her vision of the 'future client', in the hope that when the client gets there he will be pleased with the result. Goldberg explores this situation – where the therapist can envisage an outcome that is not imagined by the client – but concludes that it is still 'best practice' for the practitioner to be open about her intentions.

Disadvantages of 'hard' contracts

There are some significant disadvantages and caveats to the concept of 'hard' contracts for change. The first of these is that if a client and practitioner are agreeing that a change is desired, the client may at some level feel unacceptable the way he or she is. When many clients come to counselling with a poor self-image, it can be more important that they learn to understand and accept themselves rather than aim immediately for change. It is interesting to remember the paradoxical theory of change, which states that 'change occurs when one becomes what he is, not when he tries to become what he is not' (Beisser 1970: 88).

A possible related danger is that a contract may invite practitioner and client to be too task-focused, to the detriment of the relationship between them. Since the establishment of a *bond* (Bordin 1979) between therapist and client, involving mutual respect and trust, is an essential part of the working alliance (see Introduction) it is vital that the relationship not be ignored.

Clients may feel that only certain areas – that is, those defined by the contract – are open to examination. They may feel unseen and unheard in fundamental ways. Or they may feel that they cannot talk about deeper feelings and thoughts which might emerge in the counselling process. While there are some forms of therapy that work in a tightly structured way, most practitioners would believe that it is vital to provide a space where the client can feel free to bring anything at all to the session and not feel limited by the overall contract; also that the contract be constantly available for review and renegotiation – not set in stone but part of the clarifying process of the work. The exception would be when the contract is specifically for short-term, outcome-focused work when it is normally appropriate to limit the content of the sessions to the defined and agreed area – an approach which is summed up rather deftly by a colleague, Angus Igwe, who says 'The main thing ... is to let the main thing ... be the main thing!'

Clients may adapt to what they think the practitioner wants in order to win approval (see Kapur's 1987, work on the 'bargain relationship'). Alternatively, if they have a strong pattern in their lives of constant achievement, they may turn their contract into yet another performance hurdle to overcome. The counsellor needs to take the personality (see Chapter 8) and the patterns of the client into account when deciding whether a precise contract is appropriate. For some, simply to be in the room would be the contract of choice.

Clients who genuinely 'don't know' what they want may feel inadequate. This is particularly important: whilst many clients come to counselling with a clear idea of what their difficulty is and what in their lives they want to be different, many others do not. They come simply aware of a generalised malaise or anxiety: 'I have been feeling miserable for months and I don't know why' or, as one client put it, 'I want to know who I am.' Lapworth et al. (1993), discussing contracts, refer to another book by C.S. Lewis in which he says 'How can we come face to face with the gods until we have faces?' (Lewis 1978). In the same way, how can we come face to face with our potential self until we know the face of our present self? For these clients it could be almost abusive to ask them to state their goals clearly. An appropriate initial (soft) contract would be simply 'to explore'.

Even those clients who do seem to know what they want may not know the full significance of the change they are seeking. We human beings do not remain stuck in our difficulties for no reason. They have seemed to us like the only way of coping with life. As one eloquent man said of his mother, 'Her tears kept her company.' We need to understand fully the meaning of our choice before we can carry it through. Consequently many practitioners, as a matter of course, agree an initial contract to explore the client's situation, or to make a very small behavioural change. Then at a later stage, after the relationship is established and the client knows herself more fully, a contract for greater change is negotiated.

Clients who have been 'sent' to therapy – for example the man whose wife will leave him if he does not stop gambling – or who have unrealistic goals – such as the terminally ill client who is seeking a cure – may hurry to make contracts which are doomed to failure.

Finally, there is another caveat in relation to clients who come to therapy without a particular aim in view. It concerns first and second order change (see Introduction). Clients can make specific contracts for desired changes initially, but by definition, if they are capable of imagining them, they come from the current frame of reference and are therefore first order changes. The fundamental shift will be made only when they have risked entering that area of bounded instability between order and chaos (see Introduction), and embarked on the process of 'reflexivity' – the capacity to reflect upon themselves and their assumptions. It is essential that the contract be non-restrictive and extremely flexible, so that the client is available to his or her creativity. This is particularly true of longer term therapy, which aims at structural change, and which may lead the client into that area of bounded instability from which an unknowable outcome may arise.

Advantages of 'hard' contracts

Despite these limitations and pitfalls, there are some powerful advantages to making clear change contracts of this kind. They are as follows.

There is significant research evidence to show that they lead to success in counselling and psychotherapy outcome (see Introduction and also Sutton 1979, 1989; Rosenhan and Seligman 1984; Orlinsky et al. 1994; Asay and Lambert 1999). Clients are encouraged by the contract-making process to believe not only that they have the right to say what they want and to 'own' that want, but that they have some control over their lives, that they have options and that the power for change is in their own hands. This can have the effect of instilling hope in the client, along with the sense of personal power, both of which are identified as being factors involved in successful therapy outcome (Asay and Lambert 1999; Duncan and Miller 2000). The achievement of a contract forms a foundation for future changes. It is likely these experiences of satisfaction are associated with what Panksepp (1998) calls 'the seeking system' of the brain and actually produce biochemical rewards. Some practitioners choose to work with a broad overall goal, then use smaller, achievable 'hard' contracts as stepping stones along the way. Dryden (1989) calls these 'outcome goals' and 'mediating goals' (cf. Parloff 1967).

'Hard' contracts provide a useful yardstick for assessing the effectiveness of the work, which is essential if practitioners are to work ethically with their clients (Sutton 1989). If contracts are not being achieved this should be explored: perhaps something significant has been missed; perhaps the wrong contract has been chosen, in which case it should be renegotiated. Possibly the counsellor and client are not suited or the issues are outside the practitioner's competence. Then the counselling should be brought to a close, particularly if there is an alternative counsellor available.

'Hard' contracts also provide clarity of focus, which gives both practitioner and client something to aim for. The work of clarifying the contract is an important part of the overall work and leads to economy of time and expense in the long run. They use the power of the envisaged potential so that the client not only works consciously towards the goal but at a deeper level has already accepted the possibility of the outcome in his mind. Hard contracts also help to avoid misunderstandings and unrealistic expectations on the part of both client and practitioner, for instance that the psychotherapist actually has a magic wand which, if the client behaves well, will be miraculously waved over his head so that his life will be transformed. Contracts help to reinforce the notion that change happens because we make it happen, even if we cannot always predict all the consequences.

At the highest level a contract might describe a long-term life change. At the simplest level, it involves the client saying what she wants and the practitioner agreeing to it – or a practitioner making a suggestion which a client accepts, as in 'do you want to say more about that?', 'Yes, I have been worrying about ... etc'. Contracts help to ensure that the vulnerable client does not feel pressurised or controlled. They highlight the client's 'readiness, willingness and choice' (Mahrer 1989: 32).

The contracting matrix

The contracting matrix seeks to address some of these issues regarding the limitations of goal-led therapy, while retaining the benefits of clear contracts. It brings together different types of contract appropriate for different situations, and it invites the practitioner to hold them flexibly and lightly. The practitioner makes a contract with a client which takes account of his needs and wants, the time-frame in which they are working, his level of self-awareness and so on. The contracting matrix (see Figure 1.1) is another way of thinking about different types of contract. It is a way of organising some of these parameters into four types of agreement for the work's direction, each of which has implications for what might be required from the practitioner in terms of relationship and approach. It also addresses some of the contract-making caveats that were mentioned earlier in the chapter.

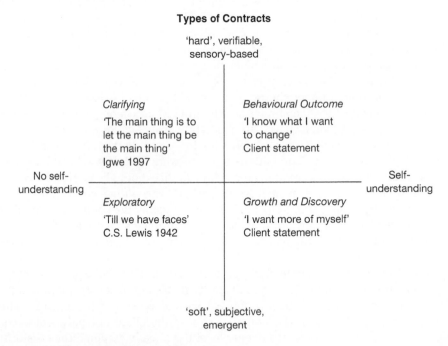

Figure 1.1   The contracting matrix

The vertical axis describes the continuum between the 'hard' contract, which is observable, verifiable, and sensory-based (see Chapter 5) and the 'soft' contract, which allows the unknown to emerge, is subjective and intangible. The horizontal axis reflects the degree to which the client does or does not understand what changes he needs to make. The resulting matrix offers four types of contract that allow the practitioner to respond to the client where he is – according to his perceived and experienced needs and wants, according to his personality type and according to his level of psychological awareness.

The *outcome-focused contract* (top right) requires of the client a high level of clarity about his problem and desired goals as well as an ability to describe those goals in behavioural terms. Clients who come to therapy, to counselling or to coaching with a clear aim – and perhaps a time-limited frame – may find these contracts most useful. For example, a newly appointed manager realised that her job involved making presentations to clients: she saw a counsellor to help her overcome her shyness and learn some communication skills; her work focused on building her confidence and working through her anxieties; she decided also to enrol on a public speaking course.

The *clarifying contract* (top left) is one offered to the client when he knows broadly what he wants, or at least that he wants clearly definable change, but he does not understand what the problem is and what he needs to do. Here the contract may be to identify the key issues and then review the direction. It fits with Igwe's guiding slogan – let the main thing be the main thing. An example of this kind of contract is the man who referred himself to a therapist in despair about his failure in relationships. His experience was that although women usually agreed to date him when he first asked them, after a couple of meetings they stopped wanting to see him. He very much wanted a long-term relationship and this was his stated contract. First he wanted to find out what he was doing to sabotage his possibilities.

At the bottom of the matrix lie two types of contract which do not articulate an observable outcome. They are for clients whose need is for a subjective internal change or development, not an externally defined one. The *exploratory contract* may be suitable for someone who can identify internal distress, such as depression or anxiety, but has neither understanding nor clarity other than a need to 'feel better'. They hardly know themselves; they may have little sense of self and therefore are certainly not capable of identifying a behavioural goal. Hence 'till we have faces'. How can we face the challenges of our lives, and decide who and how we want to be until we know who we are now? This client needs to go on an inner journey in a relationship with a trusted other, to explore the territory of her distress and her identity. The completion of this contract may possibly be followed by a behavioural, outcome-focused contract, or it may not.

Finally, there is what in TA may be called the *autonomy contract* (with the particular meaning that 'autonomy' has in TA). More widely, it might be called a *discovery contract* or perhaps an *engagement contract*. The signature phrase for this type of contract is 'I want more of myself'. This was said by a client who had been in therapy for anxiety at some time in the past. She returned to see the therapist saying that she had discovered all sorts of previously unknown aspects of herself during her last course of therapy. She had come back, not because she was in distress and discomfort but because she wanted 'more of herself'. It would have been completely inappropriate to pin her down to a contract for change. On the contrary, she wanted more of who she already was; so that was the agreement.

The process of making contracts

Various writers have described different types of contract and ways of making them (for example Holloway and Holloway 1973; Clark 1975; Goulding and Goulding 1979; Allen and Allen 1984; Bordin 1994; Stewart 1989, 1996 and Chapter 5).

The questions in Box 1.1, based on the work of James (1977) then expanded by Clarkson and Ward (personal communication) in Lapworth et al. (1993) are designed to clarify a contract for change and represent a formal style of contract making. They are therefore most suitable for making behavioural change contracts and can be explored in the course of one session or spread over a longer time. The eight stages are in themselves a form of protocol. However, the therapist will feel free to adapt them as appropriate.

Box 1.1   Making the contract for change

1   What do you want that would enhance your life?
2   How would you need to change to get what you want?
    (These are deceptively simple questions, and time is needed to explore them properly and uncover the self-damaging patterns of a person's way of living. They may need to be preceded by a much wider exploration of how life would look once the desired outcome had been achieved. It is important that the client is not expecting someone else, or life, to change but is willing to look at how they are living at present and what they are doing to maintain the status quo.)
3   What would you be willing to do to effect this change?
    (This must be couched in positive terms – i.e. to start doing something rather than to stop as in 'I will phone my friends when I am feeling lonely' rather than 'I will stop sitting at home feeling lonely.' 'I will feel and express my feelings' instead of 'I will stop smoking'. This is enormously important according to extensive research evidence that people make happen what they imagine and envisage.)
4   How would other people know when change has been made?
    (This ensures a verifiable outcome and also increases the chances of getting support and encouragement from other people.)
5   How might you sabotage yourself?
    (This addresses the client's normal ways of avoiding change and it is surprising how easily most clients can answer the question.)
6   How will you prevent the sabotage?
    (An invitation to another behavioural commitment.)
7   How will you reward yourself on completion and how will you make sure that you maintain the level of stimulus and attention that you were accustomed to getting from the old behaviour?
    (This addresses the fact that people's maladaptive patterns normally have some secondary gain in that they provide a way – albeit unsatisfactory – of getting some of their needs met.)
8   How will you spend your time when you have changed?
    (Nature abhors a vacuum. Frequently people revert to old patterns – negative self-talk, obsessing, or some other form of behaviour – because of a sense of emptiness or even loss. It is important to build in a plan for new ways of structuring the time.)

Sometimes a more organic, emergent style of contract making is more appropriate. Bordin (1994) offers a less formalised method of identifying the goal, which is particularly suitable for clients who need a period of exploration (clarifying or exploratory contracts). He stresses the importance to the therapeutic alliance of a slow and sensitive exploration of the client's situation, in which the client has the feeling of being respected and heard both for herself and in terms of her understanding of the problems and what is needed. The practitioner contributes to this with his ideas, questions and so on. Finally the practitioner suggests a goal which most fully captures the person's 'struggle' and addresses it (Bordin 1994: 15).

There are also here-and-now 'instant' contracts in order to clarify something or find a way forward in a session. Those might include such questions as: 'I have a suggestion for you, do you want to hear it?' or 'Do you want some information about that?'.

It is important to listen to the client's answer and make sure a contract is agreed before continuing. It is not necessary to make that sort of contract every time an intervention is made which diverts the process. Permission to do this is normally implicit in the positive *psychological contract.* However, it can be very useful in helping the practitioner find his way in the process or in ensuring that a client does not feel pushed or even re-abused. This sort of contract is also valuable for heightening here-and-now awareness and self-responsibility. For a deeper discussion of these 'process orientated contracts' see Chapter 6.

Tasks

The second element of the professional contract is the agreement about role or 'tasks' (Bordin 1994). Berne (1966: 20) says that the therapist describes clearly 'the limitations and potentialities of what his treatment has to offer'. This may include a description of the theory and method used, the way the therapy may proceed, and something about the practitioner's philosophy of therapy and human growth as well as its relevance to what the client wants to get from therapy. Again, practitioners vary enormously in how much they choose to make explicit. However, it should be remembered that there is considerable evidence to suggest that failed or discontinued treatment is largely caused by an unaddressed difference in expectations between practitioner and client (see Introduction and Goldberg 1977). Furthermore, Asay and Lambert, reviewing the 'working alliance', which has been shown by overwhelming research evidence to be an extremely important predictor of positive therapy outcome, state 'the element of collaboration between therapist and client including the consensual endorsement of therapeutic procedures, has been shown to be an essential part of the development of a strong therapeutic alliance' (1999: 44).

It may be especially important to give a fairly detailed explanation of the approach when proposing to work cross-culturally. The role of the counsellor or psychotherapist can vary enormously between different cultures – from advice-giving community leader in one culture, to spiritual guide in another, to awareness facilitator in a third (Grant 1994). For example, clients from some Asian and other oriental backgrounds may need a logical and rational approach while those from Western cultures may expect to address their feelings (d'Ardenne and Mahtani 1989). In therapy, the client, as well as ideally feeling a greater degree of safety, is likely to feel increased vulnerability to the power and influence of the practitioner. This may make him easily swayed by the practitioner's ideological, moral or religious viewpoint (Feltham and Dryden 1994). Clear contracting about such things helps to avoid undue influence by seeking to develop an equality of relationship while not ignoring the real or perceived power differential that exists. Another significant factor could be the different language interpretations when client and practitioner are from different cultures. The meaning of the words of a contract, the words used to describe the practitioner's roles, even the word 'contract' itself might be full of subtle shades of meaning. Clarifying them can be part of the process of interested enquiry and contact that is so necessary in a cross-cultural engagement.

In describing their role, and depending on their theoretical orientation, practitioners may say something like 'I believe that you are getting stuck in these areas because you are not bringing all of yourself to the situation and have got into fixed patterns of responding. I see my job as helping you raise your awareness of yourself and increase your options', or: 'My view is that we get into difficulties because of what we believe about ourselves and the world. My job is to help you think about your thinking and change the unhelpful patterns', or 'I believe that we get into problems when we block out natural growth processes and that given the right conditions we can rediscover those processes and allow them to develop'. Some practitioners might describe the methods they use: 'Every session we will agree together on what the focus of the session will be'; 'Each week you will make a diary of how much and when you are eating'. Some lay down very explicit guidelines for how the therapy will be conducted, for example, 'Your job is to talk about whatever is on your mind. You will find that I don't say very much; I will occasionally comment to highlight an emerging theme or issue, but mainly this is a space for you to explore'.

On the other hand, many practitioners feel that to explain the process in detail is like describing the film before you get to the cinema. For these practitioners, the client's reaction to the therapist's manner and interventions will form an important part of the work. In that case the therapist must weigh up the balance between an ethical obligation to make sure that the client is well informed about what he is 'letting himself in for', and the desire to keep the field open to surprise and spontaneity. If the practitioner chooses not to go into details about her way of working she can expect more to emerge in the *psychological contract* (see p. 21). This may be appropriate if the approach focuses largely on looking at issues of transference. If the approach seeks to minimise transference issues, one way of doing so is to be as explicit as possible about what the therapy will involve. Many practitioners choose to offer a series of three to six sessions ending with a review before offering a longer contract (Elton Wilson 1996, 2000; Chapter 11). This gives the client experience of the method of counselling and allows for a more informed commitment to further work.

The issue of touch merits particular attention. The area is complex and it is not possible to enter into a discussion here about when the use of touch may be useful and when counterproductive. Certainly, clearly negotiated contracts are essential in order to protect both parties. If a practitioner uses bodywork as part of his or her method, this must be explained and explored carefully at the outset. Some practitioners have found it useful to make an explicit, written contract about the use of touch. I am grateful to James Kepner, author (1993, 2001) and renowned body psychotherapist, for permission to include as Appendix III, his own written consent form. However, he stresses (personal communication):

The informed consent document for body-oriented psychotherapy (Gestalt Body Process Psychotherapy) is just one part of a true informed consent process for body and touch related work and should not be presented in isolation. Touch work must be done within an existing therapeutic relationship, and the consent form and its contents has to be a part of a dialogue about the rationale, use and understanding of body-oriented work as psychotherapeutic. This form should not be copied as stated and used, since its tenets are based on a particular orientation to body psychotherapy, and particular intent for the use of touch. Other therapies may use touch for different purposes and in different ways.

Breaches of contract

Whatever the practitioner's approach, the professional contract is made, along with the administrative contract, as a formal offer and acceptance of a therapy commitment. The practitioner needs to think about how to respond if the contract is broken – by either party. It is important that he is clear from the outset which agreements are part of a contract and which are simply ground rules (see Chapter 10). A breach of contract on either side is likely to be symbolic of psychological processes that must be addressed (see Chapter 2).

In theory either side has recourse to the courts if a legal contract is broken but in practice it is very unlikely that a therapist would take a client to court, even for such clear breaches as non-payment of fees. Indeed, Hans Cohn (personal communication), in somewhat humorous vein, said that the reason that therapists use the word 'contract' at all is 'because it gives them the feeling that they are in charge'. What is important is that any broken contract be addressed and sensitively explored for its implications and significance. An overemphasis on contracts may point to an excessive desire for control – a denial of human changeability. However, impatience with, or abhorrence of, contracts may imply avoidance of boundaries, of commitment and of the responsibility of choice.

Steiner (1974: 243) said that 'contracts in treatment should be regarded with as much respect as contracts are regarded within the law'. He identified four elements that he said should be common to both a legal and therapeutic contract (see Chapter 10). In fact, there are important legal dimensions to contracts in counselling and psychotherapy. These are addressed separately by Peter Jenkins in Chapter 9 (also Jenkins 1997; 2002).

The psychological contract

The third type of contract consists of the unspoken, and often unconscious, expectations that are brought to the counselling room by practitioner and client, resulting in a sort of implicit agreement which can have positive or negative consequences. It is paradoxical to use the word 'contract' in this context; it implies conscious agreements. The psychological contract, on the contrary, is usually not even in awareness. However, Berne's use of the word reminds us powerfully of the strength of such unspoken and unchosen pacts, which are at best empathic connections and at worst the enmeshment of an unrecognised transference and counter-transference symbiosis.

The 'positive' psychological contract

This is the area of the third of Bordin's (1979, 1994) elements of the working alliance: the *bonds*. From the start of the therapy, the practitioner puts a high priority on the establishment of a relationship of mutual respect and trust in which the client will feel free to share his concerns, and experience being heard and attended to. If the administrative and professional contracts are made carefully and appropriately, practitioner and client are ready to embark on whatever journey they have agreed. At the psychological level, the client may already be feeling hopeful and optimistic about what he can achieve. If the practitioner feels similarly confident, has assessed the client correctly for the course of counselling that she intends to give, and believes that she is able to offer help, an unspoken bond is developed which is likely to affect the positive outcome of the therapy. Clarkson (1992), building on the work of Winnicott (1958), refers to a 'facilitative' transference and counter-transference relationship which develops between therapist and client and involves both people's temperament, styles and preferences based on past experiences. Of obvious relevance here are the subtleties of variables in this form of relationship. This is also the realism of the right brain connection described by Schore (2003) or the 'limbic resonance' of Lewis Amini and Lannon described by Lee in Chapter 6.

The 'negative' psychological contract

There are two major ways in which the psychological contract, if not recognised, can influence the counselling in an adverse way and have unwanted consequences. The first of these is the hidden agenda: the unvoiced fears, fantasies or hopes that find a haven in the consulting room. One client may come to counselling with the unexpressed goal that it will stop her husband from leaving her. Another client appears to have come voluntarily but has actually been 'sent' by a spouse or boss (Mearns 1994). Practitioner and client may unconsciously collude to avoid some existential reality which is part of their mutual field – for example death, choice or uncertainty. Surprisingly frequently, a hidden agenda on both sides of the relationship concerns unrealistic expectations of what the therapist could and should do. If the professional contract has not been clarified with sufficient care, this hidden agenda becomes built into the therapy matrix, and both parties end up disappointed.

The second, and inevitable, unspoken expectation that the client brings will not be in his or her conscious awareness and will be based on past experience of life and relationships. Berne (1966) says that at one level people come to therapy in order to confirm their 'script'. The man who is afraid of closeness expects his psychotherapist to dominate and intrude upon him. The woman who has always allowed others to decide things for her expects to be told what to do. The friendless man who was abandoned in a children's home as a baby expects at some level not to be seen and heard. The frightened woman expects to be attacked. Clients bring their transference reactions to their counsellor or therapist and this can form part of the psychological contract. The practitioner is invited into a counter-transference which will bring about the expected outcome. If she responds to the invitation, the therapy can then be founded on this destructive bond, repeating what Wachtel (1977) calls the 'cyclical dynamics' rather than changing them. The client who fears closeness intellectualises and withholds and the therapist becomes demanding and interrogative. The passive woman is so helpless and unable to think for herself that the counsellor begins to think for her and give her instructions. The abandoned man mumbles in a monotone and talks about himself from a distance and the practitioner feels bored and switches off during sessions. The frightened woman's counsellor scares herself by feeling unaccountably murderous towards that woman. In all these situations, patterns repeat and are perhaps entrenched so that no change occurs.

Transference and counter-transference *will* happen in counselling and psychotherapy, and probably all practitioners are familiar with the phenomena. Luborsky et al. (1986) demonstrate that the relationship with the therapist or counsellor reflects the client's relationships in his everyday life. The task of the practitioner is to try and work with this without falling into a negative psychological contract. How practitioners choose to approach the issue again varies between theoretical orientations. Psychodynamic practitioners and some transactional analysts will choose to allow the transference to develop and work carefully within it. Other humanistic practitioners will see it as their task to encourage a real, 'here and now' relationship as far as possible and will therefore work to show how the transference interferes with that relationship. Some practitioners, for example cognitive–behavioural practitioners, will do everything possible to minimise the transference and if it emerges, might use it to examine patterns of thinking. And so on. What is normally true is that the more detailed and explicit the *professional contract*, the less the transference will occur. This is also true of the unconscious, unrealistic hopes of a magical cure that clients sometimes bring. What is essential is that the therapist and client address and seek to dispel the transference if it is putting what Bordin calls a 'strain in the therapeutic alliance' (1994: 18).

It goes almost without saying that practitioners too will bring some transference to the consulting room, to which clients will respond. This will inevitably contribute to the co-created psychological contract, which can be explored together with the client as appropriate and also examined carefully in supervision.

The contractual context

There are many levels to the contractual context. Administrative, professional and psychological aspects can be considered at any of the levels. First there is the level of the therapist's contract with society in whichever way he understands that; then with the organisation or agency involved (both these are discussed in Chapter 10). When these are in place, the therapist is free to negotiate the overall therapeutic goal or development contract with the client himself. He may also, depending on the nature of the work, make an explicit sessional contract at each meeting, or this may be implicit within the overall contract. And finally there are those moment-to-moment contracts known as 'process contracts', which Stummer (2002) describes as requesting permission to proceed and again can be explicit (see Chapter 5) or implicit.

Box 1.2 shows the levels of contract in the form of a list. When Brigid Proctor teaches about them she uses, with her usual flair for the spatial as well as the visual, a set of Russian dolls. Each one nestles safely inside the container of the previous one – each separate but contributing to a whole. The dolls capture the idea that the contract, at best, acts as a safe container for the creative work in the area of bounded

Box 1.2   Levels of Contracts

... with the world, society, the environment, etc.

... with the organisation and individuals in it – *the administrative contract*

... with the client regarding the desired 'developmental outcome' –
the professional contract

The Contracting Matrix

... with the client for a session

... with the client 'moment by moment'

Contracts are to be reviewed regularly and updated as appropriate.

instability (see p. 6) and that it can do that best if it itself is 'contained' by the clarity and safety of the previous level of contract.

Conclusion

This chapter has provided an overview of the different elements, types and levels of contracts which can and do occur in the therapy situation. The aim has been to offer an exploration of the range of contractual agreements which therapists and their clients make together, without being prescriptive. Whether we, as practitioners, opt for making only *administrative contracts* or whether we make an explicit contract for behavioural change, there is a common factor in our contracting. Both explicitly, and implicitly as part of the *psychological contract,* therapist and client make a mutual commitment to a relationship which will be in the service of the client's growth and development.

References

Allen, J.R. and Allen, B.A. (1984) *Psychiatry – A Guide,* 2nd edn. New York: Medical Examination Publishing Co.

d'Ardenne, P. and Mahtani, A. (1989) *Transcultural Counselling in Action.* London: Sage.

Asay, T.P. and Lambert, M.J. (1999) 'The empirical case for the common factors in therapy: quantitative findings', in M.A. Hubble, B.L. Duncan and S.D. Miller (eds) *The Heart and Soul of Change: What Works in Therapy.* Washington, DC: APA Press. pp. 33–56.

BACP (British Association for Counselling and Psychotherapy) (2000) *Ethical Framework for Good Practice in Counselling and Psychotherapy.* Rugby: BACP.

Beisser, A.R. (1970) 'The paradoxical theory of change', in J. Fagan and L.L. Shepherd (eds) *Gestalt Therapy Now.* New York: Science and Behavior Books.

Berne, E. (1961) *Transactional Analysis in Psychotherapy.* New York: Grove Press.

Berne, E. (1966) *Principles of Group Treatment.* New York: Grove Press. (Republished 1994 by Shea Press, Menlo Park.)

Berne, E. (1982) *What Do You Say After You Say Hello?* London: Corgi. (First published 1972.)

Bordin, E.S. (1979) 'The generalizability of the psychoanalytic concept of the working alliance', *Psychotherapy Research and Practice,* 16: 252–60.

Bordin, E.S. (1994) 'Theory and research on the therapeutic working alliance', in O. Horvath and S. Greenberg (eds) *The Working Alliance: Theory, Research and Practice.* New York: Wiley.

Clark, T. (1975) *Going into Therapy.* New York: Harper.

Clarkson, P. (1992) *Transactional Analysis: An Integrated Approach.* London: Routledge.

Dryden, W. (1989) 'The therapeutic alliance as an integrating framework', in W. Dryden (ed.) *Key Issues for Counselling in Action.* London: Sage.

Duncan, B.L. and Miller, S.D. (2000) *The Heroic Client.* San Francisco: Jossey Bass.

Elton Wilson, J. (1996) *Time-Conscious Psychological Therapy.* London: Routledge.

Elton Wilson, J. (2000) 'Integration and eclecticism in brief/time-focused therapy', in S. Palmer and R. Woolfe (eds) *Integrative and Eclectic Counselling and Psychotherapy.* London: Sage.

Feltham, C. (1997) *Time-Limited Counselling.* London: Sage.

Feltham, C. and Dryden, W. (1994) *Developing Counsellor Supervision.* London: Sage.

Goldberg, C. (1977) *Therapeutic Partnership: Ethical Concerns in Psychotherapy.* New York: Springer.

Goulding, M.M. and Goulding, R.L. (1979) *Changing Lives Through Redecision Therapy.* New York: Grove Press.

Grant, P. (1994) 'Psychotherapy and race', in P. Clarkson and M. Pokomy (eds) *The Handbook of Psychotherapy.* London: Routledge. pp. 75–85.

Holloway, M.M. and Holloway, W.H. (1973) *The Contract Setting Process.* Monograph No. VII in M.M. Holloway and W.H. Holloway (eds) Monograph Series. Midwest Institute for Human Understanding. pp. 34–8.

James, M. (1977) *Techniques in Transactional Analysis.* Reading, MA: Addison-Wesley.

Jenkins, P. (1997) *Counselling Psychotherapy and the Law.* London: Sage.

Jenkins, P. (ed.) (2002) *Legal Issues in Counselling and Psychotherapy.* London: Sage.

Kapur, R. (1987) 'Depression: an integration of TA and psychodynamic concepts', *Transactional Analysis Journal,* 17 (2): 29–34.

Kepner, J. (1993) *Body Process: Working with the Body in Psychotherapy.* San Francisco, CA: Jossey-Bass.

Kepner, J. (2001) 'Touch in Gestalt Body Process Psychotherapy: purpose, practice and ethics', Gestalt Review, 5 (1).

Lapworth, P., Sills, C. and Fish, S. (1993) *Transactional Analysis Counselling.* Bicester, Oxon: Winslow.

Lewis, C.S. (1942) *The Screwtape Letters.* London: Geoffrey Bles. (Reprinted Glasgow: William Collins, 1979.)

Lewis, C.S. (1978) *Till We Have Faces.* London: Fount Paperbacks.

Luborsky, L., Crits-Cristophe, P. and Mellon, J. (1986) 'Advent of objective measures of the transference concept', *Journal of Consulting and Clinical Psychology,* 54: 39–47.

Mahrer, A.R. (1989) *How to do Experiential Psychotherapy: A Manual for Practitioners.* Ottawa: Ottawa University Press.

Mearns, D. (1994) *Developing Person-centred Counselling.* London: Sage.

Orlinsky, D.E., Grawe, K. and Parks, B.K. (1994) 'Process and outcome in psychotherapy – noch einmal', in A.E. Begin and S.L. Garfield (eds) *Handbook of Psychotherapy and Behaviour Change,* 4th edn. New York: Wiley. pp. 270–378.

Panksepp, J. (1998) *Affective Neuroscience.* New York: Oxford University Press.

Parkes, C.M. and Sills, C. (1994) 'Psychotherapy with the dying and the bereaved', in P. Clarkson and M. Pokorny (eds) *The Handbook of Psychotherapy.* London: Routledge.

Parloff, M.B. (1967) 'Goals in psychotherapy – mediating and ultimate', in R.A. Mahrer (ed.) *The Goals of Psychotherapy.* New York: Appleton Century Crofts.

Rosenhan, D. and Seligman, M. (1984) *Abnormal Psychology.* New York: W.W. Norton.

Schore, A.N. (2003) *Affect Regulation and the Repair of the Self.* New York: W.W. Norton.

Smith, D. (1991) *Hidden Conversations: An Introduction to Communicative Psychoanalysis.* London: Routledge.

Steiner, C. (1974) *Scripts People Live.* New York: Grove Press.

Stewart, I. (1989) *Transactional Analysis Counselling.* London: Sage.

Stewart, I. (1996) *Developing Transactional Analysis Counselling.* London: Sage.

Stummer, G. (2002) 'An update on the use of contracting', *Transactional analysis Journal,* 32 (2): 121–3.

Sutton, C. (1979) *Psychology for Counsellors: and Social Workers.* London: Routledge and Kegan Paul.

Sutton, C. (1989) 'The evaluation of counselling: a goal attainment approach', in W. Dryden (ed.) *Key Issues for Counselling in Action.* London: Sage.

Talmon, M. (1990) *Single Session Therapy.* San Francisco: Jossey-Bass.

Tudor, K. (1998) 'Value for money?: The issue of fees in counselling and psychotherapy', *The British Journal of Guidance and Counselling,* 25 (4): 447–53.

Tudor, K. and Worrall, M. (2002) 'The unspoken relationship: financial dynamics in freelance therapy', in J. Clark (ed.) *Freelance Counselling and Psychotherapy.* London: Sage. pp. 80–90.

Wachtel, P.L. (1977) *Psychodynamics and Behaviour Therapy: Towards an Integration.* New York: Basic Books.

Wampold, B.E. (2001) *The Great Psychotherapy Debate.* Mahwah, NJ: Lawrence Erlbaum Associates.

Winnicott, D.W. (1958) *Collected Papers.* London: Tavistock.

Winnicott, D.W. (1960) *The Maturational Processes and the Facilitating Environment.* London: Hogarth Press.

PART II

Theoretical Approaches

2 The Use of Contracts in the Psychodynamic/Psychoanalytic Approach

Michael Jacobs

Although in laying down the four cornerstones of psychoanalysis (i.e., the unconscious, repression and resistance, sexuality and the Oedipus complex), Freud did not include contracts, these practical arrangements can nevertheless be demonstrated as being significant in his practice of therapy, not simply for practical reasons, but also because of the meaning that might be attached to the observance or breach of contractual arrangements. Everything has significance, according to Freud's view of 'everyday life' (1901/2002), including these practical matters. Since psychodynamic therapy and counselling takes its lead from much psychoanalytic thought and practice, it is appropriate to start with such beginnings.

Freud wrote a number of short but highly informative papers from 1911 to 1915 on technical aspects of analysis, which can be found together both in his *Collected Works* (Volume XII) and in the new Penguin classics Freud volume *Wild Analysis* (2002). In these papers he sets out a number of vital ground rules that inform the therapeutic attitude. The most obvious aspect of an explicitly stated 'contract' or agreement between an analyst and a patient is that of informing the patient of the centrality of the rule of free association – of speaking everything that comes to mind, without censoring it. The analyst is also urged to maintain similar 'free-floating attention' while listening to the patient. It is quite clear that Freud used to spell out this fundamental rule for the patient. This has some similarity to the 'professional contract' referred to in Chapter 1. It is worth noting that if psychoanalysis sometimes has a reputation for being rigid in its technique, Freud's introduction to 'rules as they apply to initiating the treatment' (2002: 45) is more relaxed:

> There will be prescriptions among [these rules] that may appear petty, and no doubt they are. The excuse for them is that they *are* just rules of the game, which gain their meaning within the context of the game plan as a whole. But it is just as well if I offer these rules as 'advice' and make no binding claims for them. (2002: 45, Freud's emphasis)

Freud includes some rather more implicit aspects of a contract, which perhaps were not spelled out unless occasion demanded it: for example, that a physician analyst should not conduct a medical examination of the patient. Yet he appears to make clear that he will always charge for a fixed time – 'Every patient is allocated a certain hour in my working day; that is his appointment, and he remains liable for it even if he makes no use of it' (2002: 48). He also makes it clear that analysis will probably be a lengthy treatment, and he advises people not to share with many others that they are in treatment, since this may subject them to hostile influences (2002: 57). Freud does not suggest that he binds patients to continue treatment for a certain length of time. He eventually recognised, through the lengthy analysis of his patient the Wolf Man, that he needed to set an ending for the analysis, and he records in one of his last papers, *Analysis Terminable and Interminable* (1937/2002), how doing this enabled a stuck analysis to proceed more therapeutically. Contracting the length of therapy comes much later in the development of psychoanalysis, as experiments with brief therapy and shorter analysis inevitably raised the issue of the importance of time-bound contracts, using the fixed ending deliberately as a means of working through issues of loss and change in a client's personal history. I return to this later.

Where there is long-term organic illness in the patient Freud makes it clear that the analyst is free to break off the treatment until the patient is recovered, so that the hour can be used by someone else. He also allows any patient 'to break off the therapy wherever they like', appearing not to interpret this as a negative reaction, but making explicit his view that to break off may well leave their problems unresolved (2002: 51). These examples from his papers on technique illustrate how much more fluid his practice was than is often assumed by those who stereotype psychoanalysis as rigid in its approach, where the balance of power appears to be in favour of the analyst rather than the patient.

A few years later we find Freud's innovative colleague Ferenczi suggesting similar guidelines for the practice of analysis, which include making agreements with patients in whom the work is progressing slowly about such matters as completing their sentences; or curbing the use of free association when it is used as a resistance; or abstinence from physical discharge of feelings, including nail-biting and sexual intercourse (Ferenczi 1955). These again appear to be contractual arrangements which are more than practical: they also serve to facilitate the analytic process. The guideline about abstinence from certain behaviours resembles the no-harm contract referred to in Chapter 7, although it must be added that such clear injunctions are not usual in the psychodynamic approach.

These early psychoanalytic papers provide different examples of the implicit, and occasionally explicit, nature of contractual arrangements, although no doubt there were others which were not so explicitly stated in writing at the time.

Contracts as a definition of boundaries

Classical psychoanalytic practice has traditionally promoted a period of assessment and history-taking before the start of the analysis proper. There has been a clear dividing line between taking a full history, and then setting out the basic rules governing the patient's and the analyst's responsibilities once the period of analysis (with its free associative method) starts. Psychodynamic therapists do not necessarily adopt such a neat distinction between the period of assessment and the start of therapy, between history-taking and defining the start of therapy itself, and what might then be expected of the client. Nonetheless they too find it essential to set out a number of well-defined parameters in the initial session(s). These are usually referred to in the literature (though not necessarily to the client) as 'boundaries': maintaining clear boundaries is a very important part of psychodynamic practice. These boundaries are made explicit to the client in agreeing the times and frequency of sessions, and the length of the contract – which may be time-limited, or may be 'open-ended'. These are clearly what Sills in Chapter 1 refers to as the administrative contract, because the client needs to know and agree these arrangements. But they are also part of what Sills refers to as the psychological contract, partly because the boundaries have the potentiality to provide a clear safety net to the client (it can be enormously helpful to know that whatever happens between sessions, the therapist will be there to listen at a definite time and day); and partly because by making the boundaries clear, any variation in them by either party (a client cancelling or a therapist taking a holiday) can then be seen as potentially evoking emotional responses, or conveying hidden meanings. Clients who cancel sessions may have good reason to do so, but it is not unknown for a cancellation to be an expression of disappointment with a therapist who has said the wrong thing the session before. Or when a therapist takes a break for holiday, this can evoke different feelings in a client: a sense of temporary loss of a necessary anchor, envy at the therapist being able to afford a break, even relief at being able to save on fees. None of these 'interpretations' are either assumed or necessarily made, but the possibilities add to the messages that everyday events might be conveying to the therapist, and which may be used to illustrate different dimensions of the client's personal responses.

There are other aspects of the administrative contract which usually feature in the arrangements made at the start of therapy. Psychodynamic therapists spell out (sometimes in writing as well as verbally) other contractual elements, such as arrangements should alteration of times be necessary (a therapist may not be able to alter the time at a client's request, but if the therapist has to alter a time the client is given as much choice as possible of an alternative hour); or notice of breaks and absences (including possible payment of fees for cancellations). These are mainly standard items in the administrative contract, although other elements may only be referred to as they arise. For example, if a client regularly tries to make contact between sessions, this may first have to be understood on an emotional level, but then discussed as a contractual arrangement (perhaps with charges for time spent on the phone). The limits upon confidentiality are often made explicit in printed material where this is given to the client, but otherwise may only arise if referred to by the client explicitly, or implicitly. The client may ask about confidentiality, which alerts the therapist to this being an issue; or may obliquely refer to concerns about trusting others with secrets, which a psychodynamic therapist would surmise may also be a concern about the therapist's trustworthiness. Similar boundaries are only likely to be stated if occasion arises for them to be stated or tested, such as abstinence from acting out in the session, including for most psychodynamic therapists desisting from touch, and in the main the therapist not sharing personal information.

The most explicit statement of boundaries is probably found within the communicative approach – an approach to the psychoanalytic form of therapy developed by Robert Langs and his followers, well described by Livingstone Smith (1991). Here the boundaries are given the nomenclature of 'the frame', which provides the setting and context for therapy. The term 'frame' is also more generally favoured in psychodynamic therapy and counselling (Gray 1994). Violation of the frame, whether by the client or by the therapist, is understood as providing a whole set of significant messages. Communicative psychotherapy is particularly concerned with therapist violations of the frame, and looks for unconscious communications by the client in response to disrespectful regard for the client. The following list is indicative of the importance of the frame for communicative psychotherapy, but it also represents aspects of what Sills identifies as both the professional and psychological contract explicitly or implicitly made by psychodynamic therapists with their clients:

A secure frame includes the following components:

1 A *secure* and *reliable* setting in which there is a fixed place, time and duration for each meeting.
2 An appropriate *fee* to ensure that the therapist is employed by and accountable to the patient.
3 Privacy and confidentiality, with no third-party intrusions.
4 A *patient-centred* therapist who does not permit his or her personal concerns to intrude into the psychotherapeutic work.
5 A therapist who refrains from any form of *coercion.*
6 A therapist who *refrains from physical contact.*
7 A therapist who will *confine his contact* with the patient to the psychotherapeutic hour and who has had *no extra-therapeutic relationship* with the patient either before, during or after the therapy. (Smith 1996: 104)

This frame is explained to the patient from the start as being for his or her protection rather than solely for the convenience of the therapist. Robert Langs' position is that too many therapists damage their patients through poor practice, which includes slack adherence to the holding of the frame.

The main difference between the communicative position and other psychoanalytic and psychodynamic therapies is the *degree* to which adherence to the frame is regarded as a *significant* unconscious communication by therapist and client to each other. The elements that Smith identifies are all very important, but can be understood rather less rigidly. For example, it is clear from the work of some counselling services that absence of a fee does not invalidate the counselling. Third-party intrusion may at times be unavoidable, although the guideline which a psychodynamic therapist follows is that such intrusion must always be communicated to the client, and its significance unpacked.

Contracts and the facilitating environment

There is a psychoanalytic stance on contractual arrangements, that in my opinion is sometimes seen in communicative psychotherapy for example, which at times appears to verge on the obsessive: if the client comes early to the session the client is seen as anxious, if late as hostile, if on time as obsessive! Negative interpretations are part of the stereotypes that psychoanalysis sometimes has to carry. Such a caricature, even if it has some truth, largely misrepresents an appreciation of the *positive* value attached to firm adherence to contracts and boundaries. Respect for the boundaries is first and foremost the therapist's task, since the time and space offered are intended to provide a secure, reliable and containing environment for clients, in which they may safely relate and explore their concerns and feelings. The contractual obligations also promise a seriousness of purpose on the part of the therapist which indicates her or his dedication to the welfare of the client and intention to represent a dependable nurturing figure. Winnicott in one of his delightful 'lists', writes of what constitutes the classical psychoanalytic setting; for example:

2 The analyst would be there, on time, alive, breathing. ...
9 In the analytic situation the analyst is much more reliable than people are in ordinary life; on the whole punctual, free from temper tantrums, free from compulsive falling in love, etc. (Winnicott 1975: 285)

Sometimes the therapist fails in some way to adhere to the contract, such as through illness, or by altering a time, often provoking an understandably negative reaction in the client. Psychodynamic therapists monitor client reactions to such therapist failures, encouraging clients to express their feelings of disappointment or even their rage, and connecting these where applicable to other experiences of broken or strained relationships.

Some clients, without such provocation, break or test the agreed boundaries, such as by asking for more time, or coming late, or acting out. Such behaviour may arise from quite legitimate requests on the part of the client, without any conscious intention to infringe the boundaries. A psychodynamic therapist considers the possibility of unconscious intent, sometimes quite quickly dismissing the possibility, or at other times waiting to see if there is further confirmation from other material of unconscious communication. When the frame is temporarily broken, it is thus possible to look for what messages the client is either consciously (but not overtly) expressing, or even unconsciously trying to convey to the therapist.

Case Example

Tim rang his therapist an hour before his session to cancel. He explained in an answerphone message that he was not well, but had hoped he would feel fit enough to come; but since he felt no better he reluctantly cancelled and recognised he would have to pay for the session. The therapist accepted this as a legitimate reason for cancelling and did not charge on the monthly invoice for the session. Tim thanked the therapist for this. Two months later Tim phoned again at a similar point before the session, saying that he had been delayed for the last two days in returning home because of work and was not going to be able to make the session. On this occasion the therapist thought that Tim could have phoned much earlier, and therefore charged him for the cancelled session. He wondered to himself whether Tim now assumed he could cancel with impunity, or indeed whether Tim was saying something else by cancelling so late. But since it did not become clear, when they met again, what this was, the therapist had to be content to collect the fee without being able to make a helpful interpretation.

Breaking and testing of boundaries may be indicative of conflicts, feelings and fears in the client which cannot be talked about in therapy. They may also reflect interpersonal issues present in the client's situation outside therapy, or earlier in life in key relationships with others.

Breaking boundaries by the client is not erroneous behaviour however, which has to be admonished. The non-judgemental attitude of the therapist remains paramount. Since the interpretation of breaches of boundaries can sometimes be heard by clients as criticism, such interpretations have to be clearly demonstrable, either backed up by other evidence or very tentatively suggested, and carefully worded and timed. When this cannot be done, all that can be said if infringements persist is something to reinforce the value of the agreed boundaries.

Other parameters

There are other aspects to the contract in psychodynamic work which are equally important. Psychodynamic therapists pay particular attention to the significance of the following.

Frequency

Psychodynamic therapists, aware of the powerful feelings evoked by the therapeutic relationship, recognise that the more frequent the hourly sessions – one, two or even more sessions each week – the greater the likelihood of either dependency upon or attachment to the therapist. In some instances it may be essential to meet more than once weekly in order to help a client to cope with distressing circumstances, or to help the client to overcome difficulties about working with deeper issues, that can be obscured by a once-weekly session. Twice-weekly sessions make for a very different therapeutic relationship compared to one session a fortnight. When the contract for frequency of sessions is arranged, this in itself gives a message to the client about their importance to the therapist. For some people, of course, to be seen frequently can initially feel threatening; for others the contract provides a sense of being cared for in a way that they may not have experienced so obviously for a long time, if at all. What a psychodynamic therapist seeks to avoid is changing the contract on a whim. Should a client normally seen once a week request two sessions, or present in such a distressing state that the therapist's concern suggests an extra session, this requires serious consideration before conceding to the request or the concern.

Case Example

Ruth had on a couple of occasions rung her therapist requesting to be seen between sessions. She sounded desperate, and the therapist offered the session each time, but on both occasions when she arrived she no longer needed the session, and the hour felt rather a waste of time. The third time the request was made the therapist declined to offer an extra appointment, giving an excuse about his availability. What emerged in the next scheduled session was that Ruth had been able to cope satisfactorily, and as the pattern of requests was looked at, the therapist recognised that each time Ruth's call had been because she had been concerned in the scheduled session that she had said something which would turn the therapist against her. She needed the extra session to ensure he was still on her side.

At the initial assessment a therapist may or may not suggest to a client that the therapist can be contacted between sessions. Such an offer may be unwise and too provocative for some clients, while for others it may provide a safety valve which in fact is never used. Whatever the frequency of sessions, there are inevitably changes when either the client or the therapist takes a holiday break. Sometimes sickness in either party also interferes with the agreed arrangements. In the case of holiday breaks, it is usual in psychodynamic therapy to agree these a few weeks before they happen, partly out of courtesy, partly because the break itself can give rise to reactions in the client which, even if negative, ultimately help the client to recognise how and why such responses arise. Sickness is less predictable, and if the therapist in particular has to cancel at short notice, the significance of this for the client is never overlooked when the sessions resume. It is a key feature of psychodynamic practice that the therapist encourages feelings about breaks to be voiced, and tries to help the client understand intense reactions in the light of their other relationships, past and present.

Times of the session need to be made clear for the benefit of therapist and client

Psychodynamic therapists endeavour to keep reliably to time. While it is possible to overstretch interpretations of a client's time-keeping, as instanced above, this can nonetheless signify anxiety or expression of discontent on the part of the client. If a client comes early or late the session still starts when agreed, and finishes when agreed. Regular infringements of the time can be seen as acting out, a concept which is important in psychodynamic work, whereby instead of feelings being expressed verbally and face-to-face, they are expressed either through an action, such as coming late, or towards a person other than the therapist when it should be the therapist to whom such feelings are conveyed. Similar concern for time-keeping arises in relation to the ends of sessions, where keeping to time not only protects the therapist from the client who inappropriately wants more, but also protects the client from the pain of staying with feelings for too long.

Case Example

Jack kept looking at his watch throughout the session. The therapist wondered (silently) whether Jack had little to say today and was anxious about the time dragging. In fact, with two minutes to go, Jack said that there was something very difficult he wanted to tell the therapist, and once he had said it he wanted to leave it behind in the room, and talk no more about it. Within those two minutes Jack was able to let the therapist know about some appalling childhood circumstances. He then left precisely on time, simply saying that he would see the therapist the following week. Had the therapist either finished early because he understood Jack to be having difficulty talking, or gone over time by asking more about the revealed material the contract would have been seriously breached. But even more, Jack would have found it difficult, if not impossible, to return to see the therapist.

Nevertheless, there may be occasions when to run over by a minute, in order to let the client complete what they are saying, is no great problem. The significance of boundaries is that they provide a standard set of limits, against which a therapist sensitively and thoughtfully handles and reflects upon any variations.

Fees

Although a number of agencies do not charge fees, some ask for donations, and some agencies work out an assessment of a reasonable amount for the client to pay for each session. In private work too, fees are a definite part of the therapeutic contract. Whenever money enters into the arrangements it is of course essential that the terms are set out clearly, including information about the likelihood of raising the level of fees when therapy is long-term, in line with inflation. These practical arrangements are no doubt common to all therapies; psychodynamic therapy may be different in the significance sometimes attached to money: the way that the client handles such matters can be seen as an expression of the client's feelings. Most clients settle fees or pay donations as a matter of course, but there are always some with whom such 'acting out' becomes an issue.

Case Example

Henry had difficulty with his donation to a counselling agency at virtually every session – even though the contract had made it clear that the cost for each session would be paid at its end. Sometimes he did not have the right change to offer the counsellor; sometimes he forgot to bring enough money. Although it was possible that Henry could have been addressing some dissatisfaction with the counsellor's work – no results, no fees – it seemed a stronger possibility that his difficulty in letting money change hands reflected the similar difficulty he had during the session in letting the counsellor have anything that could be called 'of value' about his own thoughts and feelings. The psychoanalytic description 'anal retentive' may seem a somewhat stereotypical label, but nonetheless it was an apt way of understanding Henry, which pointed to the value of trying to understand what made him so withholding.

Confidentiality

As in all therapeutic practice, it is vital to protect both the therapist and the client by the use of well-delineated rules and procedures about confidentiality. Issues of confidentiality are not always about external boundaries. Therefore a psychodynamic approach, which invariably looks for different ways of understanding a client's questions in addition to the obvious, may not necessarily lead a therapist simply to reassure a client who asks about the rules of confidentiality. Such questions may also be about the confidence the client is looking for in the therapist, and whether what is said will be treated within the session itself with the respect it deserves. Similarly questions about the therapist's background and training are legitimate for any client to ask, and should be answered whatever else of a personal nature the therapist feels it may not be right to disclose. But such questions may also be about testing the water, to see whether the therapist can be trusted to contain the client; or they may indicate a client's wish to get to know the therapist more intimately. Issues of trust as well as issues about the authority and power of the therapist, and even the wish to try to enter the private life of the therapist, may sometimes be present in these apparently matter-of-fact interactions. There are nearly always different possibilities for an interpretation, whether about the client's response to contractual boundaries, or anything else. A psychodynamic approach does not automatically assume understanding, but is always open to different meanings and to when sharing such meanings might be helpful to the client.

Aims and goals

Psychodynamic therapists are less likely than some other therapists to formulate aims and goals as part of the contract for therapy. That part of the professional contract which Sills describes in Chapter 1 does not sit easily with psychodynamic practice. However, the increasing amount of work which now has to be undertaken in short-term contracts, in primary care counselling or in employee assistance programmes for example, has meant that psychodynamic therapists and counsellors have had to give much more attention to the adaptation of their approach to a limited number of sessions. While this is not new, with Alexander and French (1946) pioneering brief therapy in the 1930s, and Malan (1976) and others researching brief therapy in the 1960s and 1970s, the emergence of psychodynamic counselling (as distinct from psychoanalytic psychotherapy), with its particular application to counselling in primary care and in employee assistance programmes, has highlighted the need for identifying an appropriate focus for the work with the client. Malan's research suggests this is essential to the effectiveness of brief therapy. Psychodynamic therapists set considerable store by the assessment procedure, which provides the opportunity to gauge the most appropriate duration and frequency of work with the client.

The focus needs to be one that is a reasonable objective within the time available, and may be clear from what the client says in the first session ('I am having problems with other people at work'). Or the client may refer to a number of issues, most of which are longer-term difficulties, but one or two could be identified as a suitable focus for brief work: here the therapist or counsellor may need to highlight the focus at the end of the first session – 'You have told me about a number of difficulties; I think in the time available we might concentrate upon… . How does that seem to you?'. The focus may need to be refined later, even in the course of short-term work.

Case Example

In the course of the early sessions of a short-term contract, deliberately arranged for a limited number of sessions because the original focus had made this feasible, the client Anne revealed a horrendous childhood, which made the therapist want to reconsider in supervision whether the agreed short-term contract was appropriate.

(continued)

(continued)

However, Anne had found it difficult to seek therapy in the first instance, not feeling she deserved help. What became clear was that it was more important for the moment to work for the remaining time on her current inability to ask for more help for herself (perhaps from a therapist who was better placed to offer long-term help) than to alter the contract to try to work with the damaging childhood experiences. The greater success might come when the request for more help came from Anne, since in her childhood she had learned that it was not wise ever to ask for anything.

In some settings short-term work is one of several options. Some agencies allow for greater flexibility, but even where a maximum contract is, for example, for two years, making the professional contract involves indicating limits. Open-ended work apparently sets no limits (although they are of course inevitable at some point). Again, this needs to be made explicit. Even if contracts are completely open-ended (more common in private practice than in institutional settings) it is often useful to agree at the start that, when the ending eventually comes, it should not be sudden on either side, but planned ahead, worked towards, and worked through. Psychodynamic therapy quite deliberately focuses on changes, losses and endings in a person's life experience, including therapy itself as another example of an inevitable ending. The opportunity to work with the potential parallels between therapy and other life experiences is a golden one which few psychodynamic therapists would want to pass up. Often the ending in open-ended work is planned for through a 'mini-contract', an agreement to end upon a particular date. One useful rule of thumb is that the time allocated to the process of ending should be about one quarter of the duration of therapy to date.

Nevertheless, even in longer-term contracts, where there is less urgency to define a focus, or where the focus can shift from session to session, it may be appropriate to set out some idea of what to expect from the therapeutic process, as the unnamed analyst does in *The Words to Say It*:

> I think I can help you. If you agree we can begin an analysis starting tomorrow. You would come three times a week for three forty-five minute sessions. But, should you agree to come here, it is my duty to warn you, on the one hand, of the risk that psychoanalysis may turn your whole life upside down, and, on the other hand, that you will have to stop taking all medication right now. ... (Cardinal 1984: 26–7)

This analyst does not mince words, and his style may appear severe. His patient, however, makes it clear just how reassuring she finds his confident stance. Contracts serve to enhance this type of containment, so vital to people in distress.

Conclusion

There are, of course, important considerations as to how all these aspects of contracts are communicated. It is not appropriate to flood a first session with procedural and contractual arrangements, and all the matters which this chapter raises. It is however important not to initiate a therapeutic relationship in which these matters have not been made clear.

Case Example

John complained to his university counsellor, who said that they would need to end counselling when he finished his degree, that she could not do this to him, because he had become dependent on seeing her. It became clear that she had not made the parameters obvious at the start, assuming at the time that John would only stay with her a short time. She then assumed that he would have understood that finishing at university meant finishing with her. Not surprisingly she had to work through even more anger and disappointment on John's part than might have been the case had she clarified all of this early on.

The main task of a therapist is to listen and to contain; and the main content of the session must be what the client brings, rather than the counsellor's concern for rules and contracts. Since such matters inevitably affect the therapeutic relationship they are essential; and the relationship may become even more therapeutic if they are talked through and monitored, including the client's responses to these necessary aspects of the work. Respectful treatment of the client as an adult who is capable of entering into a working contract is vital, even if at times in the therapy the client is encouraged to get fully in touch with a more regressed child within. Psychodynamic therapists stress the 'working alliance' as part of the therapeutic relationship – and explanations of the contract and the reasons for it are a very important part of the working relationship, which must never be neglected (Greenson 1967). Variations in response to the many aspects of that working alliance, including these contractual arrangements, contain the possibility of deepening the therapist's and the client's understanding of different aspects of human relationships. It is perhaps this that is most distinctive about the attitude of a psychodynamic counsellor or therapist to the essential administrative contract that needs to be made. Administrative matters are part of a professional approach; but a professional approach really becomes therapeutic when the psychological, psychodynamic implications of contracting are used for the benefit of the client.

References

Alexander, F. and French, T.M. (1946) *Psychoanalytic Therapy.* New York: Ronald Press.

Cardinal, M. (1984) *The Words to Say It.* London: Picador.

Ferenczi, S. (1955) *Final Contributions to the Problems and Methods of Psychoanalysis.* London: Hogarth Press.

Freud, S. (1901/2002) *The Psychopathology of Everyday Life.* London: Penguin Classics.

Freud, S. (1911–15) *Papers on Technique (Collected Works,* Vol. XII). London: Vintage, Hogarth Press and the Institute of Psycho-Analysis.

Freud, S. (1937/2002) 'Analysis Terminable and Interminable' in *Wild Analysis.* London: Penguin Classics.

Freud, S. (2002) *Wild Analysis.* London: Penguin Classics.

Gray, A. (1994) *An Introduction to the Therapeutic Frame.* London: Routledge.

Greenson, R. (1967) *The Technique and Practice of Psycho-Analysis.* London: Hogarth Press.

Malan, D. (1976) *The Frontier of Brief Psychotherapy.* New York: Plenum Press.

Smith, D. Livingstone (1991) *Hidden Conversations: An Introduction to Communicative Psychoanalysis.* London: Routledge.

Smith, D. Livingstone (1996) 'Communicative psychotherapy', in M. Jacobs (ed.) *In Search of Supervision.* Buckingham: Open University Press. pp. 102–19.

Winnicott, D.W. (1975) *Collected Papers: Through Paediatrics to Psychoanalysis.* London: Tavistock Publications. (First published 1958.)

Cognitive Therapy: A Down-to-earth and Accessible Approach

Frank Wills

Cognitive approaches have always prided themselves on being accessible and demythologised forms of therapy,[1] with more than a touch of 'common sense' (Beck 1976). It has been a hope that this was a kind of therapy that one could 'give away' in inner city areas that YAVIS-orientated (young, attractive, verbal, intelligent and successful) therapy does not always reach (Scott 1988; Beck et al. 1979). Although this notion has not been thoroughly tested, the active and commonsensical elements of the cognitive approach seem to match the expectations of less privileged clients (Ollerton 1995). Thus although the word 'contracting' is not one that is frequently used in cognitive texts, its spirit (using Murgatroyd's 1985: 38 description: 'One way to ensure that both parties begin a helping relationship with some degree of clarity about its purpose and duration') has always been a fundamental part of the cognitive approach to counselling. The cognitive therapist typically likes things to be 'on the table' rather than 'under the table.'

This chapter will focus on the tradition that has developed from Beck's cognitive therapy, though many of its arguments would also apply to CBT in general (Clark and Fairburn 1997) and other related models such as Cognitive Analytic Therapy (Ryle and Kerr 2002). Aaron Beck, however, has shown that it is built on a concern to make therapy as accessible as possible to clients (Beck 1976; Beck and Emery 1985; Salkovskis 1996).

I will show that there are two particular features that make cognitive therapy highly contractual: efforts to match the therapy to the client, and the development of a 'rolling contract'. The 'rolling contract' develops from the emphasis on eliciting continuous feedback from the client and by periodic reference to a directing individualised client 'formulation'. These activities set the focus of therapy and are therefore both the first steps of the contracting and also a framework for the process in cognitive counselling. These features can be related to the 'professional contract' described in Chapter 1.

In an early work, Beck links the accessibility of therapy to an essential cognitive therapeutic style – that of 'collaborative empiricism':

> The therapist attempts to make the treatment as comprehensible and credible as possible, so the patient can participate actively in identifying his problems and can help to develop strategies to approach each of these problems. (Beck et al. 1979: 74)

Collaboration can be helpfully linked to the way clients have sought previously to solve their problems. Apart from the generally positive, democratic aspect of client participation, a major attempt to reach consensus on the goals and means of therapy is desirable because therapist and client may begin with some daylight between their respective way of seeing things:

It is important to realise that the dispenser of the service ... and the recipient ... may envision the therapeutic relationship quite differently ... To minimise such hazards, the patient and the therapist should reach a consensus regarding what problems require help, the goal of therapy, and how they plan to reach the goal. (Beck 1976: 220)

Because the therapist often does exist in a somewhat closed 'Therapy World', surrounded and reinforced by 'people who think like us', it is part of necessary humility that she or he tries to be as clear and 'negotiable' as possible, right from the start. Counselling research appears to show that many therapies are generally equivalent in effect and are heavily influenced by 'common factors' (Stiles et al. 1986; Hubble et al. 1999; Rowland and Goss 2000). Some problems and individual clients, however, may respond to some therapies more than others, so that a careful matching process would be highly commendable. Goldfried (2000) jokes that often the therapist approaches the client thinking, 'I hope that he has the problem I treat' whilst the client is thinking, 'I hope she treats the problem I have.' An appropriate matching process might avoid unnecessary damage to the client and may additionally have the pragmatic advantage of saving a lot of wasted effort later. Thus, as the therapist begins to engage and contract with the client, he or she should have the following thoughts in the back of his or her mind: 'Does this person really need therapy?', 'Will she or he respond to what I have to offer?', 'Is cognitive therapy the most appropriate form of therapy for this client, given the problems, the client's circumstances and the goals to be reached?'. This is especially necessary because therapists are far from immune to negative automatic thoughts themselves – 'I should be able to help all clients' being a common one. Christine Padesky (1997) reminds us that we should all be ready to work with our own negative 'therapist beliefs' in this respect. Young (1988) may be correct that therapists are inclined to feel overly responsible for clients and to be somewhat self-sacrificing. These are excellent reasons for carefully matching the client's needs to what we have to offer.

Matching the therapy to the client – (1) Presenting a rationale

The matching process begins right at the start of therapy as the rationale of the therapeutic approach is explained to the client. In this, it combines elements of both the administrative and the professional contracts described in Chapter 1. The therapist attempts to keep the rationale simple and relevant to the client's situation. The therapist also keeps the rationale short – trying not to exceed three consecutive sentences without some response from the client. Relevance is sought through examples taken from the client's situation and recast in cognitive terms. The examples are discussed and the client's reactions will in themselves give useful indicators about how the client may respond to cognitive therapy (Fennell and Teasdale 1987; Sanders and Wills 2005). In the case example below, the client ('A') is a 39-year-old man who works for the Health Service. He refers himself because of 'stress at work'. Note how the client spontaneously goes into 'sentence completion' mode and signals self-recognition to the description of 'depression' – facts that encourage the therapist to move quickly into cognitive work.

Therapist:	The basic idea of this is that the way we see the world, see what is happening to us, has a big influence on ...
Client A:	How we feel.
Therapist:	Yes. There are probably different ways of seeing things and some seem to help us more than others ... If you're depressed, you seem to develop a kind of negative bias ...
Client A:	Yes.
Therapist:	... not see some of the good things ...
Client A:	Yes.
Therapist:	... and focus on the bad.
Client A:	Yes.
Therapist:	Does that make any sense to you?
Client A:	Yes, yes ... I would think so ... because I feel at one time I could take the knocks a bit more, I suppose. ... If anyone said I'd done something wrong, I used to he able to shrug it off quite easily.

The therapist can pick up the fact that the client has a sensitivity to criticism and is able to move quickly into cognitive work by asking for a specific example. Although it is only a first session, some symptom relief will usually help to secure the therapeutic process. The client offers the example of a meeting at which he'd had to present a report. He had felt very criticised and depressed and this led to his taking two days off work. Reviewing the evidence of the comments that were made, however, revealed that comments had been 80 per cent neutral, 10 per cent negative and 10 per cent *positive!*

Therapist:	So there were an equal number of positive and negative comments?
Client A:	I would say so ... but, I dunno, I seem to grasp, take hold of the negative things more.
Therapist:	Remember what we said before that one of the features of depression is that you do over-focus on the ...
Client A:	Negative.
Therapist:	I mean, do you think it is possible that happened on this occasion?
Client A:	It's possible.
Therapist:	[laughing] You're looking at me incredibly unbelievingly!
Client A:	No, no ... it probably is what happened ... it seemed though that they made more emphasis on the negative ... or at least I thought they did.

By referring back to the initial rationale, the work completes an opening cycle. The client's final comment shows that he has reached cognitive first base – he is able to regard his thoughts in this instance as hypotheses rather than facts – a good and, in the event, accurate prognosticator of good outcome!

By contrast, the next example offers an instance in which a laboured rationale quickly runs into the sand. The client ('B') is 20 years old and a regular club-goer. She is feeling suicidal, following a relationship break-up that she experienced as humiliating. The therapist tries to offer her a 'rationale story' close to her experience:

Therapist:	If you were going to a disco with a mate and she thought, 'I've got to get off with someone tonight or it'll be disaster', how do you think she'd be feeling as she went in?
Client B:	Nervous. She'd be worrying if she'd meet someone.

> *Therapist:*   Yes, that's right. If you were with her and were thinking, 'I'd like to meet someone tonight … but if I don't, I can enjoy the music, have a laugh, whatever … ' How would you feel?
> *Client B:*   More relaxed. Not so worried.
> *Therapist:*   So can you see then that the way you see things does affect how you feel about them?
> *Client B:*   Mmmm …
> *Therapist:*   And which of the two of you might stand the best chance of meeting someone, do you think?
> *Client B:*   Well, that would depend on which of us was the best looking.

The above client attended for two more sessions during which she achieved some symptom relief but, in the therapist's estimate, little lasting attitudinal change. In retrospect, the therapist appears to move on too quickly from the client's uncertain response to his question about the effect of the 'way you see things'. This does not allow for her possible doubts to be properly explored. The client's final comment, though showing an admirable realism, does indicate that the therapist might have to work quite hard at psychological change. This would not rule out a cognitive approach but may indicate the need for a more explorative approach: something that the therapist in this instance was not able to grasp quickly enough. Whilst Beck (1976) says 'Cognitive techniques are most appropriate for people who have the capacity for introspection and for reflecting about their own thoughts and fantasies' (1976: 216), this is probably true of all psychological therapies. This implies that individualised packaging should be the rule rather than the exception. Men and women seem to react equally well to cognitive therapy, perhaps because awareness of emotion is a factor equally important as access to thoughts (Safran and Segal 1990). The rationale-giving aspect of cognitive work does allow matching right from the start and the formulation concept (discussed later) allows the individualisation of therapy to continue right to the end.

Matching the therapy to the client – (2) Using collaboration

Rationale-giving can be seen as an early attempt to build collaborative agreement into the therapeutic process. The therapeutic method is itself centred on Beck's notion of 'collaborative empiricism'. The collaboration helps the therapist to 'get alongside' the client so that the sharply focused cognitive 'attack' on the problems will not be experienced as an attack on the client him or herself. As Beck puts it:

> It is useful to conceive of the patient–therapist relationship as a joint effort. It is not the therapist's function to reform the patient: rather his role is working with the patient against 'it', the patient's problem. Placing emphasis on solving problems, rather than his presumed deficits or bad habits, helps the patient to examine his difficulties with more detachment and makes him less prone to experience shame, a sense of inferiority and defensiveness. (Beck 1976: 221)

This also has the advantage of centring the therapy strongly on the client's own experience.

Working collaboratively – constructing a 'problem list' and using agenda-setting

Following collaborative assessment, a 'problem list' (Sanders and Wills 2005) is constructed which forms a provisional agreement on goals and aims in therapy. This list aims to include all the client's salient issues. It can be returned to throughout therapy, helping to 'anchor' the process. This can help prevent aimlessness and drift.

The problem list can then be used as a basis for setting an agenda for each session of the therapy. By keeping to this structure, the therapist can ensure that the session always starts by finding out what the client's actual current concerns are: 'Ideally, setting the agenda is quick and to the point … Failure to set explicit agendas frequently results in at least some unproductive discourse' (Beck 1995: 29).

It does not necessarily follow that the therapist has to work with every one of the client's issues. Research has shown that counsellors learning cognitive therapy often struggle with this point (Wills 2005). By keeping the problem list and overall therapeutic goals in mind, therapist and client can ensure that they are working on issues that will make a difference and not just on 'crises du jour'. A collaborative agenda-setting dialogue allows issues to be discussed and their inclusion on the agenda to be agreed – including a rough time allocation for different items. The therapist may have to take a lead in this process to begin with but the idea is that the client gradually takes on more responsibility for the agenda as therapy proceeds. The following extract comes from session four (of eight) with Client A:

Therapist: Let's construct an agenda for tonight then. What would you like to put on?

Client A: I'd like to go over the Daily Mood Logs, for the week before last … I didn't actually do it for last week … I didn't feel quite so bad and when I did, it was mostly the same things as the week before.

Therapist: OK, we'll go over the Mood Logs … Before we do, anything else?

Client A: Well … how do you feel these sessions are going?

Therapist: You'd like some feedback from me.

Client A: Yes, what you expect.

Therapist: So, is this about being a good counselling client? [*Both laugh*[2]] Anything else?

Client A: Yes … some advice on how to carry on.

Therapist: OK, well we'll work that into the Daily Mood Logs. There were also a couple of things I wanted to put on as well … one you've partly mentioned – sleep and exercise and so on … and the other thing was – and this is only a suggestion: would it be helpful sometime – this week if we've got time – handling criticism? What do you think?

Client A: Yes, that'd be good. We raised it last week and I've thought a lot about it. I've been trying to be less picky at work …

Therapist: Which one would you like to take first?

Client A: Mmm … Let's take the Mood Logs first.

By the end of therapy, the therapist is more in the consultant role and the client uses the sessions to check off his concerns with the consultant. As with all things, this does not always happen by the book. This is especially true when clients have significant personality difficulties – for example, with trust – so that they may see the invitation to set the agenda as some kind of 'trick'. Setting the agenda can itself become an agenda item! Collaborative solutions are, as ever, the ones to be strived for.

Collaborative choice of methods

In addition to using the cognitive rationale to assess the therapy's suitability for the client, it is also often useful to explore which of the many, and growing, tools and techniques of the cognitive therapy may be valuable to this individual client. In recent years, for example, it has been realised that some of the early models of cognitive therapy were over-rational, over-verbal and neglectful of the role of emotions (Safran and Segal 1990; Bennett-Levy et al. 2004; Hayes et al. 2004). Along with the general interest in therapy integration, cognitive counsellors have become more universal and assimilative in choice of technique. This obviously extends client choice and such choices can be included in the contract. Bearing in mind the dangers of 'hat-rack eclecticism' (Dryden and Feltham 1994), it is important to guide the use of technique by an overall formulation, an approach increasingly adopted across therapy models (Eells 1997). As Judith Beck (1995) shows, cognitive therapists can now be found using, for example, Gestalt techniques – provided they can be seen as fitting with a cognitive strategy. For example, one client held the unhelpful assumption: 'If I keep my bad feelings to myself, I won't fall apart.' Experiential sharing of these feelings helped to give powerful disconfirmation of this belief – a central strategy addressing core issues in this client's formulation.

It is often helpful to establish what kinds of psychological change a client has experienced before: what seems to help and what doesn't? It is also helpful to know what kind of change methods clients might find difficult and what 'change strengths' they might see themselves as having. At the end of the first session with Client A, I established that he liked to read. I felt sufficiently encouraged by his reception of the cognitive approach to ask if he would like to try reading a cognitively based self-help book, *The Feeling Good Handbook,* by David Burns (2000). In fact he took to the book, and the idea of bibliotherapy, well and soon bought his own copy.

The 'rolling contract' – (1) Ongoing feedback

In addition to these early types of contracting – remembering to keep them provisional and open to revision as therapy progresses – feedback from clients throughout all sessions acts as a re-contracting device. This effectively makes for therapy based on a 'rolling contract'.

Client B and I had an initial contract for six sessions. At the end of session three, she gave 'I like talking' as her end-of-session feedback. This turned out to be her last session. I wish now that I had been able to frame this as a change strategy, instead of covertly trying to think of ways of leading her to more 'elegant' (Ellis' term – see Dryden 1991) change.

Although it can often be hard to swallow, 'negative' feedback from a client is particularly useful and, if possible, should be conceptualised as the client genuinely trying to help the therapist to get on the right track. Additionally, if the client can begin to see himself or herself as helping the therapist, then this may foster a sense of self-efficacy that was previously absent. Misunderstandings occur frequently in therapy and may be mitigated by continuous feedback. Clients may need to be encouraged to make sharp yet often useful observations about the therapist. A non-defensive response, though difficult, usually reaps the greatest therapeutic rewards.

Feedback, going both ways, can also be a way of strengthening the therapeutic relationship, especially by helping issues to surface as early as possible. It is still a surprisingly rare experience for clients in any kind of professional milieu.

Therapists may sometimes need to remind themselves that there are two parties to any contract and that therapists too have rights as well as responsibilities. They should not confuse eliciting feedback with attempting to find ways of 'pleasing the client'. It is a somewhat inconvenient fact that many of the best learning experiences are not comfortable ones. This, in my view, does not justify the deliberate manufacture of discomfort but may involve learning to 'stay with' discomfort when it arises, as it naturally does in therapy. This issue can be usefully discussed at the contracting stage. A therapist who becomes inordinately concerned to prevent discomfort getting on the agenda will not get far in achieving lasting change. When working with Client A, the client kept giving feedback that, although he found sessions as a whole very useful, the (relatively brief) passages of time looking at his childhood were uncomfortable. This discomfort, 'feeling blank' and being unsure what to say, was explored. The exploration of past experience continued and eventually revealed some useful material (discussed in the next section).

This ongoing effort to explore the meaning that the client gives to therapy is congruent with cognitive therapy's concern to understand the client's attribution of meaning to all aspects of her or his life.

The 'rolling contract' – (2) Using 'formulation'

The concept of 'formulation' (sometimes also called 'conceptualisation') has taken on a central importance in cognitive therapy (Sanders and Wills 2005). This is an attempt to draw a 'map' of the client's difficulties at an early stage of therapy. This map is made collaboratively with clients and may be 'owned' by them. It is best if it is open to revisions negotiated by therapist and client in the light of events. At the start of Client A's sixth session, I gave him the formulation presented as Figure 3.1 (p. 49). He brought it back to session seven, saying that he had found it very interesting and wanted to go over it with me. It should hardly surprise us that if formulations advance our understanding, then they can be equally helpful to clients.

Therapists obviously need to be careful about how they generate these potentially powerful formulations with clients. A persuasive therapist might well, for instance, lead clients to compliance when, in reality, they are doubtful of or resistant to his or her suggestions. This is especially likely when the therapist and client are working at 'schema' level. A 'schema' is a deeper mental structure that works at a more primitive level. Early experience of abandonment may, for example, result in an 'abandonment schema'. Because schemas are often established in very early experience, they may not be encoded in language (Sanders and Wills 2005). There may rather be a hazy 'cloud' or mélange of visceral negative emotions that can be powerfully and easily triggered by seemingly innocuous events (Layden et al. 1993). Thus a client may experience feelings which may translate as 'People will always leave me' when a partner goes away for the weekend. Because schemata are early and primitive templates, they can be very resistant to change. They often have compensatory and maintenance mechanisms that may go into massive counterattack when they are challenged by events or by a therapist (Young et al. 2003). As Padesky neatly puts it: 'Being a "cheer-leader" for anti-schema may only make the client more of a cheer-leader for pro-schema!' (Padesky 1994).

The formulation can therefore become a very useful guideline to any issue that crops up either in the client's life outside the therapy room or in the therapeutic relationship within it (Persons 1989). For example, a client with a 'mistrust schema' (Young et al. 2003) held the belief that, 'No one cares about me.' When the client suddenly stopped attending sessions, I was wondering whether to take the initiative in contacting him. I considered that contacting him, though with some risk of being intrusive, would be justified by the chance to disconfirm the belief that no one cared about him. This decision was a good one because the client had arrived late for the session in question and had been too afraid to come in or subsequently contact me. With Client A, initially it proved difficult to 'get underneath' his presenting depression. He could remember that fear of criticism had been an issue in primary school but recalled his parents as being rather neutral and distant rather than critical or punitive – they didn't hinder him but neither did they help him much. This didn't seem to fit for some weeks until he said that he had reached the conclusion early in life that 'I have to do it for myself, people won't help you much.' We were then able to draw out the formulation map shown in Figure 3.1.

The formulation can act as 'the therapist's compass' (Persons 1989). Besides the role it plays in enhancing therapist and client understanding it can also help in handling process issues such as choosing interventions which link to deeper therapeutic purposes. It can also help to anticipate issues likely to arise in therapy. In Client A's case, for example, the formulation helped us to understand the role that perfectionism might be expected to and did, in fact, play in his view of himself as a client and in activities like the completion of homework. It allowed us to set one homework task requiring him to do his homework badly!

Formulation can also be seen as a stage of assessment. It is increasingly accepted that good practice assessment can be completed in a client-centred, non-stigmatising and non-labelling way and also in a way that can be transparently shared with the client (Milner and O'Byrne 1999). Formulation and its accompanying explanations can be seen as an extremely client-friendly way of achieving these aims.

The 'rolling contract' – (3) Rolling right up to the end

Considerable effort is made at the end of therapy to review all aspects of the contract and how it has worked out. One of the strengths of the cognitive approach has been

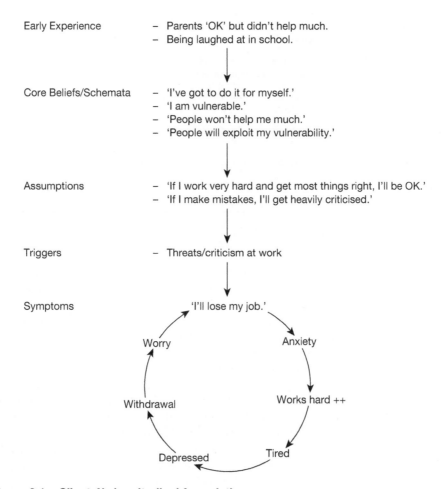

Figure 3.1 Client A's longitudinal formulation map

its ability to 'generalise' – i.e. transfer the benefits – from work during therapy to the post-therapy situation (Padesky and Greenberger 1995; Hollon et al. 1996). This can be a major factor in preventing relapse. During the process of ending the therapy, the client may be asked to work on a 'blueprint' of how beneficial change will be maintained and how future problems may be handled. This blueprint can encourage the client to 'gather in' all the most useful things he or she has learned in therapy. Going over these may result in the development of preventative devices such as 'coping cards'. The blueprint card for Client A is shown in Figure 3.2.[3]

Conclusion

The review conducted as a 'blueprint' or in some other way is the final move of the therapy. It represents the completion of the 'rolling contract' that was formed during the first session. The contract aims to make the nature, purpose and process of the

---

WHAT HAVE I LEARNED FROM THERAPY? That modifying my thoughts can modify my feelings. That I don't necessarily need tablets. That I can challenge my negative thoughts.

HOW CAN I BUILD ON THIS? I can define how I want to be – more light-hearted. I can learn to worry less. I can actively plan more pleasurable activities.

WHAT WILL MAKE IT DIFFICULT? Taking work home. Not going to work feeling 'fresh'. Getting into a cycle of 'no time', 'no motivation'.

HOW WILL I OVERCOME THIS? Reviewing the costs and benefits of positive and negative actions and thoughts.

WHAT MIGHT LEAD TO A SETBACK? (1) Problems at work. (2) Ill health.

WHAT WILL I DO IF I DO HAVE A SETBACK? Seek help early from family and friends, GP or counsellor. Read the self-help books.

Figure 3.2   Client A's 'blueprint'

therapy as clear as possible to the client. Thus the client is presented with a clear rationale for cognitive work. The rationale is developed by way of the collaborative relationship between therapist and client. It is operationalised by the construction of a problem list and by use of agenda-setting. The contract is maintained in working order by the use of ongoing feedback between client and therapist and kept on track by the development of an individualised 'formulation'. The contract is extended into the future by the use of termination strategies such as the blueprint. In summary, 'collaboration' is both a key principle of cognitive therapy and its preferred working style (Beck and Emery 1985). Much of the success of cognitive therapy may well derive from the fact that the clients use collaboration with the therapist to learn specific ways of being their own therapists. They are thus able to use therapy as a 'takeaway' service. Considerable effort therefore has been made to tailor the therapeutic relationship to the needs of the individual client, thereby maximising the possibility of delivering the promise of the individual therapeutic contract.

Notes

1 The term 'therapy' is used as a generic term for both counselling and psychotherapy.
2 This issue had been discussed before and would be again under the agenda item of perfectionism (see p. 48).
3 This is a shortened version of the actual blueprint sheet written by the client.

References

Beck, A.T. (1976) *Cognitive Therapy and the Emotional Disorders.* New York: New American Library.

Beck, A.T., Rush, A.J., Shaw, B.F. and Emery, G. (1979) *Cognitive Therapy of Depression.* New York: The Guilford Press.

Beck, A.T. and Emery, G. with Greenberg, R. (1985) *Anxiety Disorders and Phobias: A Cognitive Approach.* New York: Basic Books.

Beck, J. (1995) *Cognitive Therapy: Basic and Beyond*. New York: The Guilford Press.

Bennett-Levy, J., Butler, G., Fennell, M., Hackmann, A., Mueller, M. and Westbrook, D. (2004) *Oxford Guide to Behavioural Experiments in Cognitive Therapy*. Oxford: Oxford University Press.

Burns, D.D. (2000) *The Feeling Good Handbook,* 3rd edn. New York: Plume.

Clark, D.M. and Fairburn, C.G. (eds) (1997) *Science and Practice of Cognitive Behaviour Therapy*. Oxford: Oxford University Press.

Dryden, W. (1991) *A Dialogue with Albert Ellis*. Milton Keynes: Open University Press.

Dryden, W. and Feltham, C. (1994) *Developing the Practice of Counselling*. London: Sage.

Eells, T. (ed.) (1997) *Handbook of Psychotherapy Case Formulation*. New York: Guilford.

Fennell, M.J.V. and Teasdale, J. (1987) 'Cognitive therapy for depression: individual differences and the process of change', *Cognitive Therapy and Research*, 11: 253–72.

Goldfried, M.A. (ed.) (2000) *How Therapists Change*. New York: Guilford.

Hayes, S.C., Strosahl, K.D. and Wilson, K.G. (2004*) Acceptance and Commitment Therapy: An Experimental Approach to Behaviour Change*. New York: Guilford.

Hollon, S.D., DeRubeis, R.J. and Evans, M.D. (1996) 'Cognitive therapy in the treatment and prevention of depression', in P. Salkovskis (ed.) *The Frontiers of Cognitive Therapy*. New York: Guilford. pp. 293–317.

Hubble, M.A., Duncan, B.L. and Miller, S.D. (1999) *The Heart and Soul of Change: What Works in Therapy*. Washington, DC: American Psychological Association.

Layden, M.A., Newman, C., Freeman. A. and Morse, S.B. (1993) *Cognitive Therapy for Borderline Personality Disorder*. Boston: Allyn and Bacon.

Milner, J.and O'Byrne, P. (1999) *Assessment in Counselling: Theory, Process and Themes*. Basingstoke: Palgrave.

Murgatroyd, S. (1985) *Counselling and Helping*. London: Methuen.

Ollerton, D. (1995) 'Class barriers to psychotherapy and counselling', *Journal of Psychiatric and Mental Health Nursing,* 2: 91–5.

Padesky, C. (1994) Public lecture at the Warneford Hospital, Oxford.

Padesky, C. (1997) *Therapist beliefs in cognitive therapy*. Keynote address, European Association of Behavioural and Cognitive Psychotherapies Conference, Cork, September.

Padesky, C. and Greenberger, D. (1995) *The Clinician's Guide to Mind over Mood*. New York: The Guilford Press.

Persons, J. (1989) *Cognitive Therapy in Practice: A Case Formulation Approach*. New York: W.W. Norton.

Rowland, N. and Goss, S. (eds) (2000) *Evidence-based Counselling and Psychological Therapies*. London: Routledge.

Ryle, A. and Kerr, I.B. (2002) *Introducing Cognitive Analytic Therapy*. Chichester: Wiley.

Safran, J.D. and Segal, Z.V. (1990) *Interpersonal Process in Cognitive Therapy*. New York: Basic Books.

Salkovskis, P. (ed.) (1996) *The Frontier of Cognitive Therapy*. New York: Guilford.

Sanders, D. and Wills, F.R. (2005) *Cognitive Therapy: An Introduction*. London: Sage.

Scott, M. (1988) 'Giving away psychology in the inner city', *Counselling: Journal of the British Association for Counselling,* October: 1–6.

Stiles, W.B., Shapiro, D.A. and Elliot, R. (1986) 'Are all psychotherapies equivalent?', *American Psychologist,* February: 165–80.

Wills, F.R. (2005) 'Crossing Continents: changing from one therapy model to another during training.' Paper delivered at the Research Conference of the British Association for Counselling and Psychotherapy, Nottingham, May.

Young, J.E. (1988) 'Cognitive therapy for personality disorders'. Workshop presentation with George Lockwood, Palo Alto, CA: 1 October.

Young. J.E., Klosko, J.S. and Weishaar, M. (2003) *Schema Focused Therapy*. New York: Guilford.

Contracting within Person-centred Counselling and Psychotherapy

4

Mike Worrall

The person-centred approach to counselling and psychotherapy is an increasingly broad affiliation of approaches which share particular root assumptions. Sanders (2000, 2004) has mapped these approaches and articulated some of their similarities and differences. I write from a particular position on the map, and hope that what I write is sufficiently grounded in its principles to be recognisably person-centred, and sufficiently inclusive to be relevant beyond my own narrow position.

Although person-centred therapists do not focus on contracts in the way that some therapists do, we can nevertheless examine the way we make them for what it tells us about our attitudes to our work. For the purposes of this chapter I want to look at contracts and contracting in the light of Rogers' assertion (1957a/1990: 402) that anything we do as therapists is 'operational evidence of an underlying value orientation and view of human nature'. The contracts we make, and the way we make them, arise out of and make manifest our view of human nature. Once manifest, they define the relationship within which we work, and limit or enhance the nature and quality of our work.

I expect the process by which I contract with clients and the nature of the contracts I make, to be congruent both with my own personal philosophy and with the philosophy that underpins the person-centred approach. For that reason I want to begin this chapter on contracts by looking at person-centred philosophy and the theory of therapy that derives from it.

Person-centred philosophy

The philosophical heart of the humanistic approach in general, and of the person-centred approach in particular, is the belief that each and every human being has the *potential* for health, growth and fulfilment, and the *tendency*, latent if not evident, to realise that potential (Rogers 1967: 35). Holding this belief, I trust deeply that, under the right conditions, and without external pressure or incentive, clients will choose to move in the direction of greater health, autonomy, homonomy and creativity. This belief has a number of corollaries, the most immediately relevant of which is that a therapist's work is not to do anything to her clients, but simply to create with them a relational climate that will most effectively facilitate their self-directed exploration and development.

A person-centred contract, therefore, does not need to specify behavioural outcomes or goals.[1] I argue further that it is philosophically and therapeutically essential that such a contract be independent of outcomes. Thorne (1991, pp. 31–2) uses Lyward's term 'contractual living' to describe the experience that many clients bring to counselling, and that is often the root of their need for counselling in the first place. Briefly, this term describes people striving to fulfill their part of a perceived contract with others in order to gain approval, and in the process of this striving losing touch with their own inner capacity to direct their own lives. This contract, articulated in person-centred theory as a *condition of worth*, takes the form of a series of conditions which a client believes he has to meet if he is to be worthy of love and attention:

- I'm lovable if and only if I do well at school, don't make a mess, and always do whatever anyone asks me to do;
- I'm lovable if and only if I never speak up for myself;
- Nobody will love me if I give up my job and do what I really want to do with my life.

No one need ever have laid these conditions out on paper, or even articulated them verbally. Their power lies in the extent to which a client has internalised them as a way of making sense of his experience, and then lives by them, often without even being aware of them.

It is unhelpful for me as a counsellor to replicate this form of contract, to even the slightest degree. My client needs no further practice in living contractually. I will be more helpful if I can offer him a relationship which will itself challenge his past contractual living. This suggests that among the most helpful therapeutic strategies at my disposal is a willingness *not* to make a contract, or, more accurately, not to make one that expects, demands or values particular outcomes. One radical way of construing this is that a contract in the person-centred approach places demands on the counsellor and not on the client.

Person-centred theory

Person-centred theory suggests that we are all most effectively able to realise our potential within a particular kind of relationship (Rogers 1967, pp. 37–8). Such a relationship is characterised by the practitioner's authenticity, understanding and acceptance, and by his determination to work towards mutuality within the counselling relationship. If I profess authenticity and mutuality as important therapeutic principles, I need to incorporate them and demonstrate them actively in my work at every level and from the beginning. In practice this means that any contract I make with a client must be an authentic expression of who I am and must also encourage mutuality between my client and myself. Heyward (1993: 69) describes mutuality as:

> a way of being connected with one another in such a way that both, or all, of us are empowered – that is, spiritually called forth; emotionally *feel* able; politically *are* able to be ourselves at our best, as we can be when we are not blocked by structures and acts of violence and injustice or by attitudes and feelings of fear and hatred.

Contracts in counselling are not normally acts of violence or injustice. The counsellors who make them are not normally motivated by feelings of fear or hatred. However, implemented or imposed with any degree of rigidity or inflexibility, a contract can become a structure which blocks a person's growth and restricts the potential for mutuality within the relationship. 'Intuitively, I know that any relationship that cannot, on principle, grow more fully mutual is not a right or trustworthy relationship' (ibid.: 64–5).

A person-centred contract, then, will reflect the precise needs and wants of both my client and myself, will arise out of the nature of the relationship between us, and will both enshrine and further a commitment to mutuality. I neither impose it nor insist on it unilaterally. To this extent the contract I am advocating describes what is, rather than determines what should be. It is, if you like, a descriptive memorandum of what we have agreed to be the parameters and defining features of our relationship. And if it is descriptive, it is also dynamic, and changes as the counselling relationship it describes changes.

Person-centred practice

Assessment

Wilkins and Gill (2003) rehearse arguments for and against various forms of assessment, and clarify the difference between assessment and diagnosis. Their research suggests that whatever person-centred practitioners say they think about assessment, most of them in practice make some form of assessment before contracting with their clients. I think this is both inevitable and desirable. Before I agree to a contract with a client, I need to assess whether I am willing to engage in a counselling relationship with him. In person-centred terms, any relationship is rendered therapeutically helpful by the presence of six conditions (Rogers 1957b). Along with Wilkins and Gill (2003) I suggest that these six conditions can form the basis of initial assessment and become the foundation of any subsequent contract. For person-centred practice these six conditions provide the only contractual framework necessary between client and counsellor. We can address and resolve anything that happens between us during the course of our relationship without any other externally imposed agreement. I now want to look at each of these conditions in turn.

Psychological contact

The first condition is met when two people are in sufficient contact 'that each makes some perceived difference in the experiential field of the other' (Rogers 1957b: 96). Two people sitting together in the same room and aware of each other satisfy this condition. They have also made and fulfilled an agreement to meet, and have therefore already forged a rudimentary contact *and* contract.

Client incongruence

The second condition is that a client comes to the counselling relationship aware of some personal discomfort, vulnerability or incongruence. This is what usually prompts a client to seek counselling in the first place. He may want to make behavioural changes, or he may want to explore his way of being in the world. One of the very few counselling contracts I have been unable to agree to foundered on this condition. A woman approached me because two of her grown-up children and several of her friends were already in counselling and finding it useful. She saw the benefits they were experiencing and decided that she wanted to experience counselling herself. Over three sessions, however, she and I were unable to identify accurately or specifically anything that she wanted to change or explore. As she described her circumstances, I could see many things that I would want to change if I were her. She, however, could not. Nor did she want a space within which she could simply talk about or explore her life. Although I believe she genuinely wanted something for herself, we were unable to formulate what it was, and I had to say that I could not work with her. This woman was, in my experience, an exception. For the most part clients who come voluntarily for counselling come *because* they fulfil this condition.

Counsellor congruence

The third condition is that the counsellor undertakes to be authentic within the relationship. This is the first of the counsellor's contractual obligations. At a minimal level, this condition demands that I am at least open to myself and willing to be open to my client. At its most demanding, it is an invitation to bring as much of myself as is appropriate into my relationship with my client.

In a spirit of congruence and honesty I want to acknowledge, at least to myself and if necessary to my client, what my needs and expectations are in this relationship. How much money do I need? How little money am I willing to work for? How many hours a week am I willing or able to work? How many hours a week am I willing to work with this particular client? My answers to these questions will vary over time. Some years ago my financial position was such that I had, or believed I had, relatively little freedom to work for a reduced rate. I am now more stable financially, and more authentically willing to consider working with a client for less than my usual fee. When I was less busy, I was freer to arrange to see clients at times to suit them. Now I have other commitments, and in order to maintain my own resources to work at all, I am more careful about how many hours I work and when.

Given what I have just said about my finances, and given that I work from home and can usually fill in time relatively easily, I don't need, and therefore don't ask for, a minimum notice of cancellation. I want to start from a position of trusting unconditionally that my client makes appointments with me in good faith. I recognise that all sorts of things can happen to get in the way of someone keeping an appointment with me, and I want to accommodate this where I can. In the fifteen years that I have been working exclusively in private practice, I have had few instances of a client missing or postponing a session more than once. On the one occasion when I did work with someone who repeatedly made and then broke appointments with me, with little or no notice, I found the framework of thinking congruently sufficient to work out a way forward which suited us both. I was aware that I was beginning to feel confused, resentful and uncommitted. I didn't know from one session to the next whether she was going to turn up or not. I believed that in this frame of mind I would not be helpful to her.

At the same time I knew of her circumstances, and could understand just how difficult it was becoming for her to hold any regularity or structure in her life. Her behaviour with me was symptomatic of the current state of her life. It would not help her if I interpreted her behaviour as transference or resistance, insisted that she kept appointments, or charged her on principle for appointments she didn't keep. In the end we agreed to put our work on hold for a while. I was willing to speak on the phone for short periods from time to time, and she contacted me again six weeks later when she was more realistically able to make and keep appointments.

Empathic understanding

This condition is met when the counsellor puts aside whatever preconceptions she is carrying, and works towards understanding whatever her client is communicating as if from within her client's frame of reference, insofar as that is ever existentially possible. Whatever I might want from a counselling contract, I am aware that my client has needs too. These needs are part of her reason for coming to see me in the first place, and it is part of my professional responsibility to work towards understanding them, and her, empathically. Most of my training work and much of my supervision is monthly, and it is not always easy for me to see clients weekly. My normal practice is to make the next appointment at the end of a session. This accords both of us a high degree of flexibility, and over time has allowed most of the people with whom I work to settle into a pattern of coming to see me which meets their individual needs accurately – every ten days, fortnightly, monthly, even once every six weeks. This arrangement satisfies me philosophically, in that it honours the individual person over any preordained structure; and suits me pragmatically in that it fits more easily with the rest of what I do with my life. One client, however, because of the nature of his working week, and because he has sole responsibility for bringing up his young children, preferred to have a regular session. Agreeing to this contract with this person, I had to temper my congruent awareness of what would work well for me with an empathic awareness of what he said would work for him. On balance, I was willing to forego what I would normally want, and we contracted to meet at the same time every week, except for occasional weeks when I had to be away. If I had stuck rigidly to the way that I worked, and had been unwilling to consider working in a way more suited to him, I would have been demonstrating an unhelpful lack of empathic understanding. What we agreed arose out of a process of negotiation which in itself turned out to be therapeutically significant. This man's experience in life was that he was normally done to, had little or no power to effect change, and often felt bullied or harried into agreeing to terms that were not at all right for him. He came to see me expecting and almost prepared for the same sort of treatment. My willingness to be flexible, to listen respectfully to what he needed, to pay attention to what I needed, and to engage with him in the process of discovering a mutually satisfactory arrangement, was a new and heartening experience for him. The process by which we agreed a contract was therapeutic in and of itself.

Unconditional positive regard

This condition asks the counsellor to suspend judgement of the client, and to accept all of a client's thoughts, feelings and behaviours with equal attention and respect. I offer to accept my client unconditionally, irrespective of anything she may or may not do. This has clear implications for the making of contracts, in that it renders untenable within the approach any counsellor-led or theory-led contract that seeks to impose a direction on a client or demands from her any specific behaviour. The most profound test of this condition is probably to work with someone considering self-harm or suicide. In some counselling disciplines, even within the humanistic schools, a therapist will sometimes want to make a no-harm or no-suicide contract with a client (see Chapter 7), and might refuse to work with a client who is not willing to agree to this. Other counsellors will refuse to work with a suicidal client without the active knowledge or involvement of that client's GP or psychiatrist. Although I understand a counsellor's need for these apparent protections, such stipulations seem to me to deny a client's right to control her own life. This is philosophically untenable within the person-centred approach and is incompatible with this condition specifically. If a counsellor insists on any of these conditions, the process becomes one of unilateral imposition rather than bilateral agreement, and therefore not really contractual at all.

In contrast, Natiello (1994: 15) writes about what she calls the collaborative relationship, and describes working with a client who 'regularly went through bouts of suicidal depression'. The client was prepared to give her the gun and bullets she carried with her, on condition that she could have them back whenever she asked for them:

> Everything I believe was called into question in that moment. My mind raced ahead to a time when she might ask for the gun so she could kill herself. What was I to do? What about the law? What could happen to me? How could I breach the trust we had built? I swiftly sorted through my theoretical grounding and got back in touch with my commitment to being trustworthy, authentic, and uncontrolling in the relationship. And then I promised her – knowing in my heart that I would never break the promise – that I would return the gun when she asked.

This indicates the level of trust that unconditional positive regard demands of the counsellor. If I genuinely believe in my client's potential and tendency to move towards health, and if I also believe that the most effective way to release that potential is to be radically uncontrolling and unconditional in my acceptance of her, then the way that I act must demonstrate that.

Whether we can agree to work together or not, I want to believe and demonstrate that my prospective client deserves unconditional respect. I may not be able to meet his expectations; I may not even be able to rise to the demands of congruence and empathic understanding as I have outlined above. I can always, however, behave towards him as a person who deserves respect unconditionally. In practice, my belief in the importance of showing this level of respect often means that I am willing to work with a client even though I may have to stretch myself. In this I agree with Mearns and Thorne (1988: 31), who in a slightly different context describe a counsellor's 'preparedness to *be* manipulated' as one of the signs of a healthy relationship. And where I really cannot agree to work with somebody, two things are important: that I do not pass judgement on him as being too difficult, needy, defended or resistant; and that I offer to help him find a counsellor who will be willing to work with him.

Communication

The final condition is met when a client experiences her counsellor's empathic understanding and unconditional positive regard, to at least a minimal degree. In some ways this is the most important of the six conditions. Rogers (1967: 131) notes the need for therapists to 'receive' their clients, by which he means therapists must both understand them empathically and accept them. It is, he says, 'well to point out that it is the client's experience of this condition which makes it optimal, not merely the fact of its existence in the therapist'. Whatever my skills and attitudes as a counsellor, therapy begins only when my client experiences for himself my empathic understanding and unconditional acceptance.

The first and last conditions obviously depend to some extent on the client. The second condition depends entirely on the client. The third, fourth and fifth conditions, however, lie within the counsellor's gift. I am responsible for the presence of these qualities in my work irrespective of who my client is or what she does.

Clarity, rigidity and fluidity

Received wisdom suggests that a counsellor must be scrupulously clear about such things as how much she charges, how long she works for, and how often she sees an individual client. Wilkins and Gill (2003: 181) define a contract specifically in these largely administrative terms as 'an agreement to meet, where the meeting will take place, for how long, what the nature of the engagement may be and perhaps how many sessions there may be'. I agree. The British Association for Counselling and Psychotherapy's *Ethical Framework for Good Practice in Counselling and Psychotherapy* (2002) enshrines the importance of clarity and agreement too: 'Good practice involves clarifying and agreeing the rights and responsibilities of both the practitioner and client at appropriate points in their working relationship'. (2002: 5).

Neither received wisdom, however, nor the need to be clear about what I am offering is an excuse for me to become uncritically dogmatic about these matters, or to enter into a new counselling relationship with fixed ideas about them, unwilling to consider working in different ways to suit the changing needs of individual clients. I can be clear without being rigid. Further to this, Mearns (1994, pp. 30–1) argues that a counsellor making increasingly rigid contracts is in fact showing one of the symptoms of counsellor burnout. Framing this more positively, fluidity is one of the key values of person-centred philosophy, and one of the key indicators of mental and emotional health.

Conclusion

The person-centred approach is, above all, a way of being with another person. It is not a fixed method of counselling. Writing about what he calls 'emergent' modes of empathy, Bozarth (1984) suggests that empathic responses are most authentic and effective when they emerge idiosyncratically out of the interplay between the person of the therapist, the person of the client, and the nature of what is happening between them in a particular moment. I suggest that the same is true of contracts: they are most effective when they reflect and attend to the changing realities of an individual therapist in living relationship with an individual client. They are, in that sense, idiosyncratic to a particular relationship.

The way of making contracts that I have described is simply the way that *I* practise, informed by who I am as a person, by my understanding of person-centred philosophy and theory, by the needs and wants of each person with whom I work, and by the *Ethical Framework* to which I subscribe. It follows that each person-centred practitioner will, at best, have a way of making contracts that is unique, informed by person-centred thinking and modified by each client with whom she works.

I'm aware, as I finish this chapter, of a significant and relevant irony. I might neither have written it nor revised it if I had not agreed to do so some time ago. For the purpose of getting things done, I can see that in this instance a contract specifying a definite behavioural outcome has been helpful. The process of counselling, as I understand it, is not, however, *primarily* about getting things done. In keeping with the person-centred approach I value more highly the process of making a relationship which is authentic, mutual and personally involving. This is my primary therapeutic aim. Such a relationship often allows or encourages both client and counsellor to change how they live, and to get things done, but these changes are neither the primary focus of the counselling work nor the primary indicators of its success or failure. I see this as one of the ways in which the counselling relationship differs fundamentally from the rest of life, and as one of the elements of its therapeutic effectiveness.

Note

1   There is, of course, a difference between a client who explicitly seeks a person-centred counsellor, and one who is suffering from a specific complaint, such as a phobia, and who wants relief in the shortest possible time. Such a client may well not benefit as specifically as she would like from person-centred counselling, and might benefit more readily from a more specifically behavioural approach.

References

Bozarth, J.D. (1984) 'Beyond reflection: emergent modes of empathy', in R. Levant and J. Shlien (eds) *Client-Centered Therapy and the Person-Centered Approach: New Directions in Theory, Research and Practice*. New York: Praeger. pp. 59–75.

BACP (British Association for Counselling and Psychotherapy) (2002) *Ethical Framework for Good Practice in Counselling and Psychotherapy*. Rugby: BACP.

Heyward, C. (1993) *When Boundaries Betray Us: Beyond Illusions of What is Ethical in Therapy and Life*. San Francisco: Harper Collins.

Mearns, D. (1994) *Developing Person-Centred Counselling*. London: Sage.

Mearns, D. and Thorne, B. (1988) *Person-Centred Counselling in Action*. London: Sage.

Natiello, Peggy (1994) 'The collaborative relationship in psychotherapy', *Person-Centred Journal*, 1 (2): 11–17.

Rogers, C.R. (1957a/1990) A Note on 'The Nature of Man', in H. Kirschenbaum and V.L. Henderson (eds) *The Carl Rogers Reader*. London: Constable. pp. 401–8.

Rogers, C.R. (1957b) 'The necessary and sufficient conditions of therapeutic personality change', *Journal of Consulting Psychology*, 21 (2): 95–103.

Rogers, C.R. (1967) *On Becoming a Person: A Therapist's View of Psychotherapy.* London: Constable. (First published 1961.)

Sanders, P. (2000) 'Mapping person-centred approaches to counselling and psychotherapy', *Person-Centred Practice*, 8 (2): 62–74.

Sanders, P. (ed.) (2004) *The Tribes of the Person-Centred Nation.* Ross-on-Wye: PCCS Books.

Thorne, B. (1991) *Person-centred Counselling: Therapeutic and Spiritual Dimensions.* London and NJ: Whurr.

Wilkins, P. and Gill, M. (2003) 'Assessment in person-centered therapy', *Person-Centered and Experiential Psychotherapies*, 2 (3): 172–87.

PART III
Types and Considerations

5 Outcome-focused Contracts

Ian Stewart

This chapter is a practical guide to making contracts that will effectively help clients to achieve specific outcomes. I have drawn the material mainly from the practice of transactional analysis (e.g. Berne 1966; Steiner 1974; Woollams and Brown 1979; Stewart and Joines 1987; Stewart 1996, 2000). Interestingly, the conditions for an 'effective contract' in TA terms are closely similar to those for a 'well-formed outcome' in neuro-linguistic programming (e.g. Cameron-Bandler 1985; Andreas and Andreas 1989). This chapter includes techniques and recommendations drawn from both TA and NLP.

The bulk of the chapter will be devoted to describing a six-stage checklist that you and your client can use to develop an effective outcome-focused contract. First, however, I shall consider the definition of some key terms.

Contracts, outcomes and actions

It is important to register that an *outcome* is different from an *action*. In other words: a goal is not the same thing as the behaviour necessary to achieve it. An example will help to make this clear. Suppose one of your client's stated goals is 'to get a new job'. This says nothing at all about what he is going to *do* to achieve the goal. 'Getting a new job' describes an outcome, not a set of actions.

The next essential step in change, therefore, is to consider some actions that will help him achieve the outcome he desires. For the person wanting to get the new job, a few such actions might be:

> 'Buy the local paper and read the job adverts.'
> 'Write up my CV and have it printed out by an agency.'
> 'Read a book about doing job interviews.'

One obvious difference between outcomes and actions is that outcomes refer to states of affairs. Actions, by contrast, refer to behaviours. Another difference relates to the three time-frames of past, present and future. Action is in the present, while outcomes are in the future.

The various possible definitions of a *contract* have been discussed in Chapter 1. It will thus be clear that a *contract* is conceptually different from either an outcome or an action. In the literature of TA, it has been traditional to demand that any effective contract be behavioural – that is, that the contract be for a specific *action*. Indeed, this is central to Eric Berne's definition of a contract (Berne 1966: 362). In practice, however, the contracts that people agree upon in effective counselling are as often about outcomes as they are about actions. Indeed, in my experience, the contracts most crucial to personal change are likely to centre on outcomes rather than on actions.

Let us return to the client whose goal is to get a new job. If he and his counsellor agree a contract that simply says: 'I will get a new job within three years', they have not agreed on any action that the client will take. Yet this contract wording goes directly to the client's stated outcome. It speaks of a state of affairs that is different, in a desired way, from the existing state of affairs. Without doubt, it describes a clearly specified, observable change on the client's part. This change takes the form of an *outcome*, not an *action*.

I have therefore put forward an alternative to the traditional TA formulation (Stewart 1996: 67). I suggest the following:

1 An effective contract may be *either* for an outcome *or* for an action.
2 However, if a contract is for an outcome, it must be supported by at least one contract for an action.

Why must any outcome contract have at least one action contract to support it? Because only by *doing* something can the person interact with the world. If the person's desired outcome is 'to get a new job', he must carry out at least one action to help bring about that outcome. If he does not act, nothing new will happen.

There is another reason why effective contract making demands the formulation of at least one action contract. It is that words create experience. Thus, as the client formulates the words of an action contract, he must also internally create the experience of this change-promoting action.

In the practice of contract making, it is most usual for the person's *overall contract* to be an outcome contract. Counsellor and client will then develop a series of action contracts in the service of that overall contract. These action contracts will then correspond to *session contracts* and/or *working assignments*.

All the recommendations that follow in this chapter apply with equal force to action contracts and outcome contracts.

Six conditions for effective contract making

The treatment contract, like the administrative contract, must meet Steiner's four requirements (see Chapter 1). Once you have assured this, you and your client can go on to check six questions about the outcome or behaviour for which the client is contracting. They are as follows:

1 Is the contract feasible?
2 Is it safe?
3 Is it stated in positive words?
4 Is it sensory-based?
5 Is it finishable?
6 Is it placed in a clear context?

When you can answer 'Yes' to all these questions, you have provided the six conditions that define an effective outcome-focused treatment contract. In the sections below, I go on to discuss each of the six conditions in detail. It goes without saying that the *content* of the contract should also reflect a clear therapeutic movement on the client's part, judged in terms of whatever counselling model you are using. However, this judgement opens up different areas of discussion from the process of contract making itself and I shall simply take it as read in the remainder of the chapter.

Feasibility

A useful test of feasibility is to ask: 'Has at least one other person in the world achieved this?'. If the answer is 'Yes', then the contract may be judged feasible. It is necessary to consider carefully what the 'this' entails, taking into account the client's age, current skills, and so on. As a general guideline, be both realistic and optimistic. For a contract to be feasible, it has to speak of a change that the person wants to make in herself. It is not possible to make a feasible contract for change in someone else.

Safety

This implies both physical and legal safety. It may also raise questions of social appropriateness. For instance, suppose a woman client wants to take the contract goal of assertively choosing a man as a marriage partner. In Western social groupings, this is likely to be a safe goal. But among some other cultural groups, such action might bring disagreeable or dangerous social consequences for the client.

Another aspect of safety, less tangible but equally important to check, concerns the possible disturbance to the client's established patterns of behaviour and belief that may be entailed in achieving the contract. Many counselling models share the assumption that even dysfunctional patterns perform some positive function for the person. This may be explained in terms of 'defence mechanism', 'preserving homeostasis', and so on. Thus, when the person acts on a contract to change these old patterns, she opens herself to the abandonment of defences or the disruption of a well-established internal balance. She may, at some level, perceive this as a risk to her well-being or even her survival. In a worst case, she may act out by self-harming or harming others.

Within your own model of counselling, it is important to be aware of this potential danger and to offer the client appropriate protection against it. Within TA, for example, the counsellor would make certain not to invite a contract for script change until the client had 'closed escape hatches' – that is, taken an unconditional decision not to kill or harm self or others or go crazy (Stewart 1996: 54–8; 2000: 93–105, and see Chapter 7). In NLP, the facilitator would carry out a thorough 'ecology check' as part of the process of creating a well-formed outcome (Andreas and Andreas 1989: 81–2).

Positive wording

Frequently a person comes into counselling with the aim of stopping doing something. She will typically state her initial goal in negative words. She may want to *stop* having fights with her relations, *give up* smoking, *not* be nervous of speaking in public, to *control* her emotions or to *lose* weight. For an effective treatment contract, any such negative goals must be rephrased in positive words.

Only a positively worded contract can fulfil one of the most important functions of explicit contracting: to act as a visualisation of the achievement of the contract. It is impossible to visualise 'not something'. For example, test visualising 'not a blue elephant'. When you attempt this, you automatically make a picture of whatever follows the 'not'. Thus if, for instance, someone makes a contract to 'not be afraid', he cannot address this contract goal without continually visualising 'being afraid'.

Further, experience shows that to be effective in the long term, a contract needs to provide *at least one more option* than the old behaviour. This gives the person a positive course of action that will meet his needs at least as effectively as the behaviour he wishes to stop. Clearly, this function also can only be served by a contract that is positively worded.

Often the negotiation of a positively worded contract can itself be therapeutic. Consider what happens when your client suggests the negative contract 'I will stop overeating', and you decline to take on that contract. To move ahead from that point, you might ask your client: 'What are you going to do *instead of* overeating, that will satisfy the needs you used to satisfy by overeating?' You and he may take some time to get to a satisfactory answer to that question. But when you do, the client will have the basis for a lasting change without continual 'willpower' struggles.

Making the contract sensory-based

An effective contract needs to be *sensory-based*. This means that the contract should be stated in such a way that you can check its achievement by using any of your five senses (Stewart 1996: 78–83). Can you see, hear, physically feel, smell or taste that the contract is being fulfilled? If yes, the contract is sensory-based.

The term 'sensory-based' is drawn from neuro-linguistic programming. I prefer it to the more traditional TA formulations such as 'clear', 'measurable' and 'observable', because the operational meanings of these words are themselves unclear. Most of the techniques described below for inviting sensory-based contracts are based on the NLP 'meta-model' developed by Bandler and Grinder (1975), and on a more recent re-formulation known as the Language Model, originated by John McWhirter (workshop presentations, unpublished). I believe these models are hugely useful tools in the hands of any counsellor, for effective contract making and many other purposes.

It is worth noting that outcome contracts, as well as action contracts, can be sensory-based. Recall the example above, of the client whose outcome contract was 'to get a new job'. Obviously, it would be possible to check by seeing, hearing and physically feeling whether this person gets the new job or not. This confirms the fact that an outcome contract can be sensory-based, even though it does not speak of specific behaviours.

Of course, in order to get his new job, the person in our example will need to engage in many different appropriate actions (e.g. writing a CV, giving in his notice to his old job, looking up job advertisements, etc.). Any of these actions might themselves become the subject of an action contract. These action contracts would be *both* behavioural *and* sensory-based.

Only a sensory-based contract makes it possible for you and your client to achieve some of the main benefits of contractual method, already reviewed in earlier chapters (see for example Chapters 1 and 3). In brief, a sensory-based contract:

- makes it possible for you and your client to agree the goals and methods of treatment mutually and explicitly;
- lets you both know unambiguously when your work together has been completed, i.e. when the client has achieved her contractual goal; and
- acts as a sensory-rich visualisation of the achievement of the contract goal, for both you and your client.

Here are some checkpoints by which you can judge whether a particular statement is *not* genuinely sensory-based. By a process of elimination, you can then judge what other statements are sensory-based. At first sight, it might seem necessary to ask only the general question: 'Does this statement denote something that can be seen, heard, felt, tasted or smelt?' Indeed, this is always a useful question to start with. The answer 'No' indicates that the statement in question is *not* sensory-based. However, words are not the events they portray, and it is in forms of words that the possible pitfalls lie. The points that follow are all designed to highlight wording that *seems* to relate to sensory observation, but in fact does not.

Unspecified adjectives

For example, how about the statement 'I will become a friendly person'? At first sight, this may seem to be sensory-based: surely anybody can see, hear or physically feel whether a person is or is not being friendly? But in fact, they cannot, because the adjective 'friendly' can mean different things to different people. To me, 'friendly' behaviour may mean shaking hands on meeting. To you, it may mean hugging and paying warm compliments. Thus your sensory tests would be for a whole different set of criteria from the ones I use. Some other unspecified adjectives, familiar from the arena of contract making, are: 'warm', 'close', 'successful' and 'confident'.

You can check for this kind of unclearness during the process of contract making by asking two questions – one to yourself, the other to your client. The question to ask yourself is: 'As the client says this word, is there a chance that she could be seeing, hearing or feeling something different in her head from what I am seeing, hearing or feeling?'. If the answer to that question is 'yes' or 'maybe', then you can go on to put the second question to your client: 'So when you've got what you want, how will other people know you've got it?'. As the client answers, check her further answers in turn for unspecified adjectives. If you hear any, ask the same question about these words in turn. Continue to ask the question until the client gives you a sensory-based statement of what it is that others will see, hear or physically feel when she has achieved the change she wants.

It may often be useful to ask the same question, but ending: '... how will *you* know you've got it?'. In the same way as before, continue asking the question until the client gives a reply that expresses how he himself will employ his five senses to check whether or not he has got what he wants.

Nouns used for verbs

It is not only adjectives that are subject to this kind of unclearness. The client may often use nouns like 'feedback', 'decision', 'options', 'help', 'success', 'relationship' or 'comfort'. The common factor among nouns like these is that they denote not *things* but *processes*.

If you hear this turn of phrase, you can elicit the client's interpretation of the word by asking a question that draws her attention to the verb underlying the noun. For example: 'What do you want me to do, so that you know you're getting the kind of *feedback* you'll find useful?'; 'What do you need to find out in order that you can make the *choice* you want to make?'; 'When you've made this *decision,* how will I know that from the way you are behaving?'.

Unspecified verbs

Verbs themselves may be non-sensory-based. Examples are 'discuss', 'help', 'feed back', 'experience', 'decide', 'work on' – and, particularly relevant to contract making – 'feel', when the 'feeling' referred to is anything other than a physical sensation.

Here again, the clarifying response from you is to ask the client to define the non-sensory verb in sensory-based terms, and to stay with this line of enquiry until you and the client know what you and she will be seeing, hearing and feeling as her outcome is fulfilled. For example, suppose your client's expressed want is 'to feel relaxed when speaking in public'. You might ask her: 'How will you know when you feel relaxed?'. Your aim is to invite a reply that makes specific reference to what the client is seeing or hearing (externally or in imagination) or physically feeling.

You might then go on to ask how *you* would know that the client was 'feeling' the way she wanted to feel. The answer might refer to different observable behaviours, for example looking audience members in the eye instead of avoiding eye contact. Sometimes, you may simply agree that the client can accurately identify the internal difference in physical experience and will report that to you each time she experiences it.

Over-generalised references

Another frequent reason why a statement is *not* sensory-based is that it uses a generalised term like 'people', 'others', 'friends', 'colleagues', and so on, without specifying who in particular is meant. For example: 'I will make eye contact with people.' Without knowing *which* people the client has in mind, you have no way of checking whether or not the contract statement is sensory-based. A clarifying question from you could be: 'Which people are you talking about?'. Once again, stay with the client until he has come to a clear statement of which people he means. One useful way of identifying these people is simply to name them.

Making the contract finishable

For effective contract making you need to formulate contracts that are finishable. This term, and its converse 'non-finishable', are my own (Stewart 1996: 83–7). I use both words with their usual conversational meanings. When you think of various goals or actions for which people may make contracts, you can confirm that some of these goals or actions can be clearly *finished.* Others cannot be clearly finished, and it is this latter class that I call *non-finishable.*

It is perhaps easier to understand this distinction from examples than from definitions. Here are three examples of finishable contracts: 'To change my job'; 'To go for a bus ride on my own'; 'To say hello to two people at work today'.

Here by contrast are three statements that refer to the same content but are non-finishable: 'To look for a new job'; 'To go for bus rides on my own'; 'To say hello to people at work today'.

You can confirm first that all six of these statements are sensory-based. It is possible to check by seeing, hearing or physically feeling whether a person has got a new job, and you can check in just the same ways whether he is looking for one. The same check applies to the other two pairs of statements. (Though the third statement uses the unspecified noun 'people', you could verify by sensory checking whether these are or are not people at work.)

Let us now compare the first statement in the two sets of examples. If someone takes a contract to 'change her job', then when she does change her job the contract is clearly *finished.* If, by contrast, she takes a contract to 'look for a new job', we have no way of knowing when that contract will be finished. How long does she have to keep on looking in order to know that she has looked enough? In this example, you might suggest: 'The contract will be finished when she gets a new job, and so stops looking.' However, the original contract statement was not to *'get* a new job'; it was to *'look for* a new job'. It is that feature of wording that makes the contract non-finishable.

Likewise, when a person contracts to 'go on a bus ride', then his contract is finished when he goes on that (one) bus ride. However, a contract to 'go on bus rides' is non-finishable, since we do not know from the contract statement itself *how many* bus rides the person needs to go on before he will count it as finished.

Again, it might be possible to argue around this difficulty by suggesting that as soon as the person has done at least two bus rides, the latter contract is finished. But this does not change the fact that the contract in its original wording is non-finishable. If we assume that just two bus rides are 'enough', then we are attempting to read the client's mind.

Mary and Robert Goulding (1979: 80–1) warn of what they call 'forever contracts'. For example, a client may begin counselling by saying: 'I want to *work on* ... (some problem or other).' As the Gouldings point out, this wording is a covert device that means exactly what it says: the client will go ahead and 'work on' the problem. But he will not solve it. If he were to solve it, he would no longer be able to work on it.

In the language I am using here, the Gouldings' 'forever contracts' correspond to non-finishable contracts. The Gouldings' warning underlines one reason why it is important for a contract to be finishable: any non-finishable contract may be a strategy to avoid therapeutic change, albeit a strategy that the client is following outside of his awareness.

Another benefit of contractual method, already mentioned in earlier chapters, is that it allows counsellor and client to tell unambiguously when their work together is complete. Clearly, it is only by making a finishable contract that you and your client can fully realise this benefit.

To detect a possibly non-finishable contract statement, you can simply ask yourself the question: 'How will anybody know when the client has finished doing this?'.

If the answer is 'There's no way of knowing,' then the contract as stated is non-finishable. Bear in mind that you need to ask the question about the contract statement as the client has worded it, no more, no less. Beware of any tendency on your part to 'read in' criteria of finishing the contract that the client herself has not clearly stated.

When you do detect a non-finishable statement, you can invite the client to think up a finishable version of it by asking her that same check question, reworded as appropriate to fit the specific content of her desired contract. For example: 'Will you say how many bus rides you're going to do on your own, so you and I will know clearly you've got what you want?'; 'You say you want to make more friends. How many new friends will you need to make, so you will know you've got the contract we're talking about?' (obviously, you would also find out in this example how the client and the others would see, hear and feel that they were 'friends'); 'When you and I have finished "working on" this problem you're bringing, what do you want to have changed in your life?'.

Hanging comparatives

A particularly common form of non-finishable contract is one that contains a *hanging comparative.* This is a form of words in which the person appears to be comparing one thing with another, but does not give a standard by which the comparison is to be judged. Examples that come up often in contract making are: 'I will make *more* friends; 'I will get *slimmer*'; 'I will get *closer* to my partner'.

Even when you translate the rest of the words in each sentence into sensory-based terms, the hanging comparative would mean that there can be no sensory-specific criterion for the completion of the contract. Such statements, therefore, turn out to be non-finishable.

You might suggest that, for the client who was setting out to 'make more friends', the contract would be complete when he had made just one more friend. But so long as the hanging comparative 'more' remains in the statement of the contract, it can literally never be completed. No matter how many friends the client may make, his stated goal is always to make even 'more'.

Determining context

For effective contract making it is necessary to take account of the *context* of the contract (Stewart 1996: 97–102). The traditional TA literature on contract making makes no explicit mention of setting context, but the concept is well established in neuro-linguistic programming (Cameron-Bandler 1985: 87–8; Andreas and Andreas 1989: 244–5). I believe that NLP can offer a useful tool to TA here. To determine the context of a contract, you and your client will agree answers to the following three questions:

1 *Where* will the contract be carried out?
2 *When?*
3 Under what *limiting conditions?*

It may seem at first sight as though the issue of context is dealt with by the demand that contracts should be sensory-based. On closer inspection, however, it turns out that this is not necessarily so. Take, for example, a simple behavioural contract like this one: 'In the coming week, I will say hello to three people I haven't spoken to before.' This statement is both sensory-based and finishable. However, the contract statement as it stands misses out part of the context. The *time* dimension of the contract is indeed specific ('in the coming week'). This answers the question 'when?', but the dimension of 'where' is left unclear. Will the client say hello to three people on the upper deck of the bus, in the supermarket, at home, or just to three people anywhere?

Further, we do not know from the contract statement whether there are any circumstances in which the client would *not* carry out the contract. These are what I call 'limiting conditions'. For example, if the client is a woman, is she going to 'say hello to a new person' if that person is an unknown man she happens to pass in a deserted city street? If a man, is he going to 'say hello to three new people' in the Gents' toilet?

Here are some specific questions that you can ask to elicit the three basic modalities of context: time, place and limiting conditions.

Where?

Where is the client going to do the contracted action? Is it in some specific setting, e.g. at her work, in her home? (A check question here is: 'What is the place by name?') Or is it to be in a generic setting, e.g. whenever on top of a bus, or at some time when on the street? Or is the contract to apply anywhere and everywhere?

When?

You can investigate the time dimension of context by asking the client questions such as:

> 'By what date?'
> 'How many weeks, months, years from now?'
> 'How often?'
> 'How many times?'
> 'For how long once you have begun?'

An important aim is to elicit from the client a statement of how long (or how often) the contract statement will need to be put into action for the client to be willing to say: 'Yes, that contract is completed now.' Does she just need to do it once? If several times, how many times? If the focus is on achieving an end-point in a process (such as in a contract for reducing body fat), for how long does the target situation need to be held in place before the client will count the contract goal as having been achieved?

Under what limiting conditions?

The 'limiting conditions', of course, are already partly defined by 'where' and 'when'. Also, you will have begun to specify limiting conditions as you worked out with your client with *whom specifically* he is going to carry out the contract. Will the client carry out the contract when he is with one specific person or one specific group of people, e.g. when he is with his children, or when he is with the five people who currently work in the office with him? (Again a check question here is, 'With whom by name?') Or is the contract to be completed with a generically defined group, e.g. whenever with any workmates, or whenever he is with any people he has not met before? Or does the client specifically intend carrying out the contract with anyone and everyone?

Additional questions that may be useful are:

'What does the other person have to do first?'
'How will you know that it's time for you to do this?'
'Are there any circumstances in which you're not going to do this?'

It is as well to be cautious of agreeing statements of context like the following: 'I'll show my feelings *when it's appropriate to show them*'; 'I'll express anger to my partner *when I feel angry*'.

The common feature of statements like these is that they specify a contextual circumstance that refers only to the client's own *internal* experience, and not to anything externally observable. I call this an 'invisible context'. These 'invisible context' statements seem, and sometimes are, expressions of appropriate caution. But in my experience, they are more often cop-outs. Outside of awareness, the person is defending against therapeutic change. She is likely to discover that the occasion never seems to come when it is 'appropriate' to show her feelings, or that she seems inexplicably to have stopped 'feeling angry' just when she was on the point of expressing anger.

Useful check questions to pick up this kind of 'invisible context' are: 'If I were a fly on the wall, how would I know that the time had come when it was "appropriate" for you to show how you feel?'; 'Are you willing to show your anger even if you don't believe you feel it?'

There may be some occasions on which the client will autonomously decide to leave the context unspecified, in whole or in part. In that event, the open context gives the person more flexibility, and hence more genuine option, in deciding where, when and with whom to carry out the contract.

Conclusion

This chapter has reviewed a set of techniques that you can use during the process of contract making to help your client achieve clearly specified outcomes. As a key introductory idea, I have stressed that a contract is *not the same thing* as an outcome. Instead, a contract is a means to an end – a practical way of facilitating your client to gain the outcomes that she wants.

The chapter has offered you a set of tools to place in your contract-making toolbag. The main focus has been on the use of *language*: listening carefully to what your client is really saying, and choosing your own language with precision. The late TA trainer George Thomson (workshop presentations, unpublished), liked to teach that 'the Child is a careful grammarian'. To this I would add a favourite slogan of my own: 'What you say is what you get'.

In the language of Chapter 1, all these techniques help to transform 'soft' contracts into 'hard' contracts. This being so, whenever you consider using these practical tools, it is advisable to keep in mind the possible 'disadvantages and caveats' of hard contracts that Charlotte Sills outlines. There may be occasions when you deliberately decide to leave the contract somewhat 'soft', at least until you have developed your counselling relationship to a certain point of trust and attachment or have sufficiently clarified the issues.

Once that point is reached, then will be the time to open up your outcome-contracting toolbag. When you do, your client will be in a position to gain from the advantages of 'hard', outcome-oriented contracting. These advantages have been discussed in this and earlier chapters. But, above all, when you and your client agree a clearly specified outcome contract, you set in motion a process that empowers the client to get what he wants. 'Sabotages' and hidden agendas are minimised. The aim is to bring the overtly agreed contract as close as possible to the '"positive" psychological contract' described in Chapter 1. Focusing on a positive outcome provides the client with a powerhouse for change.

References

Andreas, C. and Andreas, S. (1989) *Heart of the Mind.* Moab: Real People Press.

Bandler, R. and Grinder, J. (1975) *The Structure of Magic Vol. I.* Palo Alto, CA: Science and Behavior Books.

Berne, E. (1966) *Principles of Group Treatment.* New York: Oxford University Press.

Cameron-Bandler, L. (1985) *Solutions.* Moab: Real People Press.

Goulding, M. and Goulding, R. (1979) *Changing Lives through Redecision Therapy.* New York: Brunner/Mazel.

Steiner, C. (1974) *Scripts People Live: Transactional Analysis of Life Scripts.* New York: Grove Press.

Stewart, I. (1996) *Developing Transactional Analysis Counselling.* London: Sage.

Stewart, I. (2000) *Transactional Analysis Counselling in Action,* (2nd edn). London: Sage.

Stewart, I. and Joines, V. (1987) *TA Today: A New Introduction to Transactional Analysis.* Nottingham: Lifespace.

Woollams, S. and Brown, M. (1979) *TA: The Total Handbook of Transactional Analysis.* Englewood Cliffs, NJ: Prentice-Hall.

6 Process Contracts

Adrienne Lee

Process contracts are those that are made moment-by-moment during the counselling or psychotherapy session as part of the interpersonal process in the here and now. They are characterised by the therapist's continuous close tracking with her client's thinking, feeling and behaviour, and by her using each change in her client's process to confirm completion and success and move on to the next contract. The usual method for eliciting this process is to ask the client 'What do you want now?' and use the reply to find some means by which the contract can be fulfilled immediately in the therapy session. Although this form of contracting is effective in individual therapy it is particularly effective in group work where the inter-personal resources are multiplied.

This chapter will describe the qualities of the process-oriented contracts. The material is mostly drawn from the practice of transactional analysis (see Berne 1966; Goulding and Goulding 1979; Ruppert and Ziff 1994; Erskine and Trautmann 1996) and its integration of Gestalt therapy techniques that focus on the cycle of Gestalt formation and here and now awareness, and techniques from NLP including presuppositions, inner alignment language patterns and reframing. I will illustrate these techniques below. The process-focused contracts are put in the context of four different stages of contracting and treatment. Guidelines for eliciting process contracts will also be presented together with examples and some annotated transcripts.

The stages of contracting

The nature and content of contracting is different at each stage of the therapeutic relationship. The success of the process contracting stage will largely be determined by the effectiveness of the two distinct stages that precede it and the one that comes after it. I shall briefly describe these stages so that the process-focused contracts are placed clearly in the context of the whole therapeutic cycle.

Stage 1: the administrative contract

Even before the therapy 'officially' begins the administrative contract stage will need to be completed. At this stage the therapist and client determine that they are indeed going to be working together and that both feel satisfied that they can give some 'mutual consideration' that is ethical and legal (see Chapters 1 and 9).

The client can more readily respond to the process question 'What do you want now?' if it is part of the mutual consideration contract. When the therapist exchanges her skills and expertise for a payment of some sort, it presupposes that the relationship can be equal in terms of gain. If the relationship is experienced as equal in this way the client is empowered and receptive to begin the dialogue and engage in the process-oriented contracts that will characterise the therapeutic journey.

Stage 2: the treatment contract

The process-oriented contracting can take place effectively within an overall treatment contract that is related congruently to diagnosis and overall treatment planning. Ian Stewart in Chapter 5 on action- and outcome-based contracts clearly delineates some qualities of the treatment contract that are drawn from TA and NLP.

The therapist who uses process contracts will usually accept a treatment contract that is softer or less specified than those described by Ian Stewart because the process contracting will not only give rise to the specifics gradually, it will also modify them in the dialogue. Ultimately they will meet the criteria Stewart suggests and will offer in the here and now clear evidence of their completion.

For example if the client's initial contract is to 'respect myself by giving myself time to be myself' the process counsellor might ask: *'And are you doing some of that now?'*. The question brings the desired experience into the counselling session instead of leaving it in some vague context that is not defined or specified.

'How are you doing it?'. This follow-up question invites the client to immediately associate into the desired state. This is a technique used in NLP to create the desired future change by neurologically and somatically accessing the experience in the present. Since the initial contract quoted above is expressed in a way that does not specify 'time' in any way the therapist has the opportunity to make use of the lack of specification to focus on the here and now – which is, after all, a 'time to be myself', for how can you *not* be yourself and *not* be in time? It is as though the therapist uses the ambiguity to draw the client out of abstract conceptualising into the concrete and clearly evidenced present moment that is part of a shared reality.

'Do you feel that you want more time now?'. Instead of asking the question 'How much time?' to achieve the necessary specificity described in TA outcome contracting, the therapist brings the question into the present and the client therefore has to put her 'want' in a frame that could either bring about immediate contract completion, i.e. by saying 'Yes', or could at least reveal the client's capacity to choose if she says 'No'.

'How much more?'. Detailed questions may follow to build on the experience of success in the here and now. These questions will model the process that can be transferred to other settings, e.g. 'When will you be doing this at home? Who do you want to be with you?'. Since the client has already achieved success in the present it presupposes that extending the experience to the world outside will also be successful. Although the client may hereby achieve the same final treatment contract that outcome-oriented counsellors might use, the process of elicitation has been an experiential rather than a cognitive process and this may be preferred by certain personality adaptations (see Chapter 8).

Stage 3: the process contracts

Having established a treatment contract the process contracts follow immediately and they relate to the treatment contract in two paradoxical ways. First, they become 'holographic' insofar as they are miniature replays of the overall treatment contract, or at least reflect and mirror it to facilitate its completion. For example, if the client's general contract is 'to make eye contact' (see Ian Stewart's example of 'over-generalised references') the process contracts will facilitate the enacting of eye contact in the here and now. This will form the blueprint for successful and confident experience with other people outside the therapy room. To use process contracting the therapist should note when the client next makes eye contact with her in the session and say, 'Now you have completed that contract what do you want now?'.

Secondly, the way in which process contracts invariably allow the overall treatment contract to evolve and transform means that the therapeutic process ceases to be a scientific or mechanical operation and instead becomes organic and spontaneous. Each new question relating to the next desired behaviour or experience takes the meaning of the original statement but subtly changes its form so that eventually the meaning also changes. To continue the example above:

'I don't mean "eye contact" literally, I mean I don't want to be afraid to see myself reflected in someone's eyes. I don't want to be hurt.'
  'What do you want instead?'
  'I want to be respected.'

When the meaning changes the client repeats the original process but in a new direction. It is rather like a plant that replicates leaves more and more abundantly; although it seems that the client has gone in many different directions, the growth has all been part of the same process and so the whole shape of the 'experience' is well balanced and has a clear overall form. In process therapy it is an important part of the therapist's job to keep the form of the whole process congruent with the treatment contract and to refer back to the latter frequently.

Stage 4: completion contracts

The organic nature of process contracts has a major limitation: contracts can go on for ever! The evolving process is obviously the experience of a lifetime, and can take a lifetime. Our metaphorical 'plant' can become a tree and the tree become a forest!

The integrity of the therapeutic relationship, however, requires a distinct space and contract for completion where the client can rest and let the learning and change impact on her life. I don't think process contracts are the same as the 'forever contracts' that Mary and Robert Goulding warn us about or the 'non-finishable contracts' described by Ian Stewart in his chapter. If the ongoing process contracts are limitless it is because they are linked. The string of pearls analogy allows us to conceptualise the separate nature of each process contract that is related to the one that comes before and the one that comes after, but that eventually can return to the beginning in a loop that can be clasped. The completion contract is the 'clasp' that will be aligned to the original treatment contract and the length of the 'string' or 'strand of contracts' will vary with each client.

'So you wanted to respect yourself by giving yourself time to be yourself, you have done that here, you have given yourself time and you have asked for what you wanted, and now that you have experienced this and go on experiencing it, what does this mean for you?'

'It means that I am important and OK just like others, and I can go on being myself.'

'Just as you are now?'

'Yes, as I am now.'

'Great. Do you feel complete?'

'Yes, complete and very satisfied, I can take time to enjoy being me.'

'Yes, you can and you are doing that now. Enjoy.'

The six qualities of process-oriented contracts

The following are ways of describing

- the basic philosophical assumptions and values of process contracts;
- the ways these are capable of being embodied in the therapeutic practice; and
- some specific guidelines for integrating them behaviourally in context.

Although there is some idea of an order for these qualities I do not propose that this is sequential and indeed the process is by its very nature a cyclical and organic one.

Acceptance of self

I am already OK.

It is important to start from the premise that whatever the client is presenting is OK. It was certainly a means once for the client to resolve a problem and in some cases was a means of survival, even though now the same behaviour or belief may be anachronistic. For example the client may have made an 'early life decision' (Goulding and Goulding 1979) 'to not show her feelings' because they were not allowed, and she was punished or shamed for showing her feelings in the family of origin.

Accepting a contract to experience and express feelings spontaneously now may imply that not expressing them is evidence of inadequacy and incompetence that is fixed in time, rather than a choice that is made each moment. Because the choice is made each moment it means that the client is OK as she is, and if something is not comfortable or unacceptable then the next 'choice' can easily change it. Because the process-oriented contracts are brought out of the context of the past and out of the context of the distant future, to the immediate future in the next moment, and the next moment, they cease to 'fix' the early decision in a time-frame and instead continuously release it into the changing 'here and now' where any judgement and shaming that may threaten self-acceptance and 'OKness' cannot hold.

Sometimes a procedure of contracting may itself suggest that the person is not OK. 'If I accept the need to change, does that mean that I am not good enough as I am?'. Although this question may not be openly articulated by the client it may be unconscious and emerge in the experience of 'stuckness' or create 'false hope' that elicits subsequent disappointment and frustration. The logic, according to David Zigmond (1990), goes rather like this:

I make a contract to change ...
  I should change ...
    I'm not OK as I am ...
      I accept myself less and less as I am ...
        My inner resistances increase ...
          STUCK.

In process-oriented contracts the idea of 'change' is softened. It is presented in moment-by-moment pieces that do not confront the client's existential position or the intrapsychic Parent that is still imposing the prohibition in the client's head. In my experience, the emphasis on new feelings and behaviour here and now, in the dialogue with the therapist or other group members, releases impasse easily and effectively because there is immediate experience of the new behaviour and immediate feedback on that experience and the consequences of the new behaviour. This immediate inner and outer processing can either permit the client to go one step further and make another process contract or enable the client to be aware of any resistance that may require a different acknowledgement and process direction. Consider the following dialogue:

'What are you feeling now?'
'I don't have any feeling at all right now.'
'What is it like not having a feeling at the moment?'

The therapist's process question both acknowledges the client's absence of feeling and implies the fact that absence of feeling is also a feeling or a sensation that can be experienced and described.

'Nothing really, a feeling of nothingness.'
'Do you want to know more about what that "nothingness" now feels like?'

This process contract question invites the client to increase her awareness of the invitation to feel and its possible consequences. (It may be advisable to repeat this question after every few interventions substituting the next feeling or thought for the word 'nothingness'.) Implicit in the therapist's question is the permission 'to feel' (Goulding and Goulding 1979) that offers a form of 'Spot Reparenting' (Osnes 1974).

'Yes.'
'Is it a sad nothingness or an angry nothingness?'

The therapist does not confront the client's distance from the feeling or the 'Be Strong' Driver (Kahler with Capers 1974) but adds the 'you have a feeling' option onto the client's 'I don't have a feeling' experience so that they don't become mutually exclusive. Both realities can be true at the same time.

'Neither of those, it feels more like a frightened nothingness.'
'Do you want to know more about why you are frightened, now?'

This contract question has brought the client closer to ownership of her feelings and she can now proceed to explore her feelings further with continued moment-by-moment contracts interspersed with invitations to take the next step. Even if the client says she does not want to know more, she now has *choice* because she is exercising it now! If she can choose *not* to be aware she can also choose to *be* aware.

'No, not really.'
'So what do you want now?'

The new process contract will now either take the client in a new direction or permit the client to retrace her steps and choose again.

Acceptance of self is an honouring experience in process contracting that also emphasises choice and the client's right to choose: there is a reason for being how you are; there is a reason for being where you are; there is a reason for what you are doing. Are these reasons still active and current? What do you want now? You have a choice now. What do you want now?

Contact

Contact precedes contract – contract makes contact.

It is easy for contracting that is based on specific behavioural formulas to become mechanistic. This can be avoided when the therapist accepts the client's reality and the positive intention behind any unconscious process. For example if the client says: 'I want to get off this world and start again!' we could say that this was 'not feasible' or 'not realistic' and invite a new contract. Alternatively, using the process contract model, we could *accept that what the client says she wants to change is actually true.*

In the above example the therapist can first acknowledge the client's reality:

'Of course you do ... the world must have been a lousy place for you up to now ... is that true?'

and then explore this experience so that it is fully accounted. It is then possible to follow gently with,

'And since today is a new start and a new beginning how do you want this new world of today to be now? ... and now?'

The process contract incorporates a 'meaning reframe' of the word 'world' in a way that allows it to be brought into the room for immediate experience. The process creates some rapport with the client's own language but it converts the concrete nouns into imagery and symbol.

If the therapist comes too quickly into an outcome contracting process there is a real possibility that the unconscious processes of the client may 'go into hiding' or that the client will become over-adapted to the perceived Parent of the therapist. We do well to be aware that many clients are shamed by such confrontation in the therapy process. Erskine and Trautmann (1996) warn us that such mismatches are experienced in the present by our clients as interruptions of contact that reflect the painful archaic internal interruptions of contact. When the client's reality or way of seeing the world is accepted and mirrored in some way by the therapist, the client experiences rapport and contact. When contact is established, contracting is integrated as part of an OK process. The relationship with the therapist becomes vitally important for the client in the same way as it was vital for the growing infant to have mirroring from her mother. Process-oriented contracts enact this mirroring without the client regressing.

Relationship in the dialogue

Resonance requires relationship – relationship permits dialogue.

The focusing on process in therapy necessitates the real responsive presence of the therapist, who needs to anticipate and be aware of her own inner feelings and behaviour in order to provide the focus and resonance for her client's process. The therapist really needs to accept how important her presence and experience are and how important she herself is in the relationship with the client in the process of change.

Emily Ruppert and Joel Ziff (1994) say that the primary principle of process work is the 'I–Thou' relationship and emphasise the need to realise 'that the contract in any relationship is an ongoing and living process which is constantly evolving'. Recent developments in neuroscience support this. In their book, *A General Theory of Love*, Lewis et al. (2001), describe the capacity of the limbic brain they call 'limbic resonance – a symphony of mutual exchange and internal adaptation whereby two mammals become attuned to each other's inner states. It is limbic resonance that makes looking into the face of another emotionally responsive creature a multilayered experience' (2001: 63).

The attachment made in process contracting is an experience of limbic resonance. The client experiences, the therapist experiences, the therapist asks, the client responds, the response creates another experience. When the therapist engages with the response, and the experience it creates, an attached relationship develops. The relationship continues to develop in the contracting process when the next question or comment grows from what has gone immediately before in an attuned, dialogic, relational way. This flow of attachment or resonance can create open and intimate dialogue and opportunity for limbic regulation and revision – in other words it can change patterns of neural activity. The same process of relatedness is stimulated intrapsychically in the client; the therapist is modelling with the client how the client may dialogue internally with themselves. The external experience of relationship and the new intrapsychic experience of relationship can then be extended successfully to others (see Figure 6.1).

Nowness

Each now is who I am.

Process-oriented contracts have already been described as a moment-by-moment procedure, but the method also makes a philosophical statement about time and empowerment. The past is established as a fixed experience that cannot be changed if all contracts concentrate on a distant future. When suggesting to the client a linear picture of time the therapist is probably also in danger of creating pathology. This may sound rather extreme, but consider how different it is when you hold the

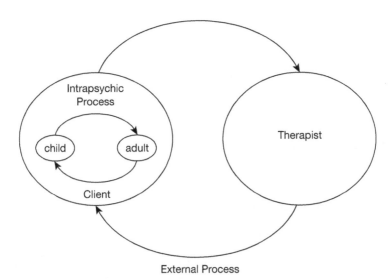

Figure 6.1   Attachment diagram (adapted from conference presentation by George Kohlreiser 1994)

basic assumption that we recreate the past in the present and so can change the past in the present. Although this is coming into vogue in the new constructionist school of transactional analysis and in more recent research about memory, it was Eric Berne himself who said that each day can be taken as an 'ego unit'.

The key to using process-oriented contracting with your clients is to keep the experience in the present and to keep asking questions that relate past experience to the present and bring future goals into the present. For example:

> 'When I was a child I was always rejected and left on my own' (Here the client has clearly restimulated the archaic pain of rejection.)
>   'I wonder what that child who was so rejected would want now if she were here? What does she want?'

The therapist begins by accepting the child in a past time-frame, transports her to the present, and then changes the tense of the verb to assume the reality of a child's presence in the room. This engagement of what transactional analysts call the Child ego state is one of the ways people bring the past into the present, often inappropriately, for it can colour the here-and-now Adult ego state, allowing the past experience to distort the evidence of the present.

> 'She wants to be cared for.'
>   'How could you care for her now?' (This moves from the disassociated state to an associated state in the present.)
> 'I don't know.'
>   'How about making some contact with her and asking her?' (Here the client is invited to engage in an inner dialogue that extends the external process-contracting to an internal or intrapsychic one. The internal dialogue may take some time and may need to be facilitated by the counsellor.)
>   'She just wants me to be here with her.'
>   'And do you want anything now?'

'Yes, I want to be with her.'
'You are already doing that. How do you feel?'

The emphasis on the present achievement of the desired experience is essential for process contracting.

'Comfortable and happy.'
'Great. And what do you want now?'
'I want to enjoy more of this.'
'Go ahead … And what do you want now?'

Organic contracting for change

There is no growth without change – no change without growth.

The organic qualities of process-oriented contracts have already been described. Perhaps all that is necessary here is to emphasise that the process needs to be kept moving and flexible so that it does not become fixed. The assumption here is that as one contract is made and then completed in the present the client is ready for the next one. The overall experience for the client is ease and success that comes with repetition. The key questions to ask the client are these:

'What do you want now?'
'What are you experiencing now?'
'And what do you want now?'
'Do you still want that or do you want something else?'
'Are you getting what you want now?'
'How will you go on getting this?'
'What needs to happen for you to get more of what you want?'
'What are you willing to do to ensure that?'
'Are you sabotaging yourself now?'
'Do you want to do something different now?'
'What are you enjoying about what you are doing?'
'Do you want to change anything else?'
'How does this new experience relate to what you first asked for?'
'What meaning does this now have for you?'
'Is that enough, or do you want more?'

Questions like these create and affirm ongoing growth, change and transformation.

Outcome or experience?

Who we may become – or who we are?

The emphasis in this form of contracting is on the present experience rather than the future outcome. It is experience that is energised and given attention and this expresses certain values that are fundamental to this process. First, that it is important to honour and enjoy and express who we are rather than what we might become. Secondly, it is the journey that is really important not the destination. It is clear that the one approach relates to 'doing' or performance and the other emphasises 'being'.

It is my belief that the therapist should not invite one of these at the expense of the other. Both the outcome and the process itself need to be honoured. The key questions, then, are 'How do we keep the outcome and the process together so that they are congruent?' and 'How do we keep the outcome and the process separate so that they don't interfere with each other?'.

A clearly defined overall outcome will be necessary to give the process shape and to build in the experience of satisfaction and pleasure that comes with completion. Gestalt therapists know well the importance of completion and pause before the new cycle of contact begins. It is therefore advisable to build in pauses and leave these gaps unfilled for a while. It is only in the 'gaps' that your client can know what she is missing and therefore access what she wants. The completion of a series of process contracts needs to be returned to the beginning contract and for the treatment contract to clasp the whole process in a meaningful whole. Often this can be achieved by asking what the present state or feeling or behaviour contributes to the original want.

Process contracting in groups

The presence of several people in a therapy group provides added resources for the process contracts. Invariably something that the client wants can be available in the present if the different relationships and dynamics of the group are used. The therapist can invite the client to use the various interpersonal resources creatively by means of the process contracts to directly experience and resolve relationship issues.

'What do you want now?'
  'I want to tell the group what happened to me when I went to see my mother on Friday'.
  'Who do you particularly want to tell that story to?'

Here the therapist confronts the possible detachment or absence of relationship by ensuring that a listener is nominated. The generalised collective noun, 'the group', sounds intimate but is in effect impersonal when there is no direct and specific contracting between individuals.

'I want to tell it to Peter.'

It is quite likely that a transferential relationship is present and in some ways is being encouraged by the client's having to choose someone. Now the telling of the story, and the relational need that can be met in the process of telling, may become more important than the content.

'Are you willing to tell Peter why it is important for you that he hears you?'

The transferential relationship can be used positively if it is recognised openly and in consciousness. This intervention also invites a new level of process contracting *between these two group members* and allows the therapist to become less dominant.

'Yes. Peter, I really want you to hear me because I don't think my father was ever around when I needed him or even if he was I couldn't be sure that he would listen or understand. I think you would, though.'

This level of insight might be unusual in an unsophisticated group but can be elicited by questions asking the client who Peter reminds her of, or to provide a guess about the reason for her choice. This might be more appropriate after the sharing has taken place. Note in this example of dialogue that the client is inviting a potential negative replay of the past if the therapist does not now establish quite clearly with the client how she will have evidence of being 'heard'.

'How will you know that Peter is listening to you and understanding you?'

In groups that are familiar with process contracting it is quite likely that Peter would ask this himself.

'I'll know you'll be listening, Peter, if you make eye contact with me while I'm talking and if from time to time you repeat back to me what you have heard me say. Are you willing to do this for me?'

Some brief negotiation may then take place between these two group members that will demonstrate that the client is *already being listened to!* The central issue may shift from the meeting with Mother on Friday to the absence of Father in the past. The healing of this in the present group process can provide both a corrective experience as well as a new perspective on the encounter with Mother that is about to be shared.

Like the unfolding of petals, the central issue is revealed gently without devaluing the separate parts. Other group members will also have their role while this particular arrangement between the client and Peter is worked out. The group members may be generalised witnesses or indeed may even become other members of the archaic or new 'family'.

The core issue will often be revealed through the choice of 'listener' and the reasons given for the choice. For example it might have provided a whole new flowering if the client had chosen a woman. After the dialogue where the client tells her story the therapist may emphasise the significance of the completion of the contract in the here-and-now process.

'Did you get what you wanted?'
'What does this experience mean for you?'
'And what do you want now?'

When using this kind of contracting in groups it is useful to nominate specific individuals rather than *go* with a process that is unstructured. Individual group members can be asked what they want while another process is going on and thus several 'pieces of work can take place simultaneously. Plenty of time needs to be given to the unfolding and the debriefing where each group member claims the relevance of the experience for themselves and also has the opportunity to 'de-role' and come into the here and now.

Ten tips for making process contracts

1 Change concrete nouns into verbs. Doing this makes the concept become more active, flexible and therefore changeable.

'I don't want any more pain, I've had enough!'
'Where are you hurting?'
'In my chest and in my stomach.'
'What needs to happen now for you to feel at ease?'

2   Turn generalised words into specific here-and-now 'testers'.

'I'm so angry!'
'Yes, and now you seem to be angry because I haven't understood you, is that true?'
'Yes.'
'And what do you want me to understand now?'

3   Turn collective nouns into named individuals.

'The family doesn't care about me.'
'Your mother? Your sister?'

'I want the group to support me in this.'
'What do you want from Peter? ... From Alice?'

4   Bring the desired experience into the present. This not only gives a specific context for the enactment of the contract; it also brings the experience into the shared reality of the present.

'How can you fulfil this now?' *or* 'Are you doing some of this behaviour now?'

5   Respond to the psychological and relational need behind each emotion.

'I feel so angry.'
'What do you want to be taken seriously? ... How can you be taken seriously now?'

'I feel so happy?
'Great! who do you want to share that with?'

'I feel so sad.'
'I'm so sorry, can I give you something you need now?'

'I feel so scared.'
'Is there some reassurance or information that you need?'

6   Change metaphor into concrete language and physiology. This allows the metaphor to be enacted in the present.

'I want to stand up for myself'
'Go ahead and stand up now.' [Encourage client to stand up.] 'What do you want when you do this?'
'I feel drained and I want some charge and energy in my life.'
'Which part of your body do you want to put your energy into at this moment?'
'My face. It feels as though I'm masked.'
'Go ahead, that's right move your lips and your eyes and your cheek muscles. Is your face energising now? What do you want now?'

7   Expand the thought/feeling/behaviour with open ended questions.

'How can you find out more about this?'

8   Accept the client's words and extend their meaning by changing the context.

'I hear that you don't like feeling nothing. Do you want to feel more of nothing or less of nothing? Is it an angry nothing or a frightened nothing?'

9   Refer back to the treatment contract. This keeps the shape and integrity of the process session.

'How does what you are doing now relate to what you came here to do?' *or* 'How is what you are doing different from what you first asked for? Do you want something else now?'

10   Notice what is happening in the present process and integrate it in the work.

'I noticed that you closed your eyes while you were saying that. What was going on for you then?'

'As you are saying this I notice that one of your hands is wrapped tightly round the other. What does your right hand want from your left hand now?'

Conclusion

Process contracting, like any other form of contracting, can become mechanistic and non-relational if not done sensitively. The dialogue and contact between therapist and client needs to be real and come from the therapist's genuine interest in the client and the client's confidence in the responsiveness of the therapist. The therapist and the client are co-creating change in the present, moment by moment. It is an energetic and intimate process that constantly unfolds to release more and more of the real self. The zen masters remind us of the profound depth and truth in simplicity and in mindfulness of the present. Process contracting honours the present fully and is not really just a means to an end. It is both the means and the end.

References

Berne, E. (1966) *Principles of Group Treatment.* New York: Oxford University Press.
Erskine, R. and Trautmann, R. (1996) 'Methods of an integrative psychotherapy', *Transactional Analysis Journal,* 26 (4): 316–28.
Goulding, M. and Goulding, R. (1979) *Changing Lives through Redecision Therapy.* New York: Brunner/Maxel.
Kahler, T. with Capers, H. (1974) 'The miniscript', *Transactional Analysis Journal,* 4 (1): 26–42.
Lewis, T., Amini, F. and Lannon, R. (2001) *A General Theory of Love.* New York: VintageBooks.
Osnes, R.E. (1974) 'Spot reparenting', *Transactional Analysis Journal,* 4: 3.
Ruppert, E. and Ziff, J. (1994) 'The mind, body and soul of violence', *Transactional Analysis Journal,* 24 (3): 161–77.
Zigmond, D. (1990) 'The making of contracts: inescapable paradoxes'. ITA conference, London.

7 Contracts and Harmful Behaviour

Geoff Mothersole

This chapter examines the place of 'no-harm contracts' in the practice of psychological therapy. Such contracts are described and are contrasted with conditions and promises. My primary focus will be on the use of contracts in the prevention of suicide and self harm, although I also refer to the use of contracts in other potentially harmful situations.

The therapeutic process can be likened to making a casserole or soup. The first task of the clinician is to ensure that a suitable pot exists, within which this can safely be done. Inevitably, there are times at the start or during clinical work when the therapeutic vessel is under threat. There is a danger of the soup spilling in a messy or harmful way. Often we can deal with potential fractures of the vessel by noting them and exploring with the client how and why they may occur. Raising the issue and seeking appropriate resolution is likely to be the most helpful response. The risk of harmful outcome is minimised by the process of talking about it with the clinician *and of feeling heard*. Whether the issue is doubt of the clinician's good will or ability, or the suicidal urges of the client, the therapeutic vessel is strengthened by the client's perception of respect, empathy and human concern from the clinician. Often, in my experience, when discussing suicide clients will spontaneously comment that they 'wouldn't do it'. Where such comments are seen as congruent in the here and now, then they may be taken as good evidence that the container is good enough.

There may be situations in which, upon reflection and after checking with the client, we are left with significant concern that the client may attempt to deal with their situation by harming themselves or someone else. We may then consider that something more is required.

The risk of practitioners experiencing a client suicide seems to be quite high, although it obviously depends on the population being worked with. Valente (1994) examining a variety of US therapists found that 15–25 per cent had had a client die by suicide. For those working with particularly disturbed populations such as nurses and psychiatrists, the figures may be higher (Kleespies et al. 1993; Valente and Saunders 2002). This highlights the need to explicitly consider the issue. Many authors have noted the widespread use of no-suicide contracts in practice (Miller et al. 1998; Simon 1999; Kroll 2000; Farrow 2002), although it sometimes seems that there is confusion in practice between contracts and promises. I believe this confusion to be unhelpful; it suggests a need for explicit training in this area, a point recognised by Range et al. (2002) and others.

Conditions, contracts and promises

In considering the value of agreements between clinician and client regarding harm to self or others, it is important to differentiate between three concepts: conditions, contracts and promises.

Conditions

First, it is possible to make client abstinence from harmful behaviours a *condition* of the therapeutic work. In such a case the clinician spells out the grounds upon which they are willing to enter into a therapeutic contract with the client. This can be extremely important when a client has a history of aggressive or violent behaviour. For example one may state clearly that any physical threats will lead to either a review of the therapeutic contract or, in more serious cases, to immediate termination of it.

Conditions for abstinence within sessions may also be considered when the client has a pattern of continual substance abuse. Given the time lag between last ingestion of the substance and its final excretion from the body, consideration may need to be given to specifying when the abstinence should begin prior to sessions. In one case I found it important to agree with a habitual cannabis smoker that they would not ingest it in the 24 hours prior to a session, thus ensuring that they were in a sufficiently drug-free state to begin the work. Such a condition is really an extension of the usual expectation that clients attend sessions fully *compos mentis.*

In my view the value of such clarity is twofold: first it helps assess whether the individual is capable of entering the therapeutic frame in a way that is containable enough. While specifying the requirements, we can observe what is going on for the client, examining any incongruities for potential sabotage on their part. If, after such attention to the process and content of the interaction regarding the requisite conditions the clinician's considered view is that the client could not reasonably be expected to hold to such a boundary, then to begin to work outside of a more containing setting would be unproductive and even unethical.

Secondly, where such a condition is made, it can be thought of as offering powerful confrontation and containment ('holding', in Winnicott's (1960) term) for the client. Equally importantly, in attending to their own physical safety, clinicians ensure that they are in a position to put their emotional energy into being therapeutic for the client, rather than being afraid and therefore at some level preoccupied and unavailable.

In addition to setting conditions on client behaviour within sessions, clinicians sometimes choose to work with an agreement that is conditional upon the client abstaining from certain behaviour outside of sessions. The classic example is substance abuses, in which a period of total abstinence from psychoactive substances is seen as a vital prerequisite to psychological work. This is not the place for a considered discussion of this topic. However, I think that it is important to base our response to such issues on thorough assessment of the problem and not to react with a knee jerk 'substance abuse equals addiction: therefore abstinence' model.

Other situations in which extra-sessional behaviour may be stipulated are where clients present a history of chaotic behaviours, associated with personality disorders or major psychiatric syndromes. Yalom (1989: 30) gives an example of making therapy conditional upon a commitment by the client to abstain from suicidal behaviour for six months stating: 'If you make any attempt – no matter how slight – then our contract is broken, and I will not continue to work with you.'

In other cases the condition is likely to focus on the clients receiving appropriate additional help. I have, for example, agreed to work with individuals with severe bipolar disorder provided that they continue to take lithium carbonate as recommended. Again such a judgement depends on thorough assessment with the client, and can be seen to have at least two effects, depending on the situation. For example with John – a client with a history of severe mood cycles and associated destructive behaviour stemming from bipolar disorder with marked borderline personality features – the requirement was, in my view, essential in confronting a potentially dangerous 'game' (Berne 1964). His pattern was to leave off medication and go into a manic depressive cycle in which the underlying tendency to polarise the involved professionals into angels and devils reached dangerous levels. In other cases my stance has not been a requirement so much as a firm recommendation, confronting the fantasy that the therapeutic process will lead to a cure of the bipolar disorder. This again is a tricky decision, requiring the balancing of a desire to be appropriately realistic and not enter into unachievable contracts that will lead to client and clinician disillusionment, with the avoidance of setting up a negative self-fulfilling prophecy (Merton 1948).

Another area in which behaviour may be addressed as part of the initial structuring of the therapeutic agreement is sexual offending. In this case the aim is to set the frame such as to leave the offender in no doubt that, whilst the therapist is respectful of them as a person, abusive behaviour will not be colluded with or accorded the usual confidentiality. Here the action is not so much a condition as a clear statement of an ethical position and of the limits to confidentiality, along with an outline of the actions that will be taken in the event of evidence of further offences. Clinically such action begins the process of challenging the cognitive distortions that occur in such offenders (see Finkelhor 1986; Salter 1988). Such work is of course highly specialised and not to be undertaken in isolation.

For obvious ethical reasons such conditions should only be made when judged absolutely necessary in order to avert serious negative outcomes to the therapeutic process. Only if there is clear and present danger that the vessel may be so flawed as to create a risk of it fracturing in a dangerous way should we consider them.

There is a major risk of the requirement being seen as a parental prohibition to be met with passivity, avoidance and even dishonesty regarding the relevant behaviours.

Often, conditions for behaviour *within* sessions are more practicable than conditions regarding behaviour *outside* sessions. This is particularly true with substance abusers, especially if one has reason to believe that they may minimise the significance of their behaviour. The condition: 'I will not work with you if *in my opinion* you are under the influence of whatever substances are relevant' is much more realistic than a general 'don't use' condition.

In general, such conditions are more likely to be required with more disturbed clients and are thus more likely to be used in specialist settings.

Contracts

In our day-to-day work we are much more likely to face situations where we do not need to impose conditions, but are nevertheless concerned. One tool that may help underpin the situation while resolution occurs is the *contract,* which can be thought of as a kind of therapeutic pit prop, shoring up the roof while the necessary work is done.

Specific contracts between client and clinician, in which the client states an intention to abstain from suicide or self harm, were first introduced into the literature by Drye et al. (1973). The most clearly articulated thoughts on the subject were for many years located within the transactional analytic framework (Drye et al. 1973; Holloway 1973; Goulding and Goulding 1979; Boyd and Cowles-Boyd 1980; Stewart 1989.) Holloway describes suicide, homicide and psychoses as 'escape hatches'. What he meant by this term is that based on our core views of ourselves we may be prone to one or all of the three behaviours as a way of escaping from the pressure, 'if things get bad enough'. The invitation for the client to commit to staying alive can be seen as a profound intervention, highlighting our individual existential choice over our life and confronting what Alvarez (1971) described as the myth that clients will be present at their own funeral.

It is important to differentiate between a *contract,* a *promise* and the *therapeutic work,* since I believe that there is some confusion about the difference. For example, Beck and colleagues (1979: 214) state: 'It is not necessary, nor even possible in most cases, to obtain a valid commitment from the patient that he will never commit suicide. A promise or "contract" to postpone suicide for a week or two may not be honoured under the pressure of a strong wish to die.' This is to confuse the notion of contract, which is a time-limited holding measure, with the therapeutic work that is needed in the longer term.

Promises

A promise is a commitment to *another person* in contrast to a contract, which involves commitment *to the self.* One of the difficulties with conditions is that they are likely to be experienced as a promise made by a less powerful supplicant to the powerful other. Such a parent-child dynamic is going to be in danger of inviting resentment or rebellion as the powerful other is responded to in a transferential fashion. In making a statement that is experienced as a promise the client may externalise their locus of control (Rotter 1966).

There may be occasions on which a promise is all that can be obtained. For example a client who feels unworthy of living, and sees the clinician as more worthy, may not be willing to abstain from suicide for their own sake, but may be willing to do so 'for' the clinician. The fact that they come to seek clinical work suggests that in some part of themselves they hold a hope of something different. This justifies seeking promises in extreme situations, since if someone continues to come they are stating that they want help. In certain cases, I believe that it can be legitimate to request a promise if that is all that will anchor the person until the issue can be dealt with.

Effective contracting

Such seeking of a client commitment to the clinician contrasts with a situation in which the client is willing to make a deal *with and for themselves,* with the clinician acting more in the role of a witness. Here the client is more likely to feel a greater degree of ownership and commitment, experiencing a greater internal locus of control of the behaviour agreed upon. The greater these two factors, the more valid the agreement will be behaviourally. Several factors help this process. First it is important that the clinician help the client clarify their answer to the question, 'who am I doing this for and why?'

Attention to the *process* of contract-setting is vital, as we note the verbal, para-verbal and non-verbal responses of the client, checking for inconsistencies and incongruence. Such incongruence may be indicated by a variety of clues, such as the linguistic structure of the client's statement; non-verbal cues (for example lack of eye contact); para-verbal cues, such as an unusual voice tone, or an over-hasty agreement with the suggestion to make a no-harm contract. A passive stance, which may be indicated by a slumped posture, and distancing, passive language needs to be checked. Thus a client who says 'I suppose so/if you want/all right then/you or one *could* ... etc.' in any way that adapts to the wishes of the clinician is likely to be feeling less ownership and commitment than someone who uses active concrete words such as 'I will', and demonstrates physical and emotional energy for the task.

An effective no-harm agreement needs to do more than just commit the client *not* to do something. Working on the principle that nature abhors a vacuum, it is important to specify with the client what action they will take instead. Such actions need of course to be relevant to the meaning that the self harm has for the client. The replacement behaviour might attempt to provide in a less damaging way some of the impact and significance of the harmful one. In respect of self harm, Layden and colleagues (1993) offer a useful list of alternatives for individuals who feel the urge to self harm. This includes writing on the skin with a soluble red pen in place of self-cutting, breaking eggs on the skin, immersing the hand in cold water, reviewing notes from previous therapeutic work and calling a sympathetic friend. To this I would also add calling the Samaritans, who are available when even the best friend may not be.

To give one example from my own practice, Andy presented in a crisis following an attempt at suicide. He committed himself to staying alive *no matter how bad he felt* via a series of weekly contracts as we dealt with his feelings of futility and depression. Towards the end of the therapy he commented how helpful he had found the contract, saying that it had served as a beacon in his time of maximum despair.

If the process is to have meaning, and be more than a token and mechanistic parroting of words geared to keep the clinician happy, it must be predicated upon a strong therapeutic bond (Bordin 1983) between clinician and client. This point is emphasised elsewhere in the literature (Simon 1999; Range et al. 2002). Where such a bond exists, the invitation to contract to stay alive is highly likely to be experienced by the client as arising from their needs and from a position of empathic understanding on the part of the clinician. This is best framed in such terms as 'I will be here (at a specified future time or indefinitely) *whatever I* (the client) *may think or feel in the meantime*' (Stewart 1989). Thus the client's pain, and the drive to act in particular ways as a result of it, is overtly acknowledged. The commitment is to refrain from certain behaviours, not to stop *feeling* in a certain way. As with any good behavioural contract, a time-frame should be set. It is best to aim for the longest achievable period. With Andy (above) a week was the longest realistic time that he could commit to. Sometimes it may be the duration of work, while in more urgent situations it may be from day to day. Either way it is essential to check and re-contract prior to the end of the stated time period. It is the clinician's responsibility to do this. Contracts must not be allowed to lapse unchecked, as this may be experienced as a 'green light' to commit the harmful act.

At the end of the process, checking and inviting restatement of the contract can add to this safety net, and be of great help in working towards deeper client ownership of the commitment. I have found it useful to ask 'How much do you believe it?' and even ask clients to rate the likelihood of keeping to the contract from 0 to 100 per cent. Where belief is low (and how low is a matter of clinical judgement depending on client circumstance), then the next question to address is 'what would need to be different for you to have more confidence in the agreement?'. Where possible, I believe that this should be raised in the session. I find it helpful to do it in a way that poses lack of client belief/commitment as a problem for us to address jointly.

In addition to checking the client's belief, the clinician needs to be constantly checking their own. If after the fullest attention has been paid, we do not believe that the client will hold to their contract, we have another series of choices: where the damage caused by slippage from the contract is wholly or largely to the client, we may simply identify, and work with, what is going on. Thus with a client who made a contract not to put themselves at risk through unprotected sex and who subsequently engaged 'accidentally' in it, the focus became the conflict between the 'rational' and the 'risky' parts of themselves. Where the risk is even more acute, as with threatened suicide, we need to think through with the client the appropriateness of other options such as extra sessions or psychiatric help. It may be of course that we decide that for ethical, clinical or practical reasons we can, or should, do no more than continue to offer our service and skill, taking to supervision and personal therapy our grandiose fantasies of being able to help everyone.

Where the risk is to another, the ethical and legal picture is more complex. In the UK there are legal requirements regarding our responsibilities to inform relevant authorities when we have evidence regarding potential terrorist offences or international drug trafficking (see Chapter 9). Beyond this the legal position is unclear, and we do not for example have legislation (unlike in the USA) requiring us to act if a third party, such as a spouse, is in serious physical danger. Ethically however, I believe that there are extreme situations in which one may wish to breach confidentiality and pass on our concern to someone we consider to be in danger. An example is where a client with a history of violence is murderously angry with a spouse and expressing an intent to use violence. Our ethical position here rests on our informing people at the start of our work that there may be extreme circumstances in which we reserve the right to act *if the client appears unable or unwilling to do so*. Spelling out the limits of confidentiality is in line with the BACP's and other codes of ethics and provides an honest and clear boundary. As we become more litigious, it may even be wise to have such conditions and limits in writing.

Research on contracts

In recent years there has been an increase in interest in the area of no-suicide contracts and some empirical research. Reviewing the field, Miller et al. (1998)

concluded that no-suicide contracts were widely used but overvalued. They made the point that of their sample of 112 US psychologists and psychiatrists, most had never had any training in this area. In a survey of 514 Minnesota psychiatrists, Kroll (2000) found that around half used no-suicide contracts with patients. Of those who did use this approach, 41 per cent had patients who had completed or made a serious attempt at suicide *after* entering a no-suicide contract. In considering this figure two things are important. First this psychiatric patient group was presumably at very high risk of suicide, and there may be issues of training and practice as highlighted by Miller et al. (1998). Nevertheless, Kroll's figures demonstrate the need to be humble in our claims about the effectiveness of no-suicide contracts.

There is little empirical work on the experience of the client. Farrow et al. (2002), in a qualitative study involving nurses in New Zealand, comment that patients find the tool unhelpful. It is somewhat unclear, however, on what basis this statement is made. On the other hand, Davis et al. (2002) found that of 135 psychiatric patients hospitalised as being at risk of suicide, most rated their no-suicide contract positively. Interestingly those with a more serious previous history of attempts tended to find the contract less helpful.

Overall, interpreting the literature is made difficult by differences in the practice of contracting, with some studies appearing to be describing conditions and promises rather than contracts as defined here. The field is ripe, as Range et al. (2002) note, for more rigorous research.

Capacity

No-harm agreements are useful when there is a conflict for the client – an impasse or struggle between opposing parts of the self. If there is no conflict, there is no need for a contract, as either the therapeutic issue has been resolved or the act is done. If the client is in the session, I assume that there is a conflict, even if there is little overt sign of it, and my job is to bolster the healthy side.

I find it useful to ask myself 'Does this person need something more?' and 'Who would the contract be for primarily?'. If, on checking with the client, it is clear that they want to be heard and that is enough for now, I would not suggest a contract.

I would of course be checking closely for suicidal thoughts and plans, and fantasies of violence or 'craziness'. Not seeking a contract is not the same as allowing the issue to drop. If I decide, upon reflection, that a contract may help me feel better at having 'done something' but would not be helpful to the client, again I would not push it. Apart from being ethically dubious there would be little point.

Where I start to consider such contracts is with individuals who have previous histories of harmful behaviours. In respect of suicide, for example, it is known (Hawton and Fagg 1988) that individuals who have attempted suicide are 27 times more likely to kill themselves eventually. Other risk factors are psychiatric and substance abuse problems, social isolation, middle/old age, antisocial behaviours and lack of specific reasons for previous attempts (Lemma 1996). It is also well established that men are two or three times more likely to kill themselves than women. In 1992, 72 per cent of suicides in the UK were men. The figures are reversed for suicide attempts (McIntosh and Jewell 1986; Lester 1990).

Suicide risk increases when individuals are coming out of serious depression, so a particular check needs to be kept at such times. It has also been found (Beck et al. 1985, 1989) that the best predictor of future suicide is the level of hopelessness exhibited by the client. When the client sees the future as unremittingly negative, we should think of suicide and consider the applicability of a contract.

With regard to violence, the picture is less clear, with past history being only somewhat predictive of future violence. A contract here is likely to be helpful when the individual acknowledges that they may become violent *and* that it is a problem.

In both cases, the best information is gained by exploring with the client their current view of their situation, and comparing this to current and past patterns. Only by careful analysis of the requisite behaviour and its antecedents can we hope to achieve a viable contract. Thus with a drinker who gets into fights when drunk, it may be pointless to have a contract about the violence at the point when it may occur. What may be more productive is a contract for earlier in the behavioural sequence, perhaps to limit alcohol intake, or avoid certain settings when in certain moods, etc. Similarly, clients with a history of psychotic episodes are only likely to benefit from contracts after they have done considerable work building their rational, self-caring ability in a way that will hold under stress. Clients who have psychotic histories with a strong biological underlay are unlikely to be helped by such contracts in outpatient settings. Indeed to imply that they may be able to make a contract could be abusive in that it implies a control that is not possible. Here again, contracts relating to how to manage themselves may be more helpful.

Assessment

I hope that it is clear by now how central assessment is to the whole concept of no-harm contracts. Unless we know what we are dealing with we run the risk of being lulled into a false sense of security. As Simon (1999) pointed out, contracts are no substitute for sound clinical judgement. Crucial to a sound assessment is previous history, especially of suicidal or overtly self-destructive behaviours. We need to make judgements about the client's tendencies to act in an impulsive manner, since any such tendency suggests that a contract might be unlikely to hold. Any history of acting in a problematically impulsive manner needs to be taken seriously. Substance use can of course have the same disinhibiting effect, and any contract needs to explicitly take this into account.

Our ability to begin to identify issues where no-harm contracts might be useful can be improved by the use of a standard measure such as the CORE Outcome Measure (see Evans et al. 2000) which contains six items that can identify risk issues. Beck's Depression and Hopelessness Inventories can provide very useful information in respect of self harm.

Our assessments should not just be of the external word of the client, but should also include examining our own motivations. The more we are acting out of fear and a desire for self protection, the more we need to question our desire to invite a contract. It is very easy to want to rush to do something as a way of avoiding looking into the intense light of powerful emotions.

Perhaps the most important factor in assessment is the realisation of the limitations on what we can offer, which are sometimes only too apparent. An example might help. Like most genuine clinical cases it is messy and can be interpreted in many ways and on many levels.

Case Example

I saw Sally in an outpatient setting whilst she was a voluntary patient in psychiatric hospital. She had a long history of depression, suicide attempts and serious self harming, the latter continuing during her hospital stay. With her full knowledge, I was in regular communication with ward staff. During the course of our work, which continued over some months, she agreed to refrain from trying to kill herself, with those agreements being discussed at every weekly meeting. She did not feel able to abstain from self-cutting, although we worked to find suitable alternatives for the times when she felt overwhelmed by her self loathing. This self harm continued, and included serious deep cuts to her arms and stomach. She told both ward staff and myself that once she had completely covered her body in scars, then she would be able to kill herself. At our final meeting she was ambivalent in her commitment to being present at our next meeting. I shared my concern with her and sought to obtain a commitment to stay alive. When it became clear that this would not be forthcoming, I let her know that I would share my serious worries with ward staff, as had been made clear in our initial agreement. I did this immediately, saying that in my opinion she was in imminent danger of suicide. Her key worker agreed that they would maintain a close watch on her, and would discuss our shared concerns when she returned. Having returned to the ward, she later went home on leave, where she killed herself.

This sad story illustrates more than just the limitations of no-harm contracting, however. It shows how the whole process of contracting provides us with an ongoing check on someone's mental state. With Sally I knew when the danger peaked and was able to do something about it, albeit sadly not enough. Without drifting too far into self-justification, the fact that I had done what I could was very helpful afterwards.

Conclusion

Contracts relating to harmful behaviours can potentially reduce the risk of those behaviours, provided that they are entered into with full reference to all the circumstances pertaining to the situation. Contracts are not a substitute for a solid working alliance, although they might (as in the case of Andy) strengthen the alliance. Neither should contracts be seen as a substitute for a full assessment and good clinical judgement. In using contracts timing is crucial, since they depend on the ability of the client to access a rational, self-caring part of themselves at the appropriate time. It is very easy for the invitation to contract to be experienced by the client as an implicit instruction not to talk about painful issues and this must be sensitively avoided.

Applied with such care, they underpin the functional side of the client against the internal pressure of their destructive urges. In bolstering this side while the work is done, they can literally be life-saving.

References

Alvarez, A. (1971) *The Savage God*. London: Weidenfeld and Nicholson.

Beck, A., Rush, A.J., Shaw, B.F. and Emery, G. (1979) *Cognitive Therapy of Depression*. New York: Guilford Press.

Beck, A., Steer, R., Kovacs, M. and Garrison, B. (1985) 'Hopelessness and eventual suicide: a ten year prospective study of patients hospitalized for suicidal ideation', *American Journal of Psychiatry*, 142: 559–66.

Beck, A., Brown, G. and Steer, R. (1989) 'Prediction of eventual suicidal in psychiatric inpatients by clinical ratings of hopelessness', *Journal of Consulting and Clinical Psychology*, 57: 309–10.

Berne, E. (1964) *Games People Play*. New York: Grove Press.

Bordin, E.S. (1983) 'A working alliance based model of supervision', *Counselling Psychologist*, 11 (1): 35–42.

Boyd, H.S. and Cowles-Boyd, L. (1980) 'Blocking tragic/scripts', *Transactional Analysis Journal*, 10 (3): 281–3.

Davis, M.S., Williams, I.W. and Hays, L.W. (2002) 'Psychiatric inpatients' perceptions of written no-suicide agreements: an exploratory study', *Suicide and Life Threatening Behaviour*, 32 (1): 51–66.

Drye, R., Goulding, R. and Goulding, M. (1973) 'No suicide decision: patient monitoring of suicide risk', *American Journal of Psychiatry*, 130: 171–4.

Evans, C., Mellor-Clark, J., Margison, F., Barkham, M., McGrath, G., Connell, J. and Audin, K. (2000) 'Clinical outcomes in routine evaluation: the CORE-OM', *Journal of Mental Health*, 9: 247–55.

Farrow, T.L. (2002) 'Owning their expertise: why nurses use "no suicide contracts" rather than their own assessments', *Australian and New Zealand Journal of Opthalmology*, 11 (4): 214–19.

Farrow, T.L., Simpson, A.F. and Warren, H.B. (2002) 'The effects of the use of "no-suicide contracts", in community crisis situations: the experience of clinicians and consumers', *Brief Treatment and Crisis Intervention*, 2: 241–6.

Finkelhor, D. (1986) *A Sourcebook on Child Sexual Abuse*. London: Sage.

Goulding, R. and Goulding, M.L. (1979) *Changing Lives through Redecision Therapy*. New York: Grove Press.

Hawton, K. and Fagg, J. (1988) 'Suicide and other cases of death following attempted suicide', *British Journal of Psychiatry*, 152: 145–53.

Holloway, W. (1973) *Shut the Escape Hatch*. Monograph. Holloway.

Kleespies, P.M., Penk, W.E. and Forsyth, J.P. (1993) 'The stress of patient behaviour during clinical training: incidence, impact and recovery', *Professional Psychology: Research and Practice*, 257–63.

Kroll, J. (2000) 'Use of no-suicide contracts by psychiatrists in Minnesota', *American Journal of Psychiatry*, 157: 1684–6.

Layden, M.A., Newman, C.F., Freeman, A. and Byers-Morse, S. (1993) *Cognitive Therapy of Borderline Personality Disorder*. New York: Allyn and Bacon.

Lemma, A. (1996) *An Introduction to Psychopathology*. London: Sage.

Lester, D. (1990) 'If women are so depressed, why don't more of them kill themselves?', *Psychological Reports*, 66: 258.

McIntosh, J. and Jewell, B. (1986) 'Sex difference trends in completed suicide', *Suicide and Life Threatening Behaviour*, 16: 16–27.

Merton, R.K. (1948) 'The self fulfilling prophecy', *Antioch Review*, 8: 193–210.

Miller, M.C., Jacobs, D.G., Gutheil, T.G. (1998) 'Talisman or taboo: the controversy of the suicide-prevention contract', *Harvard Rev Psychiatry*, 6 (2): 78–87.

Range, L.M., Campbell, C., Kovac, S.H., Marion-Jones, M., Aldridge, H., Kogos, S. and Crump, Y. (2002) 'No-suicide contracts: an overview and recommendations', *Death Studies*, 26 (1): 51–74.

Rotter, J.B. (1966) 'Generalized expectancies for internal versus external control of reinforcement', *Psychological Monographs. General and Applied*, 80.

Salter, A.C. (1988) *Treating Child Sex Offenders and Victims: A Practical Guide.* London: Sage.

Simon, R.I. (1999) 'The suicide prevention contract: clinical, legal, and risk management issues', *Journal of American Acad Psychiatry Law*, 27 (3): 445–50.

Stewart, I. (1989) *Transactional Analysis Counselling in Action.* London: Sage.

Valente, S.M. (1994) 'Psychotherapists' reactions to a patient's suicide,' *American Journal of Orthopsychiatry*, 64: 614–21.

Valente, S.M. and Saunders, J.M. (2002) 'Nurses' grief reactions to a patient's suicide', *Perspectives in Psychiatric Care*, 38 (1): 5–14.

Winnicott, D.W. (1960) 'The theory of the parent–infant relationship', in *The Maturational Process and the Facilitating Environment.* New York: New York University Press.

Yalom, I. (1989) *Love's Executioner.* London: Penguin.

8 Making Contracts with Different Personality Types

Charlotte Sills and Max Wide

In Chapter 1, Sills describes how Bordin (1994) identified *goals, tasks and bonds* as essential elements of the working alliance. Bordin's research suggested that a shared agreement about the goal of the therapeutic encounter is vital to its successful outcome, an assertion which is supported by a wealth of other research evidence. However, finding such a shared agreement – or contract – seems sometimes to be easier said than done. While some clients can readily and easily formulate their goals, others find goal-setting an excruciating experience. They either seem unable to do it, feeling trapped or in some way overlooked by the contract, or they make a contract for a particular change, then fail to achieve it, causing guilt or resentment in themselves and frustration in the practitioner. For some clients the naming of the achievable outcome is a significant part of the therapeutic process which instills in them hope and purpose. For others an attempt, as they see it, to reduce the complexity of their experience to one sentence feels at best irrelevant and at worst insulting. This problem is particularly highlighted if the therapist's preferred method of working is to agree an overall goal and then make intermediate goals or sessional contracts along the way. The consulting room can become a battleground where endless analyses of problems and solutions or discussions over failed homework assignments can overtake the counselling. In addition to all this, there is the possibility of another type of problem that can emerge gradually during the therapy – the client makes and keeps satisfactory contracts but nothing seems to change in terms of his integration and development.

Sometimes these difficulties arise from a lack of flexibility about the nature of the contract and we have found that the contracting matrix (see page 16) can be helpful in identifying different types of goal. However, we have also found that the personality style of the individual (and the therapist) can play a key part in the difficulties and it is important to take this into account. Different personalities have different channels by which they make contact with themselves and others. These channels dictate a process by which goals can be set that not only address the relevant issue but also 'feel' right to the client. In this chapter, we look at Jungian typology as a way of understanding personality types and examine its usefulness in setting an appropriate therapeutic goal.

First, however, we will briefly introduce another typology which we have found to enrich the Jungian model. Since the dawn of psychological therapy, there have been countless models that sort human personality into types or categories. Some of these are linked to developmental stages, some to defences, some to ways of managing the world, some to systems of pathology, such as the *American Diagnostic and Statistical Manual* (current edition *DSM-IV-TR®*). A version of this last type of classification is found in Paul Ware's 'Doors to therapy' (1983) which describes six personality adaptations. These are not disorders, they are ways that people adapt to and relate to the world and can therefore be useful at understanding a person's here-and-now relating. Taking three basic aspects of human experience – thinking, feeling and behaviour – Ware shows how each of these personalities has what he calls an 'open door' – that aspect of themselves which is most evident and with which they meet the world; a 'target door' – that aspect which needs to be better integrated; and a 'trap door' – the area where change will occur only when the client has 'been through' the two previous doors. One personality (categorised as *hysteric*), for example, has an open door of feeling, a target of thinking and a trap door of behaviour. Another person (*paranoid* type) has an open door of thinking, a target door of feeling and a trap door of behaviour. This has implications for the process of making contracts. The first client, even if her overall aim is to find a job that she likes (a behavioural goal), needs to be met at the feeling level and to make an initial contract about being aware of her feelings, naming them and thinking about what they mean. The choosing of a type of work, and looking for a job, comes much later. The second client needs to think through the reality of the situation first, before allowing himself to feel and then take action. Only then might it be appropriate for him to make a contract for a new way of behaving based on his uncovered needs and feelings. And so on.

Leigh and Gilbert (1992) link these 'doors', and the progression through the therapeutic process to different levels of inner conflict related to early object relations, with the 'trap door' representing the deepest and therefore least cognitively accessible level of difficulty. It follows that a client at the start of therapy would be unlikely to be able to articulate and make a contract about the ultimate change he or she may want to make in this area. She may do so out of a sense of it being required of her, but without being able to embrace it with her whole self.

The potential disadvantage of a system that uses this sort of personality typology is that it has the effect of labelling and categorising a person as having particular problems. Ware's model was later revised by Kahler (1979) who wanted to apply it in organisations and so translated the types into more descriptive rather than diagnostic labels ('enthusiastic over-reactor', 'playful sceptic', etc.). However, there is still the implication of something fixed and unchanging with this kind of taxonomy. What is more, being rather complex, it risks inviting a sort of rote application of procedures. For this reason, we are not describing it in detail. Its great strength is in heightening the awareness of the practitioner to the different ways of approaching clients so that they can deliberately choose to experiment with the different doors in order to achieve more effective contract making. It is this idea that we bring to the second typology.

Jungian typology

A method of identifying personality types proposed by Carl Jung (1971) is appealing because it uses four aspects of human functioning which are common to everyone. It describes preferences and styles rather than pathology and it provides a useful model for understanding the differences between people in a way that appreciates the attributes of all rather than finding some 'better' or 'healthier' than others. Most importantly it is a dynamic model rather than a static one, and can bring understanding to the lively flow of here-and-now communication. We find that it gives useful clues to the process of contract making – not only with clients but in organisations and also in ordinary life. Jung's ideas were developed later into more formal categories (the Myers-Briggs type indicator, 1956; or the Keirsey temperament sorter 1978), but here we are staying with the more fluid possibilities of the original.

The four functions

Jung identifies four aspects of human functioning which he called: sensing, intuiting, thinking and feeling. The first two functions concern people's way of perceiving themselves and the world and receiving information from it. The second two relate to how we make judgements and decisions about ourselves and the world. Everyone has the capacity to use all four functions but each of us has a preferred way of gathering information and a preferred way of organising it. In turn, of these preferred functions we are likely to have one function which is the strongest and most effective for us. We may then refer to ourself as a person who favours feeling or who favours sensation; or in shorthand as a 'sensation type', 'a thinking type', and so on.

Sensation types literally use their five senses (seeing, hearing, touching, tasting, smelling) to gather information and make sense of the world. This means that 'sensers' attach high importance to tangible facts. They notice details and are excellent at working through problems in a systematic and logical way. Realistic and practical, they are normally methodical and efficient though they can at times become overly concrete as their attention to facts may mean that they miss possibilities. They are grounded in the present and enjoy activities, often physical ones.

Intuitive types tend to overlook details – even becoming impatient with them as they see the world in a broader way, absorbing a wide range of data and making sense of it as an impression of the whole. When seeing the following ... sensers are more likely to see 'a row of dots' while intuitives may see 'a pause with something to follow'. Intuitives are especially different from sensers in that they are more interested in possibilities and new ideas for the future than they are in the realities of the present. Seeing patterns and connections between things, they are comfortable with change and good at initiating projects; they are exceptionally strong at knowing what should happen next. However, they are not so effective at carrying through a project in a systematic way, as the senser would do.

The thinking type, as the name implies, likes to think things through carefully in a logical and objective way. While they do have emotions, they are likely to put them on one side while they address a situation logically in order to work out the correct and fair solution. The thinker is rational, good at analysing and operates from clear and firm principles. He can sometimes appear rather unsympathetic as he deals with the facts and their consequences rather than how people feel or how they are affected.

Although the feeling type may be more free in showing emotions than the thinker, the word feeling in this case refers not to emotions but to a deeper experience of whether things 'feel right'. This means that they are likely to attach importance to subjective impressions – both their own and others. Feeling types are concerned with connection between people and are swayed in their judgements by how people feel in any situation. Their understanding of people is based on their empathy and ability to identify with others' feelings and circumstances. This empathic under-standing inevitably springs from their own experience of life, which some-times leads them to believe that what 'feels true' because it has been true in the past must be true still. They can therefore appear illogical to other people – particularly thinkers.

The four types reflect their preferences in the way they communicate. Imagine four people going into a room and then later being asked to describe that room.

The senser will focus on facts and detail. For example, 'The room is about 12 foot by 12 foot. It has two windows facing east. There is a bed in one corner, opposite a chest of drawers with a television on it. There are pictures and other decorations on the walls. On the other side of the room, there are two large chairs facing each other about five feet apart and a small, square table with a music deck on it. There are a lot of clothes on the floor and there is a slight smell of socks.'

The feeler may say: 'It's a large room, full of clutter – clothes, papers, pictures, mess. The walls are pale grey, with dark grey velvet curtains. It is an impersonal room, even though it's full of signs of life. His clothes are everywhere, heaps of CDs and so on. And the walls covered with pictures – photos of people and strange shapes. It has a nice big bed with a big duvet on it, covered in some dark material. It has chairs for sitting around. It has nice high ceilings which make it light and spacious although it is too untidy to really enjoy.' There is attention to atmosphere and impression, the focus on colours, space and subjective response. The feeler has noticed that the room's occupant is a man but probably does not know how she knows.

The thinking type may say: 'It's a bedroom, with seats in it. It's very untidy. On every surface, there are jeans, trainers, shirts and the like as well as sports clothes and equipment. The room clearly belongs to a young man who plays sport. There are few books, and those visible are related to sports or are humorous, comic type, so I assume that the person is not very academic in his interests. There are many photos on the wall – presumably of family and friends. There are also many pieces of artwork – drawings, models, etc. They are not formally presented so are proba-bly the work of the occupant.' Like the senser, the thinker pays attention to facts and details but in this case for the purpose of drawing conclusions, categorising, making sense of the contents of the room.

The intuitive type may say: 'The room is a student's study-bedroom. It's part of an old house – there's a blocked up chimney breast; if it were opened up it would make a really nice focus for the room. I wonder if the original fireplace was marble. It's got assorted furniture – probably passed on from some other room. If you put a sofa-bed in it instead of the bed and got some interesting bits of furniture it would make a much nicer space. It's probably used for sitting around playing cards or chatting as well as sleeping. If the tree outside the window was trimmed back it would have a view of the hills.' Notice the focus on links and connections, on possibilities and potential.

Nobody, of course, is purely one type. We are a unique blend of functions. Some of us are very strong in one or two functions and weak in the others. Some are only slightly stronger in one of the functions. It is further complicated by the fact that some people are introvert – in other words they tend to refer inward to their own experience to make sense of the world – while others are extravert – looking outwards and responding to others. This difference affects how the functions are manifested.

One important point that comes out of the work is that we all have a weak function, which will be the opposite of our strong one. Thus an intuitive type will be weak in sensing, and vice versa. A feeling type will be weak in thinking, and vice versa. Jung suggests that our weak function is largely in our unconscious and will therefore be least under our own control. The implication for contract making is that it would be anathema to make a contract in the area of the weak function, or to use the weak function to negotiate the contract. Thus, an intuitive type coming into therapy cannot make a contract to notice sensory details or make specific behavioural changes. At best it would feel alien, at worst impossible or imprisoning. Similarly, sensation types are so grounded in the facts that they cannot say what they want for the future or create options for themselves. Feeling types cannot think about problems and decide on solutions without feeling their way through. And thinking types cannot say how they feel (other than negatively, such as anxious or depressed) nor know how they might feel in other circumstances. Here, the work of Ware can be very useful in two ways. First, it suggests that each of us has our own particular sequence in our effective functioning. The second is that our weakest function (in Ware's terms, the trap door) cannot be addressed 'head on' and can change only after other functions have been integrated.

Each person needs to use his or her preferred function to articulate the goal they want, and gradually elicit the aid of their other functions – arriving at their inferior function in careful stages. It is a process of integration, both personally and in the contract making. The therapist can help by using interventions or comments that intentionally elicit a particular function as a step towards developing a contract. For example, to elicit:

- *Intuition*: 'Where do you see this going, how will it turn out?' 'When you know what you need to know, what will you be doing?' 'What's your hunch?'
- *Sensation*: 'What do (did) you notice?' 'What happened then?' 'What is going on in your body?' 'Notice how your shoulders are feeling.' 'Stand up and say that.'
- *Feeling*: 'How do you feel?' 'What's that like for you?' 'You seem to be feeling …' 'How has it felt/been in the past?' 'What do you know in your heart?'
- *Thinking*: 'What do you think …?' 'What are your thoughts?' 'What sense do you make of that?'

Some interventions can move from one function to the next, as in 'Tell me what you are thinking …' (sensing to thinking); 'I'm interested to know how you're feeling' (thinking to feeling). Also, note that any question actually invites thinking and a reflection or empathic response can avoid that.

Of course, the relationship between client and practitioner will have an effect on (both) people's presentation. We would describe a room differently if we were talking to our friend over coffee than we would to an estate agent. The other person's response would again affect how we continued the conversation.

The therapist may not be sure of the client's type before proceeding with making the contract. In this case, he can simply monitor the effect of interventions in the four areas; notice if the client responds with confidence or with discomfort to suggestions for behavioural change, for expression of feelings, for a thoughtful analysis or an imaginative leap. The therapist can observe the effects of the process on the client and respond flexibly.

The therapist will also have his own personality style and functional preferences, and in the back and forth of the co-created relationship there is possibility and novelty as the two people interact. A full exploration of this is beyond the scope of this chapter. Suffice it to say that an awareness of his or her own typology can assist the therapist to identify and be responsive to impasses in the contracting process. Being aware of his biases helps him to stay available for experimentation and avoid the blinkered repetition of favourite therapeutic avenues. It is a powerful argument for the necessity of a therapist pursuing his own 'inner work' of self understanding.

The use of time-frame in contract making

One aspect of the Jungian types which can be very useful to keep in mind is that of relationship to time. As we have indicated, the sensation type is very present orientated. He will therefore be quite amenable to looking at his behaviour in the present, and the evidence he has for the conclusions he draws. He will also be open to experimenting with different behaviour which he will then think about and feel. The intuitive is future orientated. She will be open to looking forwards, seeing what might be or could be, but will be most unwilling to be tied down to a specific behavioural outcome. The feeling type is attached to tradition and the past. She tends not to know what she knows. She will be able to link her present to her past through feeling connections. She needs to flesh out the experience of being herself by finding words for it. The thinker can link past, present and future through thinking. She will be able to identify causes and effects, work out what is happening, why that is going wrong and what needs to be done differently.

Approaches to making contracts with different personality types

It follows that there are different ways of approaching contracting which are sensitive to both the counsellor's and the client's relationship to time. We emphasise at this point that there is no right way of proceeding; we hope that the examples will prove helpful in illuminating certain aspects in the process of making contracts.

Making contracts with the feeling type

The feeling type tends to be focused on the past. In our experience they are unlikely to be able in the short term to make a contract that is focused on the present. Take the following example:

Therapist:	So, what do you want to get out of our work together?
Client:	Oh, I don't know.
Therapist:	[silence]
Client:	[sighs]

This is a dead end. If the therapist were to continue in this vein she would simply plug away on the same theme, becoming more and more frustrated whilst the client feels more and more inadequate. This kind of question has the effect of driving the client against his limitations, confusing the eventual goal with the stepping stone. The question has a bias toward thinking and the future. In Ware's terms therefore it jumps straight to the *eventual* goal, hitting the trap door head on. As a client once remarked, 'If I knew the answer to that I wouldn't be here.'

We have found that the best way to make contracts with 'feeling' types is to model the process of therapy in the making of the contract.

Therapist:	How are you?
Client:	Oh there's been so much going on, I don't know whether I'm coming or going. I'm being bombarded all the time with other people's demands on my time, at work and at home. If only I could find a way to stop and look after myself for a while I'd be all right.
Therapist:	You sound really distressed…
Client:	I have been – well, I am.
Therapist:	… and you were saying that if you found a way of looking after yourself you would be all right.
Client:	Oh … yes.
Therapist:	Is that what you would like to find today?
Client:	Yes.

In this exchange the focus is very different and results in an outcome that both client and therapist can work with. The therapist met the client at his contact door of feeling and in the exchange moves from the past to the present. Once the client had *expressed* what he had been feeling then he was able to move to the present, start to think about the implications of what he is saying, and identify what he needed.

Making contracts with the intuitive type

Intuitives tend to be focused on possibilities, patterns and the future. They may become impatient with details and routine procedures – even though these are the very things that they may need to learn to deal with in order to make their possibilities real. Intuitives may not respond very well to detailed behavioural contracts. However, especially if they have thinking as their second strong function, they may respond very well to being asked to name their overall goal clearly. It allows them to look forwards and envisage the future. This is well and good as long as this sort of contract – rather like salt – is used sparingly to avoid hemming the intuitive in and imposing a structure which the client may experience as punitive or ponderous.

Our example in this section is about an 'end of session' contract which some people may use to help the client determine how they might carry forward the work they have done that day.

Client: That's it. That's what's been bothering me. I've not been true to myself and what I think and feel. I've been letting other people dictate the terms and missing out on the things that make me happy and satisfied and I've been doing it everywhere, in my relationship, in my job, even playing cricket!! ... That's what I need to change.

It may be tempting to some counsellors to invite the client at this point to make a detailed contract for behavioural change wherein he would specify precisely what he is prepared to do to be 'true to himself' in each of the areas he identifies. However, that would be leaping from the strongest function, intuition, to its opposite and therefore the weakest function, sensation. The key consideration is whose agenda that would follow and whether the client would experience that as useful or whether he would feel that his great insight has swiftly been turned into a chore or an irrelevancy. This is a time to tread carefully and be guided by the client:

Therapist: What's your hunch, do you reckon you can change?
Client: Yes.
Therapist: All at once? Be true to yourself in all things?
Client: No.
Therapist: How should we proceed then? What would be most useful to you now?
Client: I guess I could pick one area, and start small. Like I *hate* being stuck out on the boundary all the time on the cricket field. I could try telling the skipper and ask him to move me in-field.

Notice that the counsellor invites the client to use his intuition to work out what to do next. The client therefore uses his greatest strength in order to think and identify a behavioural goal he can cope with. That way the 'contract' is in fact the client's *idea* – for which he has energy and enthusiasm.

Making contracts with the sensation type

Sensation types tend to be focused on the present, on real experiences and tangible facts. They may know they are 'not very happy' but not know what to do about it. They may do things according to routine or by rote and be unsure why they do them or what the possibilities for change are.

Therapist: So what do you want to do today?
Client: I want to talk about Christmas, which is keeping me awake at night. There are the things I agreed to do last week. Also I have been having terrible arguments with my daughter.

Notice in this opening that the practitioner's first question uses the contract door of facts and actions, asking the client what he wants to do and the client responds in the same vein. This at first sight is a valid contract in the sense that both parties are clear about what is to be done, but the goal is missing. The focus is on 'talking about' the present and the client seems stuck.

Therapist: Am I right in thinking that you want to cover those topics because you don't want to be awake at night, and you don't want to have terrible arguments?

Client:	Yes. Absolutely. I am worn out with it all. I want some peace and quiet.
Therapist:	I see, and do you find talking it through with me helps? Did it help last week?
Client:	Yes.
Therapist:	How does it help, do you think?
Client:	Well, I find it helps to get things off my chest. I like it when you challenge me too. People just agreeing with me or sympathising all the time is no use, it doesn't work.
Therapist:	You sound very definite about that, 'it doesn't work'. Could you describe to me what 'work' means?
Client:	Well, I feel better, more calm, more content, clearer.
Therapist:	And that's how you want to feel?
Client:	Yes!

Notice in this example that the therapist's interventions enable the client to move beyond the behavioural into thinking (her second-strongest function) and then into feeling; articulating her goal and thinking about what is helpful in getting there. The therapist's interventions help her to get there by using her strength, which lies in her talking about her experience in tangible ways. In this way she moves from the present to the past and will eventually use that reflection to plan her next step.

Making contracts with the thinking type

The thinking type can be very analytical, perhaps rather aloof; out of touch with their own feelings as well as those of others. The contract format (for example see Chapter 1, p. 18 and Chapter 5) is likely to suit the thinking type very well. A problem can arise with the thinking type, however, which is that she may be very clear in the articulation of her goals, but that process may in itself limit her. The fact that she has articulated her goals so readily means that, by definition, they are imaginable within her existing frame of reference. Nothing *really* new can happen. In Ware's terms she may get to the contract door and never move beyond it. The process of making contracts therefore would be the same as in the other examples: allow the person to use her strength to identify the contract, which in the beginning seems out of her reach.

In this example the client and the counsellor are reviewing a contract they made some time ago.

Client:	Well I think I've met most of the goals we agreed on. I have been clearer with my sister about when she can and cannot come to stay. I have made up my mind about which training course to do.
Therapist:	So you have done all the things that you said you would do?
Client:	Yes.
Therapist:	And do you think that this has enhanced your life in the way you thought it would?
Client:	Mmmm. I've done a lot of things but I'm not sure what difference it has made to how I feel.
Therapist:	How do you want to feel?
Client:	More in touch with people.
Therapist:	Have you ever felt like that?

Client: Well, when my sister and I had that talk about our lives I felt in touch.
Therapist: What was the difference then?
Client: It was sharing something together, really taking an interest.
Therapist: So how could you do more sharing?

Essentially the therapist is exploring the difference that the contract has made to the individual, enabling the client to think through the consequences of his behaviour and its impact on how he feels towards himself and others. The client is then moved to intuition to envisage a world where he would be feeling better. The contract could reflect this process, specifying some behavioural goals with the added feature of taking time to assess how he feels about what he has done.

Real change

In the last example, we warned against a 'first order change': a change that stays within the established frame of reference. In each of our examples we have portrayed a use of contracting which is aimed at helping the client to move on or encompass some part of themselves which has in some way been unavailable to them in the past. Watzlawick et al. (1970) call this second order change and illustrate it by way of what they describe as the nine-dot problem.

```
.   .   .

.   .   .

.   .   .
```

The idea is to link all the dots using one line, which can be vertical, horizontal or diagonal. Your pen cannot leave the paper and the line must not go back on itself. You will soon discover that there is no solution within the boundaries of the square shape in which the dots are first presented. The solution is to move outside the boundaries of the dots. It is this process which is at work in making contracts: the idea of meeting the client where he is, then enabling him to move outside his initial paradigm; beyond the boundaries of what he believed to be possible. Thus contracting can also mean expanding. Precisely what that new position is will vary from person to person. The consideration of different personality types may be useful in discovering it.

Conclusion

Our intention in this chapter has been to provide an overview of personality types and their tendencies in relation to making contracts. We stress that this is not the kind of information that should be used to categorise individuals in the sense of limiting them and that the approaches we describe should not be used bureaucratically, but with respect and sensitivity. We are also aware that each of the contracting sessions from which we give examples is necessarily a rather neat simplification of the real world, given to demonstrate a point. However, we believe that taking account of different personality styles can be crucial in engaging the client fully in discovering the goals of his therapy and to making relevant and effective contracts.

References

Bordin, E.S (1994) 'Theory and research in the therapentic working alliance', in O. Horvath and S. Greenberg (eds), *The Working Alliance: Theory, Research and Practice.* New York: Wiley.

Jung, C.G. (1971) *The Collected Works: Vol. 6. Psychological Types.* London: Routledge and Kegan Paul.

Kahler, T. (1979) *Managing with the Process Communication Model.* Little Rock, AR: Human Development Publications.

Leigh, E. and Gilbert, M. (1992) 'Treatment planning: an integration of the Gouldings' impasse theory and Ware's personality adaptations', *ITA News*, 34: 7–10.

Ware, P. (1983) 'Personality adaptations: doors to therapy', *Transactional Analysis Journal*, 13 (1): 213–20.

Watzlawick, P., Weakland, J.H. and Fisch, R. (1970) *Change: Principles of Problem Formation and Problem Resolution.* New York: Norton.

9 Contracts, Ethics and the Law

Peter Jenkins

Contracts for work with clients are primarily for therapeutic purposes, in order to underpin the quality and focus of the therapist–client working relationship. In this, they carry a significant *ethical* loading, as the concept of a contract also links strongly to the central philosophical principle of promoting client autonomy. However, the term contract necessarily links, in turn, to a *legal* perspective on the therapist–client work. Contract is a key component of civil law, even if many therapists seem somewhat unclear as to the exact legal status of the documents they use to guide their work with clients. This chapter will briefly review some of the differing perspectives on therapeutic contracts, their problematic status within the law, and some associated ethical and legal principles which therapists may find useful.

One of the starting points is that therapy and the law inhabit very different worlds of discourse. The law is classically concerned with objectivity, order and stability, understood in terms of normative dichotomies and within an adversarial approach. Therapy, on the other hand, is more concerned with subjectivity, ambience and change, understood from a viewpoint of relationship, context and the co-construction of meaning. Of course, even this typology smacks of either–or thinking, but it remains likely that legal and therapeutic reasoning will often tend to occupy very different spaces along this spectrum (Rowley and MacDonald 2001: 424).

'Hard' and 'soft' contracts

Within counselling and psychotherapy, views differ as to whether it is more appropriate to offer 'hard' or 'soft' contracts to clients (see Chapter 1). For example, Culley and Bond describe counselling as, by definition, 'a contractual activity'. A contract is defined as 'a specific commitment from both practitioner and client to a clearly defined course of action' (Culley and Bond 2004: 89). Mearns and Thorne, in contrast, seem to prefer a looser form of agreement between therapist and client: 'Instead of employing a provisional contract the counsellor and client may opt for a more open-ended arrangement whereby they agree to go on meeting for as long as seems necessary' (1999: 123). Finally, Egan is quite critical of the use of the term contract in therapeutic work, precisely because it carries this unnecessary loading and strong sense of legal baggage: 'Perhaps the term working charter is better than contract. It avoids the legal implications of the latter term and connotes a cooperative venture' (1998: 55). This working charter is further described as 'an instrument that makes clients more informed about the process, more collaborative with their helpers and more proactive in managing their problems' (1998: 56).

Clearly, there are very differing perspectives on what is meant by the term 'contracting' as part of therapeutic work with clients. It can be seen as a crucial process of negotiating the fine detail of therapeutic work, or in a much looser sense of making a commitment to work together therapeutically. Given the complexity and confusion surrounding the use of the term 'contract', Berne (1966) has suggested separating out the distinct aspects of the therapist–client agreement. He describes these in terms of the *administrative* or business contract, the *professional* contract, covering the goals and tasks of therapy, and the *psychological* or relational aspects of the contract. This is a useful starting point, but does not go far enough, in my view. Many of the contracts used in therapy will have administrative, professional and psychological aspects, but they do not constitute a legal agreement as such. There are precise conditions, which have to be met, in order for a therapist–client agreement to qualify as a *legally binding* contract, and it is important for the therapist to be aware of their implications.

Requirements for a contract

What are these requirements? Essentially, the parties to the contract must have legal *capacity*, i.e. through being aged 18 or over and being of sound mind. There needs to be *a firm offer and unequivocal acceptance*. There is also a clear *expectation* on the part of both parties that the agreed purpose is to create an agreement which will be legally binding. Finally, there is an element of *consideration*, or the exchange of services, normally for payment. It is the last aspect which is critical in undermining the legal standing of many therapy contracts, where the client is not actually paying for the service received. The client who is receiving counselling on a voluntary basis from a small, charitable organisation, from the NHS, or from a university counselling service, is not party to a legal contract in this narrow legal sense, however prescriptive and detailed the terms of the working agreement may actually be. It might be more accurate, therefore, to add a fourth category to Berne's suggested list of elements of the contract, namely that of a *legal* aspect, which may only apply under certain circumstances, rather than one which is assumed to apply generically to all contracts with clients.

Context of contract law

Contract law perhaps needs to be put briefly in some kind of wider context. Contract forms part of a wider set of law, namely the law of obligations, together with laws relating to tort (negligence) and restitution (McKendrick 2005: 6). Classical contract law is held to have three related threads, in that it involves a reciprocal agreement between parties, is intentionally binding under the law, and is governed by the notion of the freedom of choice of either party (O'Sullivan and Hilliard 2004: 2–3). Furthermore, the law relating to contract described here applies within England and Wales. There are significant differences applying to Scottish law with regard to contract, concerning the lack of a doctrine of consideration.

While the actual detail of contract law can easily fill imposing text books, the basic concept of a contract can be simply defined as 'an agreement enforceable at law' (Saunders 1977: 79).

Therapists using a legal contract might do so in a number of situations. The therapist might work in private practice, and contract with fee-paying clients. A supervisor may well similarly contract with trainees or students, who pay directly for supervision received. An agency may enter into a contract with another organisation in order to provide counselling, training, supervision or consultancy services, in return for payment. Finally, therapists who are formally employed by an organisation will have a *contract of employment*. The latter will have some significant consequences for their apparent freedom of action in working therapeutically with clients, which will be considered in more detail below.

Developing a contract with clients

Counsellors often ask if a contract must be written in order to hold proper legal status. Clearly, an oral contract can still be legally binding, but it may be hard to prove after the event what the contract contained, and what was agreed by both parties. A therapy contract will usually contain a number of conditions, defined as the 'business contract' in Berne's construction, or as 'express terms' in legal parlance. These will specify key aspects such as the fee, duration and frequency of sessions (see box below for suggested elements of a model contract).

Box 9.1   Elements of a model contract for therapy

- cost of sessions
- duration and frequency of sessions
- arrangements and charges (if relevant) for cancellation or holiday periods
- main characteristics of therapy to be provided
- total number of sessions and arrangements for review
- limits to confidentiality
- arrangements for termination of therapy
- cover or substitution of therapist in case of illness
- date and signature of both parties

(Jenkins 1997: 51)

Contractual terms

In addition to the express terms of the contract, as listed above, there are also implied terms (Cristofoli 2002). A high level of confidentiality, for example, may be held to apply in the therapeutic work under common law, even if not formally specified in the contract, given the special and trusting nature of the relationship between client and therapist. In addition, there is an implied term of 'reasonable care and skill' on the part of the therapist, if providing a professional service for payment, under section 13 of the Supply of Goods and Services Act 1982. The therapist offering their services to the client must maintain at least a minimal standard of competence, as judged relative to the standard of other practitioners.

From a legal and therapeutic point of view a contract provides some clarity about the nature of the service being provided, when the client may be unsure of what to expect. Beyond this, it also offers some protection to both parties, in that action can be taken should the contract not be fulfilled. The client may default on payment, or the therapist might choose to take an extended summer break without notice. An aggrieved party can, in theory, take action via the Small Claims Court, a branch of the County Court, under civil law for breach of contract in order to achieve redress. While the procedure for such actions is relatively informal and straightforward, many therapists might, in practice, be reluctant to pursue former clients through the courts. Also, even if one party is successful in winning the case, it can still prove arduous and time consuming to effect payment from an errant client, or to gain compensation from an incompetent therapist.

Another limitation to redress inherent in contract law is the concept of privity of contract. This means that a third party, that is one not directly involved in the drawing up and execution of the contract, cannot sue for breach of contract. This might be most relevant in the case of supervision. Thus a client claiming that the counselling received was ineffective, might seek to sue the counsellor's directly paid supervisor as being mainly responsible for the poor quality of the therapeutic work. However, the client does not have a right under contract law to sue the counsellor's supervisor, as this is excluded on the basis of privity of contract. Whether the client could seek to bring an action under tort law for negligence against the supervisor is also unlikely, as English law is so far generally reluctant to extend the principles of liability to third parties.

Obtaining informed consent

The legal concept of contract can be closely linked to the parallel idea of *consent*. In ethical terms, the client's autonomy is respected and exercised via the process of negotiating and agreeing a contract. Furthermore, the client needs to have sufficient information about the form of therapy on offer in order to be able to make an informed choice as to whether or not to take part. For example, the client may need to know that a psychodynamic approach used by the therapist will probably revisit childhood and early family issues, or that a behavioural approach will involve the client in actively undergoing changes of problematic routines, in order to develop their confidence and assertiveness, for example. The concept of informed consent is not, strictly speaking, part of contract law. However, it does have a bearing on the capacity of the client to make a realistic choice between undergoing alternative forms of therapy, or deciding not to have therapy, or to take medication, prior to entering into a contract. Within the wider medical field, 'consent is now a central issue in clinical practice' (Mayberry 2003: 9). While the concept of informed consent as a legal principle is stronger and more pervasive in the USA than in the UK, it has steadily been gaining ground, particularly in the context of psychological therapies provided within the NHS.

Consent has been defined as including:

- comprehension and retention of information;
- believing the information; and
- an ability to weigh the information and make a choice (*Re C* [1994]; Mayberry 2003: 93).

Contracting as a process

Within a fully developed notion of informed consent, therapists may need to discuss the possible harmful effects of therapy, as well as its potential benefits. Harmful effects to be covered might include a short-term deterioration in mood, worsening of behavioural symptoms and possible adverse effects on key relationships with a partner or family members. The concept of informed consent to therapy is perhaps more usefully viewed as part of the wider, ongoing process of *contracting* with clients, rather than linked solely to the single outcome of constructing a legal contract as such. Culley and Bond suggest that '(c)ontracting is a significant procedure for conveying the notion of your relationship with the client as a shared enterprise and not something that is "done to" clients by an expert' (2004: 16).

Reporting requirements

Therapists in many settings are increasingly bound by agency policies on managing risk to the client and to third parties, such as children at risk of abuse, or partners at risk from domestic violence. These kinds of imposed limits to confidentiality are best identified as a further category of Berne's notion of a contract, namely the dimension of agency or organisational protocols regarding confidentiality and reporting requirements. Protocols for reporting risk of child abuse, self harm or suicide, or harm to third parties belong to a fifth, separate category of the contract, the *organisational* contract. This puts the constructing of the therapist–client contract within a wider social framework, where the guidelines on disclosure and confidentiality are actually determined by agency policy, rather than negotiated individually with each client on a case-by-case basis, as might happen in the case of a therapist working in private practice.

Box 9.2 Developing the concept of the therapeutic contract

- administrative contract (details of contact)
- professional contract (tasks and goals)
- psychological contract (bonds, relational aspects)
- legal contract (status as legally binding agreement)
- organisational protocols (guidelines for reporting child abuse, self harm, risk to third parties)

(after Berne 1966)

There are, in reality, very few absolute requirements under English law for therapists to breach client confidentiality and disclose information to the authorities, except in the case of terrorism and drug money laundering. However, many counsellors and psychotherapists will work in settings such as health, education and social services, where there are clear agency protocols for reporting suspected child abuse to the authorities. In the case of counsellors working in Further Education (FE), some colleges sought to apply this obligation to report as a term of the counsellor's contract of employment. This was highly questionable in terms of the law, as this meant imposing a contractual duty to report child abuse, in the absence of any wider statutory duty to do so at that time. Independent legal opinion obtained by the British Association for Counselling and Psychotherapy clarified that the imposition on counsellors in Further Education of a contractual duty to report was in breach of their fiduciary duty of trust to the client, and conflicted with the law on confidentiality (Friel 1998; *Duncan v MPDC* [1986]). As Bond also noted in this respect, '… any contractual term that conflicts with either statute or common law … is unenforceable' (2000: 50).

Ethical principles and contractual duties

There is a potential conflict here between the ethical principles of welfare and avoidance of harm, which would support the reporting of risk of harm, and the counterposed principles of autonomy and fidelity, which would set a higher priority on empowering the client and maintaining the confidential bond with the client (BACP 2002: 6). In legal terms, as argued above, the organisational protocols that require reporting of risk or abuse, may be untenable in law, in the absence of a mandatory requirement on counsellors to make such reports. The situation in Colleges of FE remained unresolved, expressed as a clash of opposing perspectives on the role and duties of the counsellor. In a wider sense, the pressure from organisational protocols to insert reporting requirements into the contract with clients has become, if anything, even more intense. In the wake of the Laming Report (2003) into the Victoria Climbie case, and recent legislation such as the Sexual Offences Act 2003, and the Children Act 2004, the shift towards a 'reporting culture' is clearly evident, even though no statutory requirement to report abuse has yet been established. Comprehensive guidance such as *What To Do If You're Worried A Child Is Being Abused* gives a strong steer towards reporting, rather than balancing this ethical duty with a commitment to confidentiality. In essence, the Best Practice Guidance is that all practitioners working with children and families should 'refer any concerns about child abuse or neglect to social services or the police' (DoH 2003: 5).

To reiterate, therapists need to be clear that such reporting requirements may simply *be a term of their contract of employment*, rather than constituting a wider mandatory legal duty as a citizen. Imposition of such a duty has been criticised in one specific case by expert legal opinion as being both inconsistent with the counsellor's fiduciary duty towards the client, and unenforceable at law. Therapists and their professional associations need to challenge the enforcement of such terms, given the shift towards acceding to a defensive culture of reporting, rather than seeking to manage and work with client risk to self and others.

Summary

The primary purpose of contracts is to underpin therapeutic work with clients, by setting out appropriate boundaries. Berne has identified the core elements of the contract as including administrative, professional and psychological aspects of the agreement with the client. It is argued here that this concept needs to be extended to include *legal* aspects, which would apply only where the conditions for a legally binding agreement were met. In essence, a legal contract requires capacity, intention, consideration and exchange. It will have both express terms set out in detail, such as fees, time and duration, and also implied terms such as a requirement for the practitioner to demonstrate 'reasonable care and skill'. A legal contract provides clarity for both parties and some means of redress for breach of its terms by either party, usually via the Small Claims Court. It may be useful for therapists to consider the notion of informed consent, increasingly influential in some contexts such as the NHS. This is consistent with safeguarding the client's interests through an ongoing *process of contracting*, rather than an approach restricted to producing a contractual document as the main desired outcome.

It is also suggested that *organisational* aspects of the contract need to be considered separately and in addition to Berne's original categories. Organisational aspects will often define the limits to client confidentiality, in the form of an apparent duty on the therapist to report risk of abuse, self harm or risk to a third party. Therapists need to be aware that, while these reporting requirements may be part of a formal contract of employment, they can be seen as being in conflict with their fiduciary duty of trust to maintain high levels of client confidentiality, and are not necessarily supported by statutory authority in every case. Finally, it is worth recalling that, just as the map is not the territory, the contract is simply an aid to the therapeutic journey, and should never be mistaken for the terrain itself.

References

BACP (British Association for Counselling and Psychotherapy) (2002) *Ethical Framework for Good Practice in Counselling and Psychotherapy.* Rugby: BACP.

Berne, E. (1966) *Principles of Group Treatment.* New York: Grove Press.

Bond, T. (2000) *Standards and Ethics for Counselling In Action*, 2nd edn. London: Sage.

Bordin, E.S. (1994) 'Theory and research in the therapeutic alliance', in O. Horvath and S. Greenberg (eds), *The Woking Alliance: Theory, Research and Practice.* New York: Wiley.

Cristofoli, G. (2002) 'Legal pitfalls in counselling and psychotherapy practice and how to avoid them', in P. Jenkins (ed.) *Legal Issues in Counselling And Psychotherapy.* London: Sage. pp. 24–33.

Culley, S. and Bond, T. (2004) *Integrative Counselling Skills In Action*, 2nd edn. London: Sage.

Department of Health (2003) *What To Do If You're Worried A Child Is Being Abused*. London: DoH.

Egan, G. (1998) *The Skilled Helper*, 6th edn. Pacific Grove: Brooks Cole.

Friel, J.Q.C. (1998) *In the Matter of the British Association for Counselling, the Association for Student Counselling and the Association of Colleges*. Unpublished legal opinion obtained by the British Association for Counselling.

Jenkins, P. (1997) *Counselling, Psychotherapy and the Law*. London: Sage.

Lord Laming (2003) *The Victoria Climbie Inquiry*. Cm 5730. London: Stationery Office.

Mayberry, J. (2003) *Consent in Clinical Practice*. Oxon: Radcliffe Medical Press.

McKendrick, E. (2005) *Contract Law*, 6th edn. Basingstoke: Palgrave MacMillan.

Mearns, D. and Thorne, B. (1999) *Person Centred Counselling in Action*, 2nd edn. London: Sage.

O'Sullivan, J. and Hilliard, J. (2004) *The Law of Contract*. Oxford: Oxford University Press.

Rowley, W.J. and MacDonald, D. (2001) 'Counseling and the law: a cross-cultural perspective', *Journal of Counseling and Development*, 79: 422–9.

Saunders, J. (1977) *Mozley and Whiteley's Law Dictionary*, 9th edn. London: Butterworths.

Legal references

Duncan v Medical Practitioners Disciplinary Committee [1986] NZLR 1 513.

Re C (adult refusal of treatment) [1994] 1 WLR 290.

PART IV
Contracts and Contexts

Contracts, Complexity and Challenge

10

Keith Tudor

The matter of contracts and of contracting in therapy (psychotherapy and counselling) is complex. At best, the use of and reference to a contract can clarify the objectives of a therapeutic encounter or relationship for both parties. On the other hand, a therapist can use the letter of a contract, and associated professional codes, to betray the relationship and the client (see Heyward 1993). Equally, for his or her part, the client can use a contract to keep the therapy 'safe' and perhaps avoid genuine engagement with disputes, emerging difficulties and difference, and, at worst, as a basis of litigation. Moreover, as Rose (1997/2003) argues, the concept of a legal contract is not transferable to the field of therapy. Yet, despite nearly 300 years of critical theory and the more recent postmodern turn that intellectual discourse, and arguably society, has taken, the modernist conceit of contracts has, if anything, taken further and firmer root in areas such as counselling in health care. As most therapeutic work today is undertaken in agencies of one kind or another, the complexity of contracts and contracting increases.

Building on elements of two chapters in the previous edition of this book (Tudor 1997a, 1997b) this chapter seeks to clarify some of this complexity of contracts and contracting in therapy. It begins with a clarification of terms and challenges the analogy often drawn between legal and therapeutic contracts, then examines the concept of the three-cornered or three-handed contract, introducing it with reference to the social contract. The three-handed contract is used to frame a number of applications: counselling in the medical setting of general practice as well as psychological aspects of counselling in any situation where the counsellor is working with more than one person either directly, e.g. when working in organisations or with couples or families, or indirectly, e.g. when working with children. The chapter concludes with consideration of multi-handed and multi-layered contracts.

Contracts – terms and requirements

One of the problems with this aspect of therapy is that the term 'contract' is used loosely and nowhere is this more true than when the therapy takes place in an agency. A common example of this is when therapists or organisations refer to their own rules or groundrules as a contract (see Chapter 9). Eric Berne, the founder of transactional analysis (TA), which is based on the 'contractual method', defines a contract (1966: 362) as: 'An explicit bilateral commitment to a well-defined course of action.' Contracts are distinguished from rules precisely by virtue of their bilaterality: it takes two (or more) to agree.

A further consideration of rules derives from the dictum 'Never make a rule you can't enforce' (M. Turpin, personal communication, October 1988). As enforcement usually involves some sanction on the part of the therapist, such as 'If you don't agree to ... I won't work with you', it is worth therapists considering what they want to state as a rule and what sanctions they are prepared to make and, indeed, have the power to make. One practical use and effect of these distinctions is for therapists to deregulate many of their notional rules, and to negotiate erstwhile 'rules' as genuine contracts. As contracts are discussed, negotiated, agreed and re-negotiated, this process is the beginning of an engaged, co-created therapeutic relationship, marked by attunement and mutuality.

The second element of Berne's definition, that a contract makes explicit the commitment and the 'well-defined course of action' reflects the commitment of TA practitioners to open and clear communication, and acknowledges the client's part in the process of defining what he or she wants: *The Power is in the Patient*, as the Gouldings (1978) put it. The drawback of the definition and the modernist tradition it represents is the conceit that therapy can be defined and agreed in advance, in the same way that rationalists and modernists attempted to define, categorise and, thereby, control the world. An important example of this is the use of legal contracts as analogous to contracts in therapy (see Chapter 9).

In an early article in the *Transactional Analysis Bulletin* Steiner and Cassidy (1969) identified four basic requirements for contracts to be legally valid:

- mutual consent – a clear and understandable offer on the part of the therapist of what he or she will give, in return for some act or promise on the part of the client;
- valid consideration – referring to the benefit conferred by both the therapist (amelioration, cure) and the client (payment and/or attendance, active participation);
- competency – referring to the ability of the parties to enter into a contract and, therefore, mediated in the case of legal minors, and certain levels of dysfunction and intoxication; and
- lawful object – referring to the broader consideration that, as Steiner and Cassidy put it (1969: 31): 'The contract must not be in violation of law or against public policy or morals'.

Writing in the context of UK law, Jenkins (see Chapter 9) identifies similar requirements or conditions:

- legal capacity;
- firm offer and unequivocal acceptance;
- clear intention of the parties to create a legally binding agreement; and
- consideration of exchange.

Significantly, Steiner and Cassidy introduce their discussion of these requirements by stating (1969: 29) that: 'Inasmuch as these requirements have been historically evolved from innumerable litigations, over hundreds of years, they may be accepted not only as legally necessary, but socially desirable as well'. This is significant in that they acknowledge the litigious and, therefore, defensive origins of the contract as defining the exchange of services between people. Secondly, the requirement of having a 'lawful object' is one which encourages conservatism and social conformity. There are many examples of therapists working, as it were, at the margins of society, sometimes in violation of the law and against public policy, if not morality, for example when working with some asylum seekers whose legal status may be in dispute, or when discussing or giving advice on aspects of sexual health or sexuality with and to teenagers. A third implication of these requirements is that they promote a legalistic view of therapy. In his discussion of therapists' use of contracts, Jenkins (1997 and see Chapter 9) discusses the distinction between the *express terms* of a contract, such as those which define frequency of contact, length and cost of therapy sessions, and *implied terms*, such as confidentiality. He cautions:

> The fact that terms *appear* on a contract does not mean that they are *legally part* of the said contract. Terms need to be *incorporated* into the contract, which is usually done by each party signing the document which sets out the terms to be included. (1997: 49)

This is therapy by clauses. One of the problems of applying any theory to an application other than the one for which it was developed is what Rogers (1959: 193) refers to as 'the magnification of error. The same is true for the 'theory' of legal contracts. As Rose (1997/2003: 29) puts it:

> The contract, especially over the period of the 1980s in Britain and the United States, was seen as a mechanism that established equivalence between two parties. The classical legal notion of a contract is of an exchange freely and mutually entered into by equals, which is binding on both parties, and specifies that certain goods or services should be provided by one party in exchange for a specified price or other consideration.
>   A moment's thought, I think, is sufficient to indicate that the contract in therapy is not of that sort. It is a pseudo-contract ... the relation is more tutelary than contractual.

Therapy – and certainly any therapy based on a therapeutic relationship – is not and cannot be based on a simple exchange of 'service' for consideration such as a fee, for further discussion of which see Tudor and Worrall (2002). The notion that it is promotes a mechanistic view of therapy; a cautious, defensive and impotent therapist; and a passive, consumerist view of the client who, in this defensive and litigious frame of reference, ends in seeking legalistic redress for rights wronged. Inevitably, the potential for reductionism and rigidity is increased manifold when there are several parties involved.

Having offered some deflation and deconstruction of the concept of contracts and of the inflated use of the analogy between the legal and social world and the psychological world, I now examine its use and usefulness in describing the complexity of relationships when contracts are more than bilateral, setting this in the broader content of the social contract.

Three-handed contracts

Given the increased complexity of relationships involving more than two people and the increased possibilities for misunderstanding and miscommunication, it is

Figure 10.1   The three-cornered contract (English 1975)

useful to consider a model for contracting which goes beyond bilateral agreements. In 1975 English developed the 'three-cornered contract' (Figure 10.1), originally in the context of being invited to run training workshops, as an antidote to, as she viewed it, 'various additional and mutually contradictory expectations [on the part of] participants based on subtle promises that have been made deliberately or unknowingly [by the organisers]' (1975: 383).

By simply drawing this diagram trainers or therapists may clarify the different and, often, differing expectations the various parties to a contract may have.

As therapists we have a three-handed contract involving the professional associations, bodies and institutes of which we are members. As citizens we have a similar relationship with society, a relationship which the French philosopher Jean-Jacques Rousseau (1712–1778) described as a social contract.

Social contracts

The concept of a *social contract* derives from the eponymous work by Rousseau, who argued that the existence of the state is the outcome of a covenant or contract between people. The need for a governing state arises from the historical fact and psychological reality of possession and possessions, the consequent inequality of wealth, and the need, therefore, for a system of law. Hence people agree, or do not agree, to live under a political system. Rousseau believed that it was possible for people to be members of a (political) society and, at the same time, to be free (Rousseau 1968). The English philosopher Thomas Hobbes (1588–1679), on the other hand, argued that people have to choose between being ruled and being free (Hobbes 1962). This reference to two philosophical arguments about the necessity of society and the role of the social contract between its members is pertinent to the position and role of 'societies' or associations of therapists.

One person, the client, 'possesses' a problem. Another, the therapist, possesses certain experience, knowledge, training and skills. There are inequalities in this relationship and, it is argued, that there is therefore a need for a system by which the relationship is governed. Hence the parties agree to abide by a framework or code of ethics, an agreement which often forms part of a less or more formal business contract for therapy. That such codes provide a consultative framework for therapists, within which they are still free or at liberty to consider and make decisions about practice, reflects Rousseau's belief that we are free and, at the same time, choose to be 'governed'. In the UK, this is, at present, through self-regulation. The Hobbesian view of society, liberty and governance is represented by those in the field of psychotherapy and counselling who see frameworks and codes as rules of governance rather than principles of guidance, and consider that therapists cannot be free within them. They also eschew organisations such as the British Association of Counselling and Psychotherapy (BACP) and the United Kingdom Council for Psychotherapy (UKCP) and the regulation of counselling and psychotherapy (see, for instance, Mowbray 1995).

The UKCP has, as one of its aims, the statutory regulation and registration of psychotherapists, and the present UK government supports this, a position which represents a Hobbesian view. On the other hand, there are now a number of organisations in the UK which offer accreditation schemes for therapists. This subverts the notion of one 'great power' or player in this scheme and represents more freedom of choice, à la Rousseau.[1] Also, in this tradition, since the first edition of this book in 1997, the BACP has replaced its 1996 *Code of Ethics* with an *Ethical Framework for Good Practice in Counselling and Psychotherapy* (BACP 2002), which seeks to reflect more of an ethical diversity by considering and inviting the practitioner to reflect on his or her values, principles, and personal moral qualities.

Within the social organisation and a social model of therapy, the challenge for the therapist is to square the circle (or triangle) of regulation/self-regulation, being governed and being free, having rights and having responsibilities, recognising also that these are issues for clients, with whom we share citizenship (see Tudor and Hargaden, 2002).

Power relations

Developing English's original concept of 'great powers', Micholt (1992) describes four types of three-cornered contracts, originally developed as regards the supervisory relationship, each of which may be used to illustrate the impact of different power relations between the parties involved. These provide useful visual representations of the subjective experience of both interpersonal and organisational dynamics.

The equilateral triangle of Figure 10.2 represents an equal and healthy psychological distance between the three parties to this contractual supervision relationship in which 'great powers' may be an organisation or a counselling course.

Figure 10.3 represents an uneven triangular relationship in which the therapist is nearer to the client than either is to the organisation. In itself, this may not be a bad thing or a problem; it is, nevertheless, worth noting and, at worst, may encourage an 'I'm OK, You're OK, They're not OK' position (Berne 1972/1975) on the part of the therapist and client, and a collusion between them which may be disempowering for both or subverting of the organisation. For their part, the 'great powers' concerned may or may not encourage this type of triangulation.

In Figure 10.4, X and Y are a couple where X is already in therapy and Y has reluctantly agreed to come to couples therapy. Although the therapist is not X's own therapist, he is experienced as a 'great power'; the subjective experience or

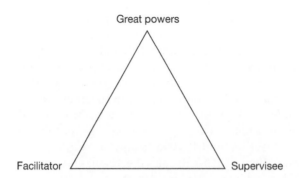

Figure 10.2   Three-cornered contract (Type A) (based on Micholt 1992)

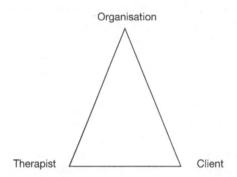

Figure 10.3   Three-cornered contract (Type B) (based on Micholt 1992)

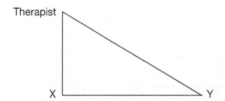

Figure 10.4   Three-cornered contract (Type C) (based on Micholt 1992)

imago of the parties involved and the dynamic between them is represented by Figure 10.4. The relative emotional literacy (Steiner 1984) of the two partners may make it more difficult for the couples therapist to work with both X and Y together, and this may well form a part of his initial assessment of the couple (see Boyd and Boyd 1981). In this situation, there is also a danger of Y experiencing the therapist and her partner as persecuting her and thus this three-handed relationship is vulnerable to the Victim-Persecutor-Rescuer drama described by Karpman (1968).

Finally, in an example applied to working with children, Figure 10.5 shows the parent as the 'great power' and the therapist on the same level as but at a distance

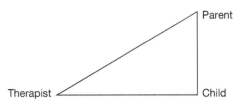

Figure 10.5   Three-cornered contract (Type D) (based on Micholt 1992)

from the child. Whilst the relative closeness of the parent and child may be healthy, the therapist, at the same time as being invited in to work with the child is kept apart. Equally, there is a danger that in her work with the child the therapist becomes the 'great power' or influence, such that the parent is marginalised and put on the same level as the child, thus undermining the family structure.

In the second half of this chapter, I draw on Berne's (1966) three levels of contract (as described in Chapter 1) – the administrative contract, the professional contract and the psychological aspects of the contract – as an organising framework at the institutional level within which I consider examples from practice in different contexts: the administrative context of therapy, more commonly referred to as counselling in general practice; the professional context of an EAP; and an example of the psychological aspects of contracts in the context of couples therapy.

The administrative context – counselling in primary care

The administrative contract is concerned with the practical demands of the counselling, as distinct from the professional contract, which is to do with the potentialities and limitations of the treatment or service offered (Berne 1966). I develop the example of counselling in primary care, predominantly in general practice, to illustrate and to distinguish between the two levels of contract.

Administratively, in this context, the three-handed contract involves the counsellor, the General Practitioner (GP) or GPs, and the relevant 'great power', such as the local PCT, which may fund counsellor attachments and placements in general practice. Following and developing Berne's observations, the administrative contract includes the following:

Relevant law directives and policies

In this context this refers to UK law and directives; national policy, such as the NHS Quality Agenda; and local policies and protocols about professional standards in primary care, such as the policy that counsellors in general practice should be accredited or eligible for accreditation. Since the first edition of this book almost ten years ago, and the growth in the numbers of counsellors both generally and working in general practice (see Mellor Clark, undated) this bar has been raised in that, nowadays, adverts often stipulate that counsellors should be qualified, accredited and even have academic qualifications, as well as necessary experience.

Of course, this excludes certain counsellors and student counsellors, especially those who take a more critical view of accreditation and registration. The concept of the three-handed contract may help to identify differences and contradictions between various relevant and governing policies, especially for the student counsellor whose other two 'hands' comprise the GP practice or PCT, and the training provider or Institute. In this context, some written agreement or contract between all three parties concerned can be facilitative in clarifying lines of responsibility, accountability and communication. This is particularly useful when people confuse administrative issues with professional or theoretical disagreements and prejudice (see Tudor and Worrall 2004).

Purpose

This includes some description of the nature and purpose of the counselling offered. The Royal College of Practitioners, for example, publishes an information folder on *Counselling in General Practice* (Staveley 1992), and the BACP has published a report on *Counselling in Primary Care* (Mellor Clark, undated). Any agreement about purpose should also include something about the nature, amount and duration of the counselling offered, as well as the general workload of the counsellor, including any meetings they are expected to attend. Of course, by definition, an *agreement* or an *agreed* contract is bilateral, and requires mutual consent and valid consideration. Thus, it should be made clear whether particular policies and protocols are, in effect, rules, or whether they form part of a contract, in which case they are open to discussion. Again, this is especially important in the light of differences between theoretical orientations which influence ideas about practice and purpose. There's no such thing as a neutral protocol. Also, whilst the main purpose and focus of the counsellor's work is to counsel clients, she may also be expected to provide support to staff and, again, this purpose should be explicit.

Finance

This includes the relevant financial arrangements regarding fees or salary, and the mechanism of payment. Again, the three-handed contract is useful in clarifying these issues. All parties need to consider the implications, advantages and disadvantages and ethics of various administrative options as regards the counsellor's employment status: being employed as salaried member of staff; being employed on a sessional basis; or being self-employed. The then British Association for Counselling (BAC) produced guidelines on the employment of counsellors in 1992, and specifically on the employment of counsellors in general practice (Ball 1995).

Personnel

In Berne's framework, this includes all parties to the contract, and incorporates consideration of other personnel involved, such as other counsellors and the relationship between them. In the present context it also refers to personnel matters such as the health and safety of the counsellor, the employers' duty of care, liability and insurance. It is generally considered to be good ethical and professional practice to have professional indemnity insurance which covers professional indemnity, public liability, libel and slander, and product liability. The issue for counsellors in primary care is whether they are covered by the PCT's or the general practice's own medical insurance; and, even if they are, whether they need their own cover in this context and, if so, whether the PCT pays their insurance premium. In its information sheet on 'Guidelines for the Employment of Counsellors', the BAC (1992) clearly states that 'employers should provide professional liability cover for the counselling service'.

Facilities

This includes room arrangements and their significance. Is there a separate counselling room? If so, is this suitable for the type of counselling offered in terms of being soundproof? If not, what are the implications of the counselling taking place, say, in a GP's consulting room? Counsellors are used to having set and uninterrupted time, which may be different from the culture of a busy general practice. Counsellors in primary care have administrative needs. Is there any secretarial support for the counsellor? If so, to what extent, and on what conditions? If not, are there expectations of the counsellor to administer their own work?

Equipment

This refers to the 'equipment' or provisions the counsellor needs in order to do their work, such as training, supervision, and personal and professional development. Different PCTs and general practices take different approaches: from those which fund the training and supervision of practice counsellors, their time and travel costs, to others which contribute nothing to costs other than that of employing the counsellor. Given the open-ended demand and inevitable financial constraints on the NHS, and the constantly changing state and organisation of it, this situation is likely to continue or become more acute. Nevertheless, just as counsellors in higher education argued for a minimum number of hours of supervision, which led the then British Association for Counselling to make this a monthly requirement of one and half hours (J. Bell, personal communication, June 2005), so counsellors employed in primary care could and perhaps should argue that this is part of their maintenance or 'equipment'. There is a clear contractual argument here, and one which is commensurate with other staff who need to maintain their professional status. If PCTs want and recruit counsellors who are accredited, then they need to support counsellors to maintain their membership and eligibility for accreditation or registration. Again, the three-handed contract is helpful in identifying and clarifying such expectations and the provisions or lack of provisions for fulfilling them.

Administration of practice

Additional to Berne's considerations, this concerns the specific administration of the counselling within the primary care setting, including:

- Referrals. On what basis are they made? Here the counsellor has an important role in discussing with the GPs what she can and cannot do, given the usual limitations of time and resources. How are referrals made? What does the GP say to the patient/client? This is crucial in terms of any expectations the client may have of the counsellor and from counselling.

- Notes and records. There is no current legal requirement on counsellors to keep notes or records. Bond (2000) summarises the arguments in favour of and against, as well as the legal implications of record-keeping; the BACP's (2002) *Ethical Framework* encourages but does not require counsellors to keep notes. This, of course, may be superceded by institutional or organisational requirements on counsellors to keep notes and to keep them in certain forms, requirements which again may be understood in the frame of the three-handed contract. Assuming that the counsellor does keep notes or records of sessions, then the client should be made aware of this. Counsellors employed by PCTs come under the auspices of the Access to Health Records Act 1990 and the Data Protection Act 1998. Jenkins (2002) reviews this changing area of legislation, policy and procedure, also with reference to the Human Rights Act 1998 and the Freedom of Information Act 2000. There are administrative as well as professional implications to: the client having access to her records; the availability of the counsellor's notes to other professionals, such as the GP; the combining of the counsellor's records and/or notes with the client's medical records; and the security of such records.
- Monitoring and evaluation. This follows on from the issues of notes and record-keeping, in that some records are kept for monitoring and evaluative purposes. Thus the nature and purpose of notes and records, as well as the specific information the counsellor is required to collect or collate, all needs to be discussed by and/or made explicit to all parties to the administrative and professional levels of contract.
- Referrals onward. GPs and counsellors refer clients on to other professionals. Given that many counsellors in primary care and general practice are working in the administrative context of a limited number of sessions, and depending on the client's continuing needs, the counsellor may consider referring her on to a counsellor in private practice. If the counsellor himself also works in private practice, they may be in a position to take clients from the general practice. Given the potential confluence of interests, this needs to be discussed *in advance* by all parties to the administrative contract.

The professional contract – Employee Assistance Programmes (EAPs)

An EAP is a programme or scheme whereby an organisation (the employer) buys in counselling for its employees, either directly from a counsellor or counsellors, or, more usually, through another organisation which acts as a broker between the employer and the counsellor, and as a guarantor to the employer for the programme and the counsellors. Such an arrangement thus involves a four-handed contract between the organisation/employer, the employee/client, the EAP, and the counsellor/s. Figure 10.6 shows an extension of the three-handed contract, which offers a framework for a series of contracts or, at least, a way of conceptualising the relationships between the parties involved.

Berne (1966) suggests that after the administrative aspects of the contract are settled, the professional goals of the therapy need to be agreed. These are discussed and elaborated with reference to the example of an EAP.

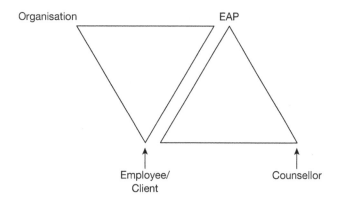

Organisation   EAP

Employee/
Client   Counsellor

Figure 10.6   **The four-handed contract applied to EAP counselling**

- The professional goal of the therapy. All parties to such a contract need to be clear about the goal, nature and purpose of the therapy, as well as the benefits and limitations of the counselling offered. Berne (1966, 1972/1975) talks in terms of different stages of 'cure': social control, symptomatic relief, transference cure and script cure. The difference between these is particularly relevant as the different parties to the EAP may have different views about the purpose and outcome of the 'assistance' to the employee. As Berne (1966: 16) puts it: 'The local meaning of such terms should again be agreed upon even at the risk of appearing pedantic, for this is preferable to being vague'. However, in this context, being clear with all parties about goals may be problematic, especially for the client/employee. Whilst an employer may have the goal for the employee of social control and symptomatic relief, and the maintenance of levels of functioning or an early return to work, the employee may want more support, understanding, therapy and time.
- Values. According to the BACP (2002), one of the fundamental values of counselling and psychotherapy is ensuring the integrity of practitioner–client relationships. However, in the context of an EAP, the counsellor–client relationship is inevitably influenced by the context: the client is referred by the employer, who may well have views about what the employee needs, as has the client. The employer funds the counselling through the EAP, which, in turn, has its own expectations of the counsellor and of the counselling, as well as certain administrative procedures regarding forms, feedback and accountability. Thus, integrity and relationship is mediated by the context. Another value, that of increasing personal effectiveness, again may clash with the expectations and needs of the employer. In the BACP *Framework* and other codes and frameworks, especially in the West, client autonomy is viewed as a core value. One major implication for the counsellor's professional support for client autonomy in the context of an EAP is the potential for conflict between the client/employee and the employer. Fostering a sense of self that is meaningful to the person (another value identified by the BACP) may be at odds with the employer's aim to foster a sense of identity with work and a common task. In this, autonomy describes only a part of our human tendency to actualise. Another value, that of enhancing the quality of relationships between people, represents another trend, that of homonomy or a sense of belonging (Angyal 1941; see Tudor and Worrall 2006).

Whilst it might not be possible or desirable to make all the contracts explicit, the framework of the three- or four-handed contract again offers the therapist a way of mapping both the parties and their relationships, and of acknowledging the social and ulterior, psychological levels to each relationship or possibility of relationship. For further discussion, specifically of EAPs, see Berridge et al. (1997).

Having clarified the administrative and professional levels of the contract, the therapist, according to Berne (1966: 20), 'is free to devote himself to the psychological aspects of the contract which become part of the therapeutic struggle.' In the next part I explore some aspects of this struggle in the context in which the therapist is working with more than one person directly.

The psychological contract – couples therapy

Interestingly and perhaps significantly, there is almost no mention of contracts or contracting as such in the literature on working with couples across a number of approaches, for example, Crowe and Ridley (1990) and Bubenzer and West (1993). Schröder discusses contracting briefly, commenting, strangely and without any substantiation, that 'explicit contracts ... may foster dependence' (1989: 62–3). The exceptions to this gap in the literature are, unsurprisingly, given their respective backgrounds in transactional analysis, Bader and Pearson (1988) and Gilbert and Shmukler (1996). Bader and Pearson discuss the contractual process in some detail, arguing that 'ideal contracts will have ... mutually agreed-upon objectives with a high motivation for achieving them'(1988: 55), whilst recognising that many couples will have difficulties in mutuality, clarity of objectives and motivation, and that the clarification of the contract will be the initial focus and work of the couples counselling. Gilbert and Shmukler (1996) discuss contracting in brief therapy with couples.

Developing the three-cornered contract, the contractual relationship between the couples therapist and the couple is represented in Figure 10.7.

Figure 10.7 represents the relationship between three people, that is, one couple and the couples therapist, in which two contracts are acknowledged and elaborated. First, it is recognised that the couple have a contract between them, whether explicit or implicit, legal (as in a marriage) or social (as in a relationship), although this distinction is changing with a number of countries and states recognising the legal status of gay or same-sex relationships (see Stonewall 2005). The couple also bring some understanding of why they have come to counselling, although this understanding and the respective motivations of the individuals may well differ, and this is often the starting point of couples therapy. At this stage, the couples therapist may use various techniques from couples and family therapy, such as focusing, formulation and tracking (Minuchin 1974), and circular questioning (Selvini Palazzoli et al. 1980), as ways of facilitating the initial therapy contract. The second contract represented in Figure 10.7 is that between the couples therapist and the couple. It is an important, if obvious, point that in couples therapy the therapist is working with the couple, that is, the relationship, and not doing therapy with an individual in front of his or her partner. On this, Boyd and Boyd

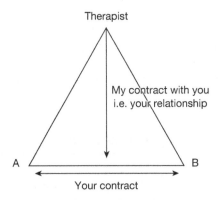

Figure 10.7   The contractual relationship in couples therapy

Figure 10.8   Psychological aspects of the contract in couples therapy

(1981) offer a transactional model of relationship therapy in which they identify, at the diagnosis and assessment stage, certain dysfunctions in the relationship as indicating the need for individual rather than couples therapy.

Taking one of Berne's points about the nature of communication, that 'the behaviorial outcome of an ulterior transaction is determined at the psychological level and not at the social level' (1966: 227), his third rule of communication, I take contracts to have both an explicit social level, that is, what is stated *and* an implicit psychological level, that is, what is not stated but often wished. The psychological aspects of the contract in couples therapy is represented in Figure 10.8.

The dotted lines of the arrows in Figure 10.8 between A and B, from A to the couples therapist and from B to the couples therapist, represent the psychological aspects or level of the contract. These are the ulterior transactions or hidden agendas of both parties to the couple: A may want the couples therapist to tell B that he is 'the problem', B may want the couples therapist to tell A to get off his back. By doing so in the meeting with the couples therapist, A and B are reflecting a process in their relationship. In this situation, the principal task of the couples therapist is to maintain the position of being therapist to the relationship, represented by the vertical arrow in Figure 10.8, rather than getting drawn into any psychological 'games' (Berne 1964/1968), and to make the psychological contract explicit.

When doing couples therapy, the psychological contract is often quite directly accessible as both parties are present. In the context of therapeutic work with children, matters are made more complex by the absence usually of one of the parties to the administrative and professional contract, that is, the parent.

Multi-handed, multi-layered contracts

As discussed with regard to EAPs, the concept and logic of the three-handed contract extends to situations in which there are more than three parties. A therapist in training, for instance, has a number of administrative and professional relationships: with the training course or institute, with their clients, and with their supervisor. Page and Wosket (1994) represent these relationships, thus:

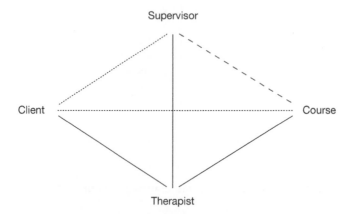

Figure 10.9   Relationship structure in trainee supervision (Page and Wosket 1994)

With the different lines representing different direct and indirect relationships, this is a clear representation of a number of relationships and inter-relationships: in this example, three, from any one person's point of view. With this number of parties, such multi-handed relationships may be represented either in this way or in multiple versions of the three-handed relationship (see Figures 10.6 and 10.10), which incorporates the EAP's counsellor's supervisor.

However, as the number of parties to a contract increases, or the particular issue becomes more complex, such inter-relationships become increasingly difficult to hold together either conceptually or in practice; and hence there is a greater need for clear processes (contracting) by which clear agreements (contracts) are made.

In order to visualise this I draw on the analogy and image from computing language of hypertext, literally, text 'beyond' text. The example of the contractual relationships between the counsellor in general practice, the client/patient, the GP and the PCT may now be represented as in Figure 10.11.

The advantage of this hypertext version is that it represents all the contractual relationships affecting all parties in any given situation. Figure 10.12 shows an expanded version based on the same situation.

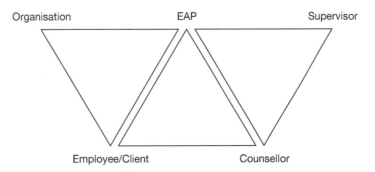

Figure 10.10   Multi-handed contract applied to EAP counselling

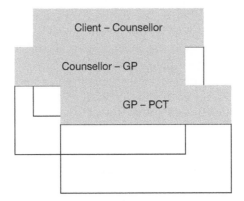

Figure 10.11   Three-handed contractual relationship in general practice (hypertext version)

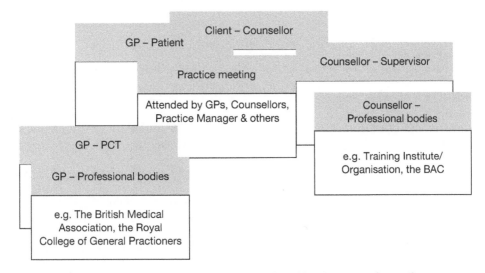

Figure 10.12   Multi-layerered contractual relationships in general practice

The relative location of the hypertext boxes in Figure 10.12 is important in that they represent the relationships, and their inter-relation, in practice. All the boxes overlap the client; the practice meeting overlaps the client/patient, the GP and the counsellor; and so on. At any one time and as regards specific issues, such as the funding of counselling in general practice, different parties will be involved. This hypertext view of contractual relationships in therapy is particularly useful in clarifying situations in which there are many parties and many layers to the relationships (such as in working in organisations, in training and in supervision, and in supervision of supervision).

Conclusion

The therapist is often dealing with a multiplicity of therapeutic and administrative relationships. Three-handed, multi-handed and multi-layered contracts are useful representative models in which the parties to such relationships, the administrative and professional levels, and the psychological aspects of contracts, as well as the implications of different settings for counselling and psychotherapy, may all be identified, considered, negotiated, defined, explored, re-negotiated and concluded. The concept of the contract in therapy remains useful, but only when it is separated from inappropriate analogies and expectations, and deconstructed.

Note

1   The organisations are: the Association for Christian Counsellors, the BACP, the British Association for Sexual and Relationship Therapy, the British Psychological Society, the Confederation of Scottish Counselling Agencies, the Federation of Drug and Alcohol Professionals, the United Kingdom Register of Counsellors, and the United Kingdom Association for Humanistic Psychology Practitioners, as well as the Independent Practitioners' Network which offers an alternative structure for validating and monitoring therapists, counsellors and others in the field.

References

Angyal, A. (1941) *Foundations for a Science of Personality*. New York: Commonwealth Fund.

Bader, E. and Pearson, P.T. (1988) *In Quest of the Mythical Mate: A Developmental Approach to Diagnosis and Treatment in Couples Therapy*. New York: Brunner Mazel.

Ball, V. (1995) *Guidelines for the Employment of Counsellors in General Practice*, (revised edn). Rugby: BAC.

Berne, E. (1966) *Principles of Group Treatment*. New York: Grove Press.

Berne, E. (1968) *Games People Play*. Harmondsworth: Penguin. (Original work published 1964.)

Berne, E. (1975) *What Do You Say After You Say Hello?* London: Corgi. (Original work published 1972.)

Berridge, J., Cooper, C. and Highley, C. (1997) *Employee Assistance Programmes and Workplace Counselling*. New York: Wiley.

Bond, T. (2000) *Standards and Ethics for Counselling in Action* (2nd edn). London: Sage.

Boyd, L.W. and Boyd, H.S. (1981) 'A transactional model for relationship counselling', *Transactional Analysis Journal*, 11: 142–6.

British Association for Counselling (1992) *Guidelines for the Employment of Counsellors*. Information Sheet 9. Rugby: BAC.

British Association for Counselling (1996) *Code of Ethics and Practice for Counsellors*. Rugby: BAC.

British Association for Counselling and Psychotherapy (2002) *Ethical Framework for Good Practice in Counselling and Psychotherapy*. Rugby: BACP.

Bubenzer, D.L. and West, J.D. (1993) *Counselling Couples*. London: Sage.

Crowe, M. and Ridley, J. (1990) *Therapy with Couples*. Oxford: Blackwell Scientific Publications.

English, F. (1975) 'The three-cornered contract', *Transactional Analysis Journal*, 5: 383–4.

Gilbert, M. and Shmukler, D. (1996) *Brief Therapy with Couples: An Integrative Approach*. Chichester: Wiley.

Goulding, R. and Goulding, M. (1978) *The Power is in the Patient*. San Francisco, CA: TA Press.

Heyward, C. (1993) *When Boundaries Betray Us: Beyond Illusions of What is Ethical in Therapy and Life*. San Francisco, CA: HarperCollins.

Hobbes, T. (1962) *Leviathan* (edited by J. Plamenatz). London: Collins. (Original work published 1651).

Jenkins, P. (1997) *Counselling, Psychotherapy and the Law*. London: Sage.

Jenkins, P. (2002) 'Transparent recording: therapists and the Data Protection Act 1998', in P. Jenkins (ed.) *Legal Issues in Counselling and Psychotherapy*. London: Sage. pp. 45–56.

Karpman, S. (1968) 'Fairy tales and script drama analysis', *Transactional Analysis Bulletin*, 7 (26): 39–43.

Mellor Clark, J. (undated) *Counselling in Primary Care in the Context of the NHS Quality Agenda: The Facts*. Paper. Rugby: BACP.

Micholt, N. (1992) 'Psychological distance and group interventions', *Transactional Analysis Journal*, 22: 228–33.

Minuchin, S. (1974) *Families and Family Therapy*. London: Tavistock.

Mowbray, R. (1995) *The Case Against Psychotherapy Registration*. London: Transmarginal Press.

Page, S. and Wosket, V. (1994) *Supervising the Counsellor*. London: Routledge.

Rogers, C.R. (1959) 'A theory of therapy, personality and interpersonal relationships, as developed in the client-centred framework', in S. Koch (ed.), *Psychology: A Study of Science, Volume 3: Formulation of the Person and the Social Context*. New York: McGraw-Hill. pp. 184–256.

Rose, N. (2003) 'Power and psychological techniques', in Y. Bates and R. House (eds) *Ethically Challenged Professions*. Ross-on-Wye: PCCS. pp. 27–45. (Original work presented 1997.)

Rousseau, J.-J. (1968) *The Social Contract* (translated by M. Cranston). Harmondsworth: Penguin. (Original work published 1762).

Schröder, T. (1989) 'Couples counselling', in W. Dryden, D. Charles-Edwards and R. Woolfe (eds) *Handbook of Counselling in Britain*, London: Tavistock/Routledge. pp. 58–72.

Selvini Palazzoli, M., Boscolo, L., Cecchin, G. and Prata, G. (1980) 'Hypothesizing-circularity-neutrality: three guidelines for the conductor of the session', *Family Process*, 19: 3–12.

Staveley, R. (1992) 'Appointing a counsellor', in M. Sheldon (ed.) *Royal College of General Practitioners Clinical Series on Counselling in General Practice*. London: RCGP Enterprises.

Steiner, C. (1984) 'Emotional literacy', *Transactional Analysis Journal*, 14: 162–73.

Steiner, C. and Cassidy, W. (1969) 'Therapeutic contracts in group treatment', *Transactional Analysis Bulletin*, 8 (30): 29–31.

Stonewall (2005) *Countries that Recognise or Proposed to Recognise Same-Sex Relationships*. Information available at: www.stonewall.org.uk/information_bank/ partnership/international/137.asp

Tudor, K. (1997a) 'A complexity of contracts', in C. Sills (ed.) *Contracts in Counselling* London: Sage. pp. 157–72.

Tudor, K. (1997b) 'Social contracts: contracting for social change', in C. Sills (ed.) *Contracts in Counselling*. London: Sage. pp. 207–15.

Tudor, K. and Hargaden, H. (2002) 'The couch and the ballot box: the contribution and potential of psychotherapy in enhancing citizenship', in C. Feltham (ed.) *What's the Good of Counselling and Psychotherapy? The Benefits Explained*. London: Sage. pp. 156–78.

Tudor, K. and Worrall, M. (2002) 'The unspoken relationship: financial dynamics in freelance therapy', in J. Clark (ed.) *Freelance Counselling and Psychotherapy*. London: Sage. pp. 80–90.

Tudor, K. and Worrall, M. (2004) 'Issues, questions, dilemmas and domains in supervision', in K. Tudor, and M. Worrall (eds) *Freedom to Practise: Person-Centred Approaches to Supervision*. Llangarron: PCCS Books. pp. 79–96.

Tudor, K. and Worrall, M. (2006) *Person-Centred Therapy: A Clinical Philosophy*. London: Routledge.

Choosing a Time-limited Counselling or Psychotherapy Contract

11

Jenifer Elton Wilson

The problem with short-term contracts

For many practitioners in counselling and psychotherapy, the prospect of placing a time limit upon a therapeutic commitment is still seen as both unwelcome and uninspiring. Short-term contracts are often limited to the pragmatic agreements of the *administrative contract* with some attention being paid to the impact of these time limitations upon the *professional contract* but little or no thought being given to the use which could now be made of the *psychological contract* (see Chapter 1). It is as if the imposition of a time boundary paralyses the talent, knowledge and emotional investment of the practitioner. Not only has time become limited but restrictions in meaningful contact, in 'depth' of therapeutic work and in outcome are automatically assumed to operate. Above all, the practitioner fears the resentment and disappointment of the client who is, through cruel circumstance, being offered a second-class engagement. This could be a case of projection. Talmon (1990) wrote with sympathetic understanding about practitioners' own needs to be intimate, to learn from their clients and to feel secure professionally and financially. This last is not merely included from cynicism but with an attitude of generous transatlantic pragmatism.

During the last 50 years an articulate, and often illustrious, minority of therapists have declared their conviction that brief therapy can be, for many clients, both efficacious and a preferred option. As early as 1946, Alexander and French were warning against the drift within psychoanalysis towards an uncritical acceptance that several years were needed to achieve relief from any form of neurotic distress. They promote and describe a psychoanalytic therapy which is both 'economic' and 'flexible'. Alexander warns against encouraging the patient to sink into a comfortable, dependent and regressive and long-term transference neurosis:

> the patient must never be allowed to forget that he came to the physician not for an academic understanding of the etiology of his condition but for help in solving his actual life problems. (Alexander and French 1946: 34)

They urge psychoanalytic practitioners to use the emotional force of the therapeutic experience only as a pressure towards the goal of returning the 'patient' or client, as soon as possible, to an improved and healthy external lifestyle. Towards this end, they encourage practitioners to be creative and positive towards termination and to introduce 'interruptions' (Alexander and French 1946: 35), of at least 18 months, to the analytic encounter so as to enable the client to experiment with their new emotional learning in 'real life' (1946: 40):

The therapeutic maxim of an economical psychotherapy, therefore, must be to allow as little regression as the patient can stand, only that procrastination which is unavoidable, and as little substitution as possible of transference gratifications for life experiences. (Alexander and French 1946: 34)

There have been many psychoanalytic experiments with brief therapy since 1947. The roll-call of eminent practitioners promoting a less lengthy version of analysis includes Balint (1957), Malan (1975), Sifneos (1979), Davanloo (1980) and Freud himself (1905, 1909). Finally there have been the inspiring, somewhat existential, insights provided by Mann (1973, 1981) in support of a fixed closing date for therapy. In spite of all this, and the demands of a restricted economic climate, the attraction and superiority of long-term engagements still dominate the psychoanalytic terrain.

Within the practical, goal-orientated and diligently researched field of cognitive-behavioural therapy, time-limited contracts are standard. Theoretical and empirical support is found in the work of the strategic family therapists (Minuchin 1974; Selvini Palazzoli et al. 1980; Watzlawick 1983; Haley 1976), the highly structured approaches of Ellis' Rational Emotive Behaviour Therapy (1970) and Beck's Cognitive Therapy (1976) as well as the hypnosis-based work of Milton Erickson (Erickson and Rossi 1979). Literature arising from this theoretical base describes the therapist as a skilled change artist (see Cade and O'Hanlon's 1993 *A Brief Guide to Brief Therapy* for a summary). Solution-focused therapy (de Shazer 1988; O'Connell 1998) is probably the best known approach to short term work within this overall approach, although it cannot really be described as a guide to forming time-limited contracts since most solution-focused practitioners do not make formal contracts but work from session to session.

A combination of psychoanalytic and cognitive insights is offered by the innovative and highly structured approach to time-limited practice of Cognitive Analytic Therapy (CAT), developed within a psychiatric setting by Ryle (1990). Originally based on a 12-session limit, this highly flexible and practical approach has, where appropriate, expanded the number of sessions available, and has been successfully applied to patients diagnosed with borderline personality disorder. It seems likely that the growth of a more generic, integrative approach to all forms of psychological therapy will be closely connected with the development of effective time-conscious practice.

Most counselling and some psychotherapy practice in Britain has been heavily influenced by the humanistic tradition within the parameters of an (often hidden) agenda aimed to achieve problem-solving and active change through cognitive-behavioural strategies. The central concept of the person-centred practitioner is the efficacy of the unrestricted offer of a therapeutic relationship. The work of Carl Rogers has contributed to our increased understanding of the interpersonal factors operating in a therapeutic relationship which, in themselves, offer the essential, if not perhaps sufficient, conditions for psychological change. However, one of these very conditions, of unconditional positive regard (Rogers 1967: 283–4) for the natural growth processes inherent in clients in receipt of therapeutic benevolence (see Worrall, Chapter 4 in this book), appears to militate against clearly stated limitations of time and direction. The implication is that to impose time boundaries as a condition upon a client would flout this firmly held belief and nullify the beneficial effects of counselling or psychotherapy.

In juxtaposition to these assumptions, counselling in Britain has always been firmly wedded to the tradition of making clear and explicit contracts which are inevitably grounded in some form of conditionality. Contractual agreements are conditional upon agreement about the nature of the services being offered (BACP 2005: 71–6) including availability, the degree of confidentiality offered, and practitioners' expectations of clients regarding fees, cancelled appointments and any other significant matters. This dissonance between the humanistic theoretical roots and the day-to-day practice of counselling may lie behind the discomfort felt by many practitioners, particularly those working in agencies and institutions where time limits are inevitable. A usual response is to sigh deeply and accept a less than perfect situation with as good a grace as possible. The administrative contract becomes focal, pushing the psychological and the professional contracts to the periphery. Inflexible time limits are accepted reluctantly, made central and struggled with.

There is also another well-established training route for practitioners within the British psychoanalytic tradition, most usually described as 'psychodynamic counselling'. Now that the main counselling organisation in the UK has changed its name from the British Association for Counselling to the British Association for Counselling and Psychotherapy, it is probable that a psychodynamic approach, or an integration between psychodynamic and humanistic approaches will become the major influence on practitioners. In the psychodynamic approach, the central concept has been the understanding and interpretation of transference phenonema, arising through the development of a therapeutic relationship. In spite of the pioneering work done within the psychoanalytic tradition by Alexander and French (1946), Malan (1975), Davanloo (1980) and others, the notion of long-term therapy as the only real 'gold standard' for effective therapy has persisted and permeated the field of 'psychodynamic counselling'. Ending is usually perceived as being appropriate only when the client has attained a profound level of intra-psychic transformation. To work in a context where there is a restriction of time due to limited resources can be perceived, by those holding to this belief system, as a cruel deprivation of the client's real need for therapy. A way round this dilemma has been found by Mann's (1973) inspiring adaptation of psychoanalytic thinking through which he emphasises the importance of developing a mature ego through reality testing and the acceleration of insight provided by the acceptance of ending as an existential given. This is a solution to the guilt felt by those who feel themselves to have benefited from the ongoing and long-term therapy which was central to their training. A body of training in brief therapy has been developed around these concepts. However, for those psychoanalytically influenced practitioners, who have not encountered Mann's (1973) approach, a similar response to work in a time-limited context to their humanistic colleagues is usual. They take on the brief work as a necessary evil, and hope to provide some supportive insights in the time available.

Thus, all these theoretically based belief systems tend to generate negative attitudes to any form of 'brief' or 'short-term' counselling. These attitudes are very likely to be picked up by the recipients of counselling or psychotherapy, at a non-verbal level, as they leak through the practitioner's body language and their rather despairing and half-hearted approach to the work in hand. Both clients and practitioners are ill served by this stance, and it is unnecessary. A therapeutic contractual commitment, which focuses on a time limit, is one which can provide the basis for an imaginative, flexible and rewarding piece of work, emphasising quality and intensity rather than quantity and patience.

However, there is another aspect to many of the planned time-limited contracts in the UK. The time limit is experienced by the practitioner, and possibly the client, as one that is imposed by some external agency, itself obedient to some impersonal overall provider of the necessary financial and practical resources on which the agency relies. Most Employment Assistance Providers (EAPs) as well as some, but not all, NHS primary care settings, university counselling services and low cost counselling agencies are likely to impose specific time limits. For some reason, most of these agencies seem to have arrived at six sessions as the ideal time boundary. To my knowledge, there is still very little research support for this particular number of sessions, which may have been originally based on some psychotherapists' practice of allowing a few sessions to build a reasonable working alliance before committing themselves and their clients to ongoing work. Alternatively, one could suspect that this amount of sessions has been adopted by service providers for financial budget-driven reasons. Nevertheless, there is valid research evidence that the 'dose-effect' of 10 to 20 sessions does seem to be indicated as the point at which immediate change through counselling or psychotherapy begins to level off, only to begin to accelerate again after 25 to 40 sessions have taken place (Howard et al. 1986; Seligman 1995). As Seligman (1995) points out, this research supports the effectiveness of psychotherapy in general, in that long-term therapy, where available, seems to show increased improvement.

Where possible, practitioners using a time-focused and positive approach to an externally imposed time-limited contract are advised to negotiate for as much flexibility as possible within the parameters of the resources available to their employing agency. This does not mean continuous requests for extra time. If the first session is handled well and the immediate needs and preferences of the client are explored without prejudice, practitioners are likely to find that many clients do not need even as much as the six sessions often allocated. As indicated below, clients 'in crisis' (Elton Wilson 1996: 13) or 'visiting' (de Shazer 1988: 87–88; Elton Wilson 1996: 13) may even find that first session enough in itself, or perhaps return for a couple more sessions to resolve the feeling of crisis or their decision that counselling is not for them at this time. Talmon (1990) has developed a two-hour 'single session' approach to his practice but advises that this works best if offered with indications of a generous availability of more time, if needed. Regrettably, the administrative needs of service providers may preclude any such flexibility and, in such cases, practitioners will need to work as flexibly as possible within the time available, perhaps by offering fortnightly sessions where a slower pace of change is indicated. An optimistic belief in the power of an attentive, focused and intense engagement, made available in every session and at every moment will provide the conditions within which almost all clients can experience and use the quality, if not quantity, of skilled psychological therapy. If this optimism cannot be genuinely adopted within these externally stipulated short-term contracts, then there is an almost ethical requirement for the unwilling practitioner to find other forms of work where ongoing longer-term contractual commitments are the norm.

How to make, use and enjoy time-limited contracts

Contrary to some of the pessimistic assumptions described above, the practitioner working successfully in short-term engagements needs to be supported by a positive and ethically consistent set of principles in dealing with the administrative aspects of the overall contract. Where these basic precepts have been established and shared between client and practitioner, the concentrated application of the professional elements becomes a fascinating exercise of the practitioner's skills in interaction with the client's search for relief from emotional distress. Meantime, at the psychological level, the short-term practitioner is managing the most profound levels of existential dread in themselves as well as in their clients. To surf through these three levels of contracting demands a higher level of proficiency in all practitioners but can also provide a greater fulfilment.

First principles of the short-term administrative contract

Work with abundance rather than poverty

If the counsellor or psychotherapist is relaxed and flexible in their offer of a brief period of therapeutic work at this time, then their clients' confidence will be enhanced. Above all, it is important to avoid giving an impression that therapy is a commodity subject to rationing. It is important to remember that, no matter how rigidly the number of sessions may appear to be controlled by the external context, the client's life lies ahead of them with its potential for personal development. There are other therapeutic contexts and other helpers, not least the client's own internal search for a meaningful existence. In many contexts, there is some flexibility with regard to the length of contract. Where resources are scarce, efficiency is more likely to result from an administrative agreement that allows a gradual firming up on the agreed time limit of the contract. The approach recommended here entails the offer of an introductory number of sessions with a mutual opportunity to try out working together before deciding whether to continue ('a mini-commitment and a review' (Elton Wilson 1996)) as a standard and experimental precursor to therapeutic engagement.

Case Example

Freda had never been to see a counsellor before. She felt ashamed and excited at the same time as the counsellor enquired about her recent visit to the doctor's surgery. She had arrived in tears, become agitated and angry when offered some pills and then felt too frightened and shaky to drive home alone. She told the counsellor that she had so many problems that it was difficult to know where to begin, or what to say. She would need so much time to sort herself out. The counsellor seemed to understand her embarrassment and confusion, listening carefully to her jumbled account of her daughter's new flat and her husband's business problems and the way they both were freezing her out. The counsellor suggested they continue to meet on a weekly basis and that after three meetings they could decide whether to continue. Freda had found it surprisingly pleasant to be able to talk non-stop to this patient stranger.

Commit yourself to the process even if it is only a one-session mini-mini-commitment

This is the second principle underlying a successful administrative contract in short-term counselling or psychotherapy. Substituting the word 'commitment' for the more formal legalistic word 'contract' indicates the personal investment required by client as well as by the practitioner. Where time is limited, a mutual agreement to work together wholeheartedly is arguably crucial, even though the aim may be only to explore whether therapy is necessary at all. A mini-commitment can be described as a 'crucial period of exploration with each session important in itself, clear in content, focus and resolution' (Elton Wilson 1996: 16). Wherever possible, and where there is enough flexibility in the definition of short-term practice, a mini-commitment of three to six sessions is likely to offer enough time for client and practitioner to engage in a working alliance, to define the main issues and to begin working together. If, however, the setting prescribes only six sessions in all, then it is still advisable to divide this time between the mini-commitment of, say, three sessions culminating in a review of the work done so far, and a decision whether and how to use the remaining sessions. The more motivated and committed a client is to the therapeutic process, the fewer sessions need to be offered before review. Conversely, where serious doubts remain as to a client's motivation, it is often better to offer the full measure of six mini-commitment sessions. Focusing and treating each session as important in itself are ways of ensuring that, if the client decides to discontinue at review, practitioner and client will have experienced some worthwhile work.

Case Example

Fred found his first visit to a psychotherapist very difficult. He had expected to come away with some answers. He told the therapist about his failure to get promotion at work and his feelings of anger with his boss. The therapist asked about his social life, his childhood and even his drinking habits. Fred felt sure that there was some way in which he could have been told what to say to the boss, or even how to put in a complaint. He had not expected to discuss his own private affairs. He felt surprised and challenged when the therapist suggested meeting for another month or so, naming their last session as a date five weeks away. Fred agreed reluctantly and said that he hoped the next one would be more useful.

Always assess for need and motivation

Ideally, this contractual commitment will have developed out of a careful process of assessment at an initial 'intake' interview. However, in many contexts clients are referred for counselling or psychotherapy as a last resort, or as an alternative to another form of treatment. Even where adequate assessment has taken place, it is advisable to use the first meeting between counsellor and client as a form of mutual assessment, a time to check what this client needs at this time, and what this counsellor could offer right now. Clients *in crisis* (Elton Wilson 1996: 13) are likely to need a practical focus on immediate coping and survival. Any discussion of time, place, fees or the number of sessions on offer will take second place to the investigation of support in the environment, referral to other forms of professional help and safety issues. Where appropriate or possible, a follow-up session will be necessary, within the next day or so.

Case Example

Chris had asked to see the occupational health counsellor as soon as possible. She could not understand what was going on. She felt breathless and anxious all the time and was unable to concentrate on anything. She was not sleeping or eating properly. She became angry and embarrassed as she told the counsellor of the stranger in the street who had seemed totally mad and grabbed her wrists, pulling her into a shop doorway. She had kicked out at him and managed to struggle free. She had tried to forget the incident, came into work as usual and told nobody of the shameful event. The counsellor was serious and concerned. She went through the story in detail and asked what would help Chris feel safe again. She offered her phone to Chris so that she could phone her parents and arrange to go home for the weekend. She would see Chris again on Monday to repeat the relaxation exercises and to discuss again Chris' decision about informing the police.

Other clients may be 'visiting' (de Shazer 1988: 87–8; Elton Wilson 1996: 13) the practitioner out of cautious interest as to whether counselling or psychotherapy might be useful to them. This ambivalence will need to be respected and explored before any firmer contractual agreements are made. For both these categories, counsellors may find a single session is all that is necessary, which could mean that more sessions are available for clients who are fully motivated and interested in contractual commitment.

Case Example

Conrad enjoyed his meeting with the counsellor in the GP's surgery. He had known for some time that his difficulty with eating out was in some way connected with his painful memories of the interminable and tense family meals he had endured before his father had finally left home. It was very interesting to link this to the sleepless nights he was experiencing now. However, he still had to face the firm's Christmas outing and he would be relying on the pills to get him through. There were other more painful memories about the past which he was not willing to revisit. The counsellor seemed to understand and accept these fears. Maybe he would go back to see her in the New Year.

The research evidence regarding the powerful effect of the first 10–20 sessions of psychological therapy, otherwise known as the 'dose effect' (Howard et al. 1986), has already been mentioned. Where possible, the counsellor using a time-limited approach would be well advised to use this information by offering a *time-limited commitment* of approximately six to eight further sessions after the mini-commitment, so that the duration of the entire therapeutic engagement between practitioner and client, at this stage of the client's life, is likely to have an upper limit of 15 sessions. Ideally, the practitioner would discuss this contract using the language of calendar dates rather than numbers of weeks so as to avoid an impression of time being rationed.

Accept and work with the concept that time is limited

The exact number of sessions is not the defining characteristic of time-limited counselling or psychotherapy. A 'time-focused' commitment (Elton Wilson 1996) can be distinguished from other forms of contractual commitment in the following ways:

1 Time itself is focused because there is a *specific closing date,* agreed between practitioner and client.
2 The extent and nature of psychological work undertaken is focused by the area of concern experienced by the client at this *stage of their personal development.*
3 Therapeutic concerns are focused onto a particular *focal theme,* which can be verbalised by the counsellor and recognised by the client.
4 Aims and ambitions are focused because there is an *agreed purpose* for this particular commitment. (Elton Wilson 1996: 90)

In making effective short-term administrative and professional contracts, these four distinguishing characteristics of short-term counselling or psychotherapy should be invoked during the mini-commitment, confirmed at review and remembered in every session right up to the agreed closing date.

Be realistic and consider the context

Surprisingly, some of the straightforward administrative considerations influencing a short-term commitment are sometimes ignored by practitioners until after the therapeutic engagement has begun. Discussions of confidentiality and its limits are even more necessary when referral to another service is a possibility. With a shorter time to work together, the use of mid-week telephone contact could be considered positively. Absences and cancellations are much more significant if the total engagement is agreed to terminate on a specific date some six to eight weeks ahead. Decisions need to be made at the outset as to whether meetings are to take place for a specific length of time or for a number of sessions, and whether a missed session is counted in or out of the contractual agreement.

Where counselling or psychotherapy is brief, fee structures may need to be considered carefully, especially by those in private practice where the practitioner is dependent on the security of fees arising from long-term work. Talmon (1990) suggests that a higher fee could be charged for skilful focused and effective brief therapy, since the overall financial investment of the customer is reduced, whether this is a private individual or a funding agency. In the latter case, the practitioner's relationship with a funding agency needs to be very clear. How much freedom does the practitioner have to be flexible within limits as to the number of sessions offered? Can the practitioner decide about weekly or fortnightly sessions? Can crisis containment sessions be offered? Is the client likely to be able to attend on a regular basis even in the short term? How will the practitioner fit their longer-term work around this time-limited commitment? All these questions are typical of contextual realities, which are better resolved before offering a short-term commitment.

Application of the professional contract

This is an agreement to work together with a particular focus

Where time is short, it is imperative that the practitioner engage openly in a joint project with the client. The client is motivated and in some form of psychological distress. The practitioner offers to work in alliance with the client in order that they might together understand the meaning of the present distress and plan together a way through to a more satisfactory style of living. The vague explorations of an uncommitted client, the 'visitor' mentioned above, are best suited to an open-ended contract rather than a time-limited context. However, even where goals are imprecise, the contractual agreement can be framed as work together, perhaps in search of a more clearly visualised aim.

Case Example

Freda told her counsellor that she felt confused and frightened. Her husband seemed to want her out of the way and her daughter had made it clear that she could manage without Freda's anxious phone calls. She sometimes thought of going back to her parents' home. At least she could be useful to them and support them in their old age. The counsellor asked who Freda turned to when she herself needed to be supported. Freda looked surprised and then began to weep as she told the counsellor that she was always the helper. She had no idea how to ask for help – maybe that was her problem. The counsellor pointed out that, in seeking out a counsellor, Freda had already done something different. Would Freda like to use their time together to tell more of her story and then, with increased understanding, they could together explore the present situation? Freda's face relaxed as she began to tell the counsellor how much she missed the work she had given up when her daughter was born.

Negotiate goals which are small but powerful

Working in a shorter and fixed time-frame, it is essential to discuss and then revisit, especially in a review session, the aims of client and practitioner. Clients may present unrealistic generalised wishes, which represent a somewhat miraculous escape from the present painful experience. Counsellors or psychotherapists, working in the candid co-operative manner recommended for short-term contracts, are well advised to explore and elucidate the best likely outcome which both participants can work towards. This needs to be described as an actual experience manifested in behaviour, feeling and thought rather than in purely psychological terms. Ideally, these aims should be realisable and modest, a beginning for the rest of the client's life and not a final solution.

Case Example

Fred had found his first three therapy sessions much more useful than he had expected. He felt that he had been taken seriously for a change and his anger at being passed over for promotion had been heard. Now he had begun to be interested in his role in the office and with his workmates. He realised he was in many ways a perfectionist and found it difficult to work alongside others with less exacting standards. Fred announced to the therapist that a change of job was in order – he needed to become his own boss. The therapist suggested that they could use the remaining sessions to examine the implications of this decision and its link to Fred's experience of being the 'lonely hero'.

Focus on a central issue

This is the most dominant and essential activity of the short-term practitioner. Whatever the problem which has brought the client to seek counselling or psychotherapy, it is likely to be linked to a learned pattern of response in stressful or challenging situations. Even where the emotional disturbance appears to belong deep inside the person, with no apparent external link or cause, it is likely to be a way of surviving the present even though, as a strategy, it is not working very well. Respecting the symptoms and making sense of them with the client's co-operation is an essential part of a contract to work together. The practitioner remains contractually dedicated to the discovery of an underlying and powerful pattern to be offered up respectfully as an insight for the client to use or reject in their own process of change. The central issue usually arises from the 'in here' process and clarifies the pattern formed 'back then' in the past which is now influencing the client's present life 'out there' (Jacobs 1988: 105) as well as shaping the future 'in view' (Elton Wilson 2000). Clarifying this 'kite of insight' (Elton Wilson 2000) enables a clearer contract to be agreed if the client chooses, with this understanding to work, with practitioner as ally, towards a broader range of strategies for survival.

Case Example

As Wednesday approached, Freda would experience a mixture of excitement and dread. The counsellor seemed so kind and accepting and yet Freda found herself admitting to such strange longings, like the fantasy about renting a room by the day so that she could spend time all by herself, for instance. And the counsellor would continually return the conversation to Freda's feelings and wishes, especially when Freda was describing the difficulties experienced by her daughter and her husband. It was uncomfortable to realise how much resentment she had been hiding and how much guilt lay behind her dutiful expressions of anxious concern. The fourth time they met, Freda noticed that the counsellor seemed pale and tired. She felt frightened and suggested that they finish early so that the counsellor could get home in good time. The counsellor did not take up the offer but asked Freda to be aware of her own

(continued)

(continued)

tensions – what was she reminded of at that moment? Freda's voice became sharp and shrill as she told the counsellor about her mother's constant illnesses which had meant that, even as a teenager, Freda stayed in most evenings. She never had the opportunity to gad about like her daughter was doing. She had put her mother's needs first. And, as the counsellor added quietly, learned how to suppress her own needs and wishes.

Work together within a variety of therapeutic relationships

The primary mode of relationship necessary for time-limited practice is the 'working alliance' (Gelso and Carter 1985: 161–9). Without this emotional bond to work together on agreed tasks towards agreed goals, there is likely to be very little achieved within a limited period of time. This necessary level of trust and respect between client and practitioner needs to be established early in a therapeutic engagement involving any series of regular sessions, no matter how brief and exploratory. Where there is likely to be no acknowledged alliance, it is better to refer a client elsewhere or to encourage time out for further contemplation. A surprising discovery made by many short-term therapists has been the beneficial influence of the rapid transference of intense interpersonal patterns by the client onto the practitioner who has a time limit. It is as if the client's awareness of time limitation encourages swift re-emergence of the unsatisfactory past experiences which are feeding emotional discomfort encountered in the present. In time-limited work, the practitioner initially allows and welcomes this eruption from the client's past, no matter how unreal and inappropriate. Once in the room and available to challenge, the assumptions underlying the transference reaction can be explored by client and practitioner and the repetition confronted. Where, however, there is a real component to the client's experience of the practitioner, it is best to fully acknowledge and deal with any obstruction to the working alliance arising from the 'real relationship' (Gelso and Carter 1985: 183–91). As each relationship modality is encountered, the contractual commitment is tested and may be strengthened.

Case Example

Fred had only two sessions left now, and he looked at his psychotherapist with real dislike. How could this big quiet man with his posh accent ever really understand what it had been like to be a small scrawny boy growing up on a housing estate where gang membership was the only passport to acceptance? He decided to shock the therapist by describing how he had learned the hard way about pleasing the older boys. They had used him for errands, and then for sex. His only way out had been to study hard, even though his brothers sneered at him as a swot. Fred had won a scholarship

(continued)

(continued)

to the local grammar school and then somehow managed to get to university. He had dreams of getting to the top, making lots of money and then retiring. But nothing had changed – he was still expected to do all the dirty work. He was the one who made sure that the books balanced and who chased up the bad debts. Fred's therapist looked sad as he responded to the painful story. He said he understood better now how important it must seem for Fred to avoid the danger of all social relationships by burying himself in his work. He commented upon Fred's courage in disclosing so much to himself, a comparative stranger with a different history. Fred relaxed. He had not expected this level of respect from a man who seemed so much older and more successful than himself.

Managing the psychological contract

Use every moment of contact to build trust

Where time is short, the hidden agenda of client and practitioner may be to avoid too intense an encounter so that it will not be painful to terminate at the agreed time. This is counterproductive to short-term work, which depends on a high level of motivation and willingness to take psychological risks. Without this subtle agreement to work closely together at the cliff face of the client's problematic central issue, the most powerful insight, cathartic facilitation or experiment in behaviour change is likely to be ineffective. The beneficial psychological contract is founded on a silent acknowledgement that practitioner and client are in this journey together up to the very last moment.

Facilitate fears as well as hopes

At the psychological level, there is always likely to be strong resistance to change. The client has, after all, managed so far to survive, no matter how unsatisfactory the means whereby this has been achieved. Counselling or psychotherapy itself is likely to be a risky business with attached apprehensions which may not have been revealed. Practitioners are known to encourage discussion of family and friends. There have been accounts of practitioners taking advantage of their clients' vulnerabilities. A common phrase is that clients 'undergo' therapy, which implies a prescribed but unpleasant experience. It is important to encourage clients to articulate their fears about their commitment to therapeutic work in all contractual agreements, whether short or long term. A brief experience of therapy is particularly vulnerable to sabotage from unexpressed anxieties.

Accept high expectations at first, and stay firm through disillusionment and retreat

Time-limited therapy often attracts optimism in clients. There can be an inbuilt assumption that the limited number of counselling or psychotherapy sessions on offer is all that is needed to make a crucial difference to the difficulty being experienced by the client. These positive expectations, especially when matched by the practitioner's own belief in the efficacy of short-term therapy, are, in themselves, predictive of a positive outcome, and enhance the contractual commitment between participants. However, the practitioner is well advised to prepare her/himself, and where possible the client, for a lowering in the client's hopeful anticipation of immediate relief during the 'middle' (Peake et al. 1988: 224–5) or 'midpoint' (Mann 1973: 35) phase of the psychotherapeutic commitment. At this stage, the time-limited practitioner reminds the client about the contractually agreed closing date, reveals or revisits the central issue focused upon and the agreed goal of this piece of work. In a highly flexible setting, this return to the original contractual agreement may lead to a new contract. However, the benefits of flexibility should be calibrated against the beneficial pressure of an impending closing session. There is a danger that practitioner as much as client is seeking to avoid the existential anxiety which any time limit can activate, and which is a powerful reminder of the necessity to take responsibility for finding a meaningful existence within an essentially finite life situation.

Case Example

Now that they were almost over, Fred was ready to admit that he had needed these six therapy sessions. He realised how lonely and dull his life had been up to now, and he was excited to find that going out for a drink with his colleagues after work was really enjoyable. They seemed to enjoy his dry sense of humour and Fred had agreed to join a fell-walking expedition being organised by one of the women. However all this was very superficial compared with the relief of being able to talk to someone without having to perform, and someone who knew about his past. Fred's therapist acknowledged that Fred might still need a safe place to experiment with this new expanded sense of self-esteem and to lay ghosts from the painful past. He suggested that Fred contact an organisation which offered support groups for male survivors of sexual abuse. This would not only be somewhere to talk more openly, but would also be an opportunity for Fred to celebrate his achievements, past and present. Fred said he was interested but that this sounded a scary prospect and he had felt disappointed not to be offered some more sessions here. There was a silence and then Fred laughed. It seemed that he was allowing himself to rely on another human being after all. The therapist was appreciative as he commented upon the immediacy and frankness of Fred's response. He offered Fred the opportunity to come back for a follow-up session in a few months' time. Maybe they could discuss the group again then.

Offer warmth with non-possessiveness

At the psychological level, a belief is shared by client and practitioner that counselling or psychotherapy must provide a nurturing and empathic environment within which the client can achieve relief from psychological pain. This is not usually discussed contractually but remains an assumption which is based on a reasonable level of evidence within all the main theoretical orientations (Fiedler 1950). The short-term practitioner is likely to covertly enter into an unspecified contract to provide compassionate sensitivity but is also contractually committed to combine this warmth with a high level of non-possessiveness. The agreement underlying all short-term counselling or psychotherapy is to work within the intimacy of a thera-peutic relationship which is dedicated to its own dissolution in service of the client's progressive resolution of their problematic life issues.

Believe in the efficacy of time-limited practice

It is in this area that even the most skilful use of short-term counselling or psy-chotherapy can founder. The client will swiftly pick up on any suppressed or hidden doubts held by a practitioner. To work within a time-limited commitment effectively means to fully accept the limitations, to use them and to trust the client's own self-healing process to continue outside and beyond the professional commitment. If practitioners cannot let go of their doubts and their own dislike of limitations of time, then it is better for them to continue working with energy and enthusiasm in a less demanding but equally satisfying manner where time limits are not imposed either by the setting, by external circumstances or by the client's own preference.

References

Alexander, F. and French, T.M. (1946) *Psychoanalytic Therapy: Principles and Applications*. New York: Ronald Press.

BACP (British Association for Counselling and Psychotherapy) (2005) *Talking Therapies: An Essential Anthology*. Rugby: BACP.

Balint, M. (1957) *The Doctor, his Patient and the Illness*. London: Pitman.

Beck, A.T. (1976) *Cognitive Therapy and the Emotional Disorders*. New York: International University Press.

Cade, B. and O'Hanlon, W.H. (1993) *A Brief Guide to Brief Therapy*. London: Norton.

Davanloo, H. (1980) *Current Trends in Short-term Dynamic Therapy*. New York: Aronson.

Ellis, A. (1970) *The Essence of Rational Psychotherapy: A Comprehensive Approach to Treatment*. New York: Institute for Rational Living.

Elton Wilson, J. (1996) *Time-Conscious Psychological Therapy – a Life Stage To Go Through*. London: Routledge.

Elton Wilson, J. (2000) 'Integration and eclecticism in brief/time-focused therapy', in S. Palmer and R. Woolfe (eds) *Integrative and Eclectic Counselling and Psychotherapy*. London: Sage.

Erickson, M.H. and Rossi, E.L. (1979) *Hypnotherapy: An Exploratory Casebook*. New York: Irvington.

Fiedler, F.E. (1950) 'A comparison of therapeutic relationships in psychoanalytic, nondirective and Adlerian therapy', *Journal of Consulting Psychology*, 14: 436–45.

Freud, S. (1905) 'Fragment of an analysis of a case of hysteria', in *The Complete Psychological Works of Sigmund Freud*. Vol. X. London: Hogarth, 1958.

Freud, S. (1909) 'Notes upon a case of obsessional neurosis', in *The Complete Psychological Works of Sigmund Freud*. Vol. X. London: Hogarth, 1958.

Gelso, C.J. and Carter, J.A. (1985) 'The relationship in counselling and psychotherapy: components, consequences and theoretical antecedents', *Counseling Psychologist*, 13 (2): 155–243.

Haley, J. (1976) *Problem-solving Therapy*. San Francisco: Jossey-Bass.

Howard, K.I., Kopta, S.M., Krause, M.S. and Orlinsky, D.E. (1986) 'The dose–effect rela-tionship in psychotherapy', *American Psychologist*, 41: 159–64.

Jacobs, M. (1988) *Psychodynamic Counselling in Action.* London: Sage.

Malan, D.H. (1975) *A Study of Brief Psychotherapy.* London: Plenum Press.

Mann, J. (1973) *Time Limited Psychotherapy.* Cambridge, MA: Harvard University Press.

Mann, J. (1981) 'The core of time-limited psychotherapy: time and the central issue', in S. Budman (ed.) *Forms of Brief Therapy.* New York: Guilford Press. pp. 25–43.

Minuchin, S. (1974) *Families and Family Therapy.* Cambridge, MA: Harvard University Press.

O'Connell, B. (1998) *Solution-focused Therapy.* London: Sage.

Peake, T.H., Borduin, C.M. and Archer, R.P. (1988) *Brief Psychotherapies: Changing Frames of Mind.* London: Sage.

Rogers, C.R. (1967) *On Becoming a Person: A Therapist's View of Psychotherapy.* London: Constable.

Ryle, A. (1990) *Cognitive-analytic Therapy: Active Participation in Change.* Chichester: Wiley.

Seligman, M.E.P. (1995) 'The effectiveness of psychotherapy: the *Consumer Reports* study', *American Psychologist,* 50: 965–74.

Selvini Palazzoli, M., Boscolo, L., Cecchin, G. and Prata, G. (1980) 'Hypothesising–circularity–neutrality: three guidelines for the conductor of the session', *Family Process,* 19: 445–53.

de Shazer, S. (1988) *Clues: Investigating Solutions in Brief Therapy.* New York: W.W. Norton.

Sifneos, P.E. (1979) *Short-term Dynamic Psychotherapy: Evaluation and Technique.* New York: Plenum.

Talmon, M. (1990) *Single Session Therapy.* San Francisco: Jossey-Bass.

Watzlawick, P. (1983) *The Situation Is Hopeless, But Not Serious.* New York: Norton.

12 Therapy Contracts with Trainee Practitioners

Brigid Proctor and Charlotte Sills

It is a rare situation when a client is 'required' to have counselling. Occasionally, it may be a provision of a probation or prison order, or part of an ultimatum by a disgruntled spouse. It is a strange fact that the single largest group of 'enforced clients' consists of those whose counselling or psychotherapy training makes 'personal therapy' a requirement of the course. As a training requirement, such therapy/ counselling is different in kind from that which is freely sought as a result of 'choice, change, or confusion reduction' (Gilmore 1997). This requirement, though widespread, is a subject of ongoing professional controversy and there has been insufficient research into its efficacy. We believe that there are varied and valid intentions behind the tradition, and that what is lacking is clarity of purpose and contract.

The purpose of this chapter is to argue that the personal counselling or therapy that students are required to have as part of accredited training should be spelled out in terms of a three-cornered contract or working agreement (English 1975 and see Chapters 1 and 10). This agreement would be made between the course managers of each training course, their trainees, and the prospective counsellor/therapist of each trainee, within the relevant Code or Framework for Ethical Practice (see Figure 12.1). Such an agreement would vary according to the stated intentions of each training organisation. Within each organisation the intentions need to be agreed by each participant to the contract.

A three-cornered puzzlement

The therapist

From our experience as supervisors and supervisor consultants we have come across counsellors and therapists who are puzzled by the particular practical and ethical issues which can arise when they are working with trainees. The kinds of questions raised are: 'How can I work with someone who is just coming because they are required to do so?' or 'I have real reservations about my client who is a trainee on a counselling course. I don't think she is a *danger* to clients but I do think she is very confused and confusing. The training course appears to want no contact with their students' counsellors. What is my position in relation to the Ethical Framework?'

The client

We have also met trainees who are uneasy or dissatisfied with their counselling/ therapy while they are in training. A trainee may say 'My counsellor and I have had some disagreements and she seems to be hinting that she doesn't think I am "ready" to take on clients' or 'I don't think my therapy is being helpful to me. Will it affect my assessment if I decide to change therapists?' or 'I was really pleased to have an excuse to go into therapy and my therapist was great. However, she used interventions and techniques which were not in the same tradition as my training. We agreed she would tell me about them as we went along but we forgot, and we never had a review except at finishing.' When any of these concerns were explored, it usually seemed that client (trainee) and counsellor/psychotherapist did not have a shared agreement about the purpose of the experience. They were uncertain about their roles and responsibilities – and in some cases, rights.

The course

Some training courses have not thought thoroughly about these issues. Others have, but are relying on unspoken assumptions about the purpose and practice of the therapy requirement. The presumed contract has never been spelt out. Trainers may say: 'Of course, personal work is a key element of training', or 'Our students are all required to have therapists who are on our list. Both students and therapists understand that the therapy is entirely confidential under any circumstances. We would never speak with a therapist about a student' or 'The therapy is an integral part of the assessment process and the trainees know this'. What may not be spelt out are the course's expectations, or the trainees' and the therapists' rights and responsibilities in these situations.

Unresolved professional tensions

Such questions weave in and out of various unresolved tensions within the wider profession. These tensions will surface in any arena where unspoken assumptions are being enacted. Trainees, their therapists and their trainers can get caught up in them. In this particular context, examples of these tensions might be:

- unspoken or conflicting assumptions about the nature of 'healthy' living or 'psychopathology';
- what formal or informal assessment of 'personal' suitability and readiness to practice should be taking place;
- whether experiencing a counselling process which is in the same tradition as the training is necessary for good practice or merely perpetuating unexamined traditions;
- whether blanket confidentiality is always ethical in organisational settings;
- what the connection/distinction is between a therapeutic process and a learning process;
- should training courses be primarily educational and devolve any therapeutic intent to personal counselling/therapy?
- should courses see personal development and healing as *the* major learning experience?
- is experiencing personal vulnerability in a therapy dyad (or group), and surviving, a necessary component of developing counselling/therapeutic empathy, competence and confidence?
- if one of the purposes of the requirement is to gain experience of being a client, might therapy throughout training be unhelpful for trainees when they offer

time-limited counselling to clients; would, say, six sessions from time to time be more appropriate – or adequate?
- what are the professional and economic implications of counsellors/therapists relying on a steady stream of trainees as 'required' clients who go on to do the same when they are qualified; or what are implications if that requirement were altered?

and, perhaps most importantly,

- is the purpose of training therapy to support trainees in a difficult training process, or to benefit their clients? Or both? And, if so, how?

These tensions are real – we do have differing beliefs and agendas in our profession. It is appropriate that they be aired and, where possible, 'worked through' in a time-honoured manner. Deciding that trainees should not *have* to experience being in some sort of client role will not send the tension away. Neither will continuing a practice in which intentions are unclear.

Resolution through shared action – the three-cornered contract

Informed consent at course level

We do not propose that there should be a uniform professional agreement about the purpose and practice of required trainee counselling/psychotherapy. Indeed, because of the huge variation in approaches and methods taught in different training courses, there could not be such uniformity. We are suggesting that it should become standard practice that each training course engage in the task of thinking out and devising an appropriate tri-partite contract between training course, trainee and prospective counsellor/therapist (see Figure 12.1). This contract will involve defining the *administrative* and *professional* contracts at the organisational level (Berne 1966 and see also Chapter 10) so that they are clearly understood by all parties.

Such a contract would make clear:

- the purpose of the requirement within the overall values and theoretical orientation of the course;
- the nature and extent of the requirement – linked to that articulated purpose;
- the procedure for making individual counselling/psychotherapy arrangements;
- the procedure for initiating the three-way contract;
- the rights and responsibilities of trainee, counsellor/therapist and training course, for monitoring and reviewing that the stated purposes are being met;
- the feedback loop (if any) between the partners to the agreement, and the purpose of the feedback (assessment? confirmation of attendance? ethical dilemmas?);
- the course of action for dealing with difficulties or disputes between any of the parties; and

- whether the trainee is to demonstrate how the experience of being a client has helped her in the overall stated purpose and if so, how that can be accomplished appropriately.

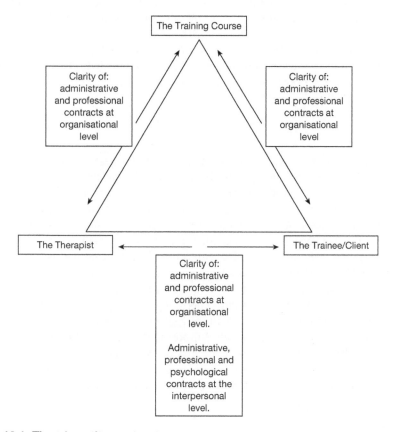

Figure 12.1: The tri-partite contract

We suggest that such a contract would establish sufficient agreement in the aims of the process and the 'rules of engagement' for trainee and therapist to give free and informed consent to work together; and for training courses to support and challenge this important component of learning and development.

Required personal therapy – a rationale for 'integrated education'

We suggest such a contract because we believe that any requirement for trainees to have their own counselling/psychotherapy as part of training must have a purpose which is integrated into the overall educational experience. We offer here our own rationale.

Life and learning as therapeutic

All our life experience has the potential for being therapeutic – that is, it can lead to living 'more satisfyingly and resourcefully' (the original BAC definition of counselling). Our belief is that the entire design of a training course should be based on encouraging personal and interpersonal development as an active intention. Such learning is usually also therapeutic. Since the stated intention of most courses is to prepare and enable trainees to practise as counsellors and psychotherapists, some of the aspects of the course will be necessarily focused elsewhere. The counselling/therapy requirement potentially offers protected learning and therapeutic space geared to each trainee's needs.

Experiential

Viewed educationally, personal therapy is clearly not a part of the didactic component of the course. Neither is it primarily skills practice or discussion (although dialogue will be the method and learning will be taking place about 'client skills'). It is, rather, a part of the experiential component – trainees are required to engage in a structured experience from which they are expected to learn something useful for their training. All experiential work is offered for a purpose. The purpose may be *specific*, for instance, 'We want you to develop the ability for empathising with "role-vulnerability" by being in client role and experiencing the power variable'; or it may be *general*, 'It is our experience that trainees usually find out about their own accustomed interpersonal patterns through experiencing therapy, and we want to ensure that each has that opportunity'; or 'Counselling training is usually stressful and we want to enable you to have appropriate support and challenge through that process.'

Therapists often say that they notice a link between a course where the personal development component is engaging and integrated, and the trainee who can use and integrate their therapy experience into their development.

Reflective

Some people argue that thinking about and articulating one's learning from therapy in some way dilutes the power of it. We believe, on the contrary, that as an experiential part of the course, it necessarily involves a stated expectation that the trainees not only *have* the experience, but also that they *reflect* on it in the light of some overall educational purpose: 'I personally found it to be intrusive when my therapist said … I wonder if that is just me or whether different clients experience it differently'; or 'I am realising that I automatically protect myself from experiencing anger by feeling sorry for people who treat me badly. I am experimenting with what other options I have in my personal life. I wonder how this insight might affect my practice as a psychotherapist.' It is this expectation of focused reflection (stated or assumed) that marks the difference when a dentist undergoes root canal treatment or a doctor has a cancer scare as an incidental life experience. Both will be helpful to their patients only to the extent they consciously relate their experience to their intention for developing skill with patients. For us, therefore, it would be congruent to require some demonstration by a training therapist of this reflection in, for example, a learning journal, or at least in regular review between client and therapist.

Modelling a private and peculiar practice

The therapeutic, or helping, alliance is a peculiar concept. It has aspects which resemble other alliances – friendships, teacher–student, doctor–patient, parent–child. For all clients there will be a 'first time.' Clients differ widely as to the extent that they understand what the proposed alliance entails. They may see it as potentially terrifying or shaming, be taken by surprise at unexpected exposure or understanding, or just be desperate to talk, rant or weep. Most cannot give 'informed consent' at the first meeting – only when they have had a taster of what the words mean in practice. We can think of no other way to appreciate the complexities, advantages and pitfalls of such an enterprise than experiencing it. In addition, it offers a model for practice, which, like all models, can be swallowed whole, rejected or used with discrimination.

Offering a 'healthy' environment for change

It is now universally accepted (supported by much research – see Introduction and Chapter 1) that of the factors most significant in determining successful outcomes of psychotherapy, it is the quality of the therapeutic relationship that is the most important. There is further evidence from the world of neuro-science, as fMRI scans demonstrate, how it is in relationship that we learn to regulate our affect and manage our experiences, and that this can happen only with another person who is really open to our feelings. It seems to give support for the long-held belief that our clients cannot work through issues that their therapists have not addressed.

Another way of expressing all this, perhaps, is to say that a therapist's most important 'tool' is herself. It would seem to be important, therefore, to try to ensure that the tool is as clean, well-oiled and serviceable as possible. Differing models have different languages for describing this condition. A person-centred counsellor might define it as being congruent; a TA practitioner script-free and autonomous; a CBT therapist might aspire to right thinking and so on. But whatever the definition of the condition, generally all the approaches advocate it as a desirable way of living and propose counselling and psychotherapy as a way of so 'becoming'. We owe it to our clients to try and achieve it – or at least to have tested out whether it works for us!

The contract between the course and the trainee

Any course will develop its own rationale which might agree with or differ from ours; in any case the course needs to be clear about its own position and the requirements and expectations that arise from it. All the areas described above need to be clarified including issues such as:

- what is the intended aim of the therapy?
- who will be appropriate therapists for trainees and must they be of the same orientation as the course?
- the duration of the therapy required, and why?

- what, if any, will be the requirement to demonstrate the effectiveness of the therapy (for example through a reflective essay or journal)?
- will there be any communication between the course and the therapist?
- will the therapy form any part of the assessment?
- to whom could either party turn in the event of an ethical or professional dilemma arising? And by what processes will resolution be sought?

The contract between the course and the therapist

Once the course has clarified its reasons for requiring therapy and agreed them with the trainee, a contract can be made between the course and the therapist which will give the same information. This could be in the form of a standard letter to be presented to the therapist that sets down the course's aims and any requirement for demonstration that they be met. The course may even provide details of the syllabus so that the therapist can understand the particular approach that the trainee is learning. This contract is *inviting the therapist to be part of an intentional learning journey* with the trainee/client. The letter could ask the therapist to confirm that he or she is willing to take on a client in these circumstances.

The contract between the therapist and the client

The therapist and client are then free to negotiate the contract for their engagement. This will involve the 'private' administrative and professional agreements as to the time, fees, setting etc, as well as the goals and tasks. In normal circumstances, agreeing the tasks would include a brief description of the theory of change involved in the approach, and how the therapy would proceed (see Chapter 1). However, with a contract between therapist and trainee, the conversation needs to go further. Before agreeing a personal direction for the work, the two parties need to reflect on the obligations of the course requirements and how they might be met.

'Health' or 'freedom from neurosis' has been defined by the course approach in terms that trainee/client and therapist can use to set goals and review the work. This could form the basis of part of the agreement. The particular methodology can be discussed and it's implications. This consciously adds a dimension to the endeavour by making the relationship a forum for learning about therapeutic practice. The partners in the learning relationship may agree to set aside some time in each session, or once a month, to discuss the *process* of the therapy. How is it unfolding? What interventions of the therapist were most useful in furthering the therapeutic task? What is the client learning about being a client (a new client? an experienced client?) in this experience, and is the insight particular to him or might it be transferable?

This sort of exploration would be entirely compatible for some approaches to therapy. A relational approach, for example, sets store by intersubjective experiences in the consulting room or by the development of transferential dynamics. There could be an explicit agreement to reflect upon the relationship that is developing between the two of them. CBT practitioners would also find a 'feedback' discussion wholly appropriate, as might person-centred therapists. Other practitioners may need to find different ways of integrating the experience into the trainee's learning.

Therapist and client also need to acknowledge and discuss how the therapy will be different from a usual one. There may be a loss of freedom, in a sense, in a requirement to reflect on learning. What will be the impact on the client? He or she will also certainly have feelings about being 'obliged' to undertake such a private and intimate journey, when not prompted by 'choice, change, or confusion reduction' (Gilmore 1997).

The psychological contract

Chapter 1, in addition to describing the administrative and professional contracts, explores what Berne (1966) calls the *psychological* contract. This refers to the hidden wants and needs that lead to an unspoken – frequently unconscious – bargain between participants in an agreement. At the institutional level this may arise from the culture of the training organisation and convey itself to the therapist. For example, the therapist may pick up from one organisation the subtle impression that she is being relied on to deliver unwelcome messages about a trainee's suitability. Or conversely, she may sense from another organisation which is reluctantly adhering to UKCP section requirements for personal therapy, that if she gets her name on the list of recommended therapists, in return she must do nothing to 'rock the boat'. So challenging the box-ticking trainee to engage meaningfully in the therapeutic journey is subtly discouraged. It is useful for all parties to be alert to such 'contracts'.

At the level of therapist and client, again the therapist would do well to examine the possible unconscious aspects of the working agreement, aspects that would not exist in ordinary circumstances. This may include, for example, passing the time in order to fulfil requirements or intellectualising so that the theoretical learning about practice takes over from the experiential. The therapist subtly colludes in the idea that being present equates to meaningful work or that a demonstration of how much is being learned theoretically is a substitute for real insight. When the therapeutic engagement involves the present or future livelihood of both parties, a scrupulous attention to the psychological level is vital.

Conclusion

As long as the requirement for training therapy exists, it should be properly contracted. All parties need, mutually, to understand the intention of this experiential component of the training. Some courses may require some account of the learning which has accrued for their trainees. Others will want to have some agreed review that checks if the (expensive) experience is being beneficial and leads to the hoped-for results. All should know their rights and responsibilities in the enterprise; and courses should be aware of a responsibility to monitor whether participants are operating within the agreed ethical framework. Clearly, as Moses might have said, man does not live by contracts alone. There will always be misunderstandings and confusions; there will always be transference and counter-transference. However, ensuring clarity of understanding about the purpose, aims and circumstances of required therapy can do much to avoid a wasted experience.

References

Berne, E. (1966) *Principles of Group Treatment.* Oxford University Press.

English, F. (1975) 'The three cornered contract', *Transactional Analysis Journal*, 5: 383–4.

Gilmore, S. (1997) *The Counsellor-in-training.* New York: Appleton Century Crofts.

13 Contracting in Supervision

Brigid Proctor

'The most important thing I have learned from this first session of supervisor training is that I intend to ask my own supervisor if we can have a clearer working agreement.' This comment, or one similar, is heard frequently from supervisors-in-training. It highlights the need for supervisors and their supervisees to think intentionally about the best use of precious supervision time. It is also a reminder that a working relationship should be based on clearly agreed expectations.

In such remarks, counsellors are referring to the overall contract that their supervisor makes (or as is frequently the case, does not make) with them for their supervision relationship and working alliance. In creating this working agreement, both parties clarify and negotiate the tasks, roles, responsibilities, rights, ground rules, assumptions and styles which will guide and prioritise their work together. This process of clarifying and negotiating has both task and relationship implications. The working agreement which is arrived at as an interim contract for the work is the end product. The opportunity to meet and know each other better, as practitioners and as human beings, allows for the sharing of information about styles, preferences, passions, aversions and so on – the pointers as to what will foster this relationship or delay its development into a fruitful working alliance.

This initial contracting process weaves a container for the work together, and also sets markers by which both parties can guide and prioritise their direction at points of choice or confusion. It ensures that each participant is clear as to their responsibilities, and their freedoms.

One-off contracts

In addition to the overall *working agreement* there are other contracts which it can be useful to make in supervision, as in counselling. A *session contract* determines the agenda for a specific supervision session. Within that, *mini-contracts* allow for negotiating what both parties want from any individual item of work within the session. We will return to these contracts later in the chapter. Like the outer doll in a nest of Russian dolls, the working agreement both shapes and contains all the other contracts negotiated within it.

Creating the working agreement

The specifics of the agreement and the manner in which the supervisor conducts the negotiation will vary widely. For instance, a supervisor who is very new to that role, negotiating with a group of beginning trainees, will rightly have different preoccupations to an experienced supervisor negotiating supervision with a pair of student counsellors; or the same supervisor agreeing a contract with a newly independent free-lance counsellor. Thus the negotiation will involve attention to at least three key variables:

- context – e.g. agency, free-lance, training;
- developmental stage – of supervisor and supervisee; and
- form – individual, group, peer, etc.

A further variable – the theoretical orientation of the supervisor and, where there is a difference, the supervisee – will influence the style, priorities and specifics of the agreement.

Basic understanding

From the outset, it is crucial that both parties have arrived at some agreed understanding of the shared task: and what, consequently, are the roles and responsibilities of each. Each supervisor needs her own thumbnail description, which encapsulates task and process and makes purposes clear. The supervisee, however, may or may not have his own developed ideas and experience of supervision. An initial clarifying and negotiating of these basics defines everything that follows. Inskipp and Proctor (1993, 1995) offer a framework for helping supervisors and supervisees develop their own definition. Page and Wosket (1994) offer a cyclical model. Michael Carroll (1996) after having quoted various definitions, opts for describing seven supervisor tasks, they are:

- to create the learning relationship;
- to teach;
- to counsel;
- to consult;
- to evaluate;
- to monitor professional/ethical issues; and
- to work with administrative/organisational aspects of client work.

Professional bodies have been remarkably unclear about the professional contract they are in with supervisors. It has been left to practitioners, writers and trainers to ponder the proper rights and responsibilities of supervisors and supervisees. The then BAC in 1995, for example, created a new *Code of Ethics and Practice for Supervisors* and asserted that 'the primary purpose of supervision is to ensure that the counsellor is addressing the needs of the client'. Since then, the Association has opted for the *Ethical Framework for Good Practice in Counselling and Psychotherapy* (2000) which subsumes all previous Codes of Ethics. This places responsibility for good practice very clearly on all members of the BACP, whatever their professional role, and spells out what values, principals and personal qualities such good practice is based on and entails. The three paragraphs addressed specifically to '*Supervising and Managing*' (paras 25, 26, 27) require '*practitioners to be responsible for clarifying who holds responsibility for the work with the client'.* It also states that there is a *'general obligation'* to receive supervision/consultative support independently of managerial relationships. Supervisors have *'a responsibility to maintain and enhance good practice ... to protect clients from poor practice and to acquire the attitudes, skills and knowledge required by their role'.*

My current working definition of supervision is: 'A working alliance wherein the counsellor can offer an account or recording of her work, reflect on it, and receive feedback and, where appropriate, guidance. The object of the alliance is to enable the counsellor to gain in ethical competence, confidence, compassion and creativity so as to give her best possible service to her client.' Three central tasks emerge from this definition. The *normative task* entails the sharing of responsibility between supervisor and counsellor for monitoring the counsellor's competent and ethical practice; the *formative task* entails sharing responsibility for the professional development of the counsellor; and the *restorative task* entails reminding the counsellor to take care of herself and support the continuing renewal of energy and faith in her work.

Whatever your definition, your basic belief and understanding underlie any other negotiations, and it should be clear what they are. This may seem an obvious assertion, but through experience I know how much supervision has been undertaken without such a shared framework. There are many disparate traditions in counselling and psychotherapy, and many supervisors and counsellors have never encountered any but their own. Clarifying and arriving at a shared understanding prevents, at best, confusion and, at worst, disempowerment of the supervisee.

Content

Having established a shared basic understanding of what supervision is, there are a number of issues which need negotiating and clarifying, either before getting underway or in the early stages of the alliance. Table 13.1, adapted from Inskipp and Proctor (1993), divides these into

- the administrative contract – cost, place, etc.;
- professional and personal information (including the working context) which may affect *the professional contract* and the task and process of supervision;
- ground rules – what is expected by both parties about the way the work is done; and
- items that could affect the alliance, which either party wishes/is prepared to disclose at this stage.

Any of these will affect the implicit or explicit *psychological contract* which will develop throughout the alliance.

There is no way that all the material in the table can be negotiated in a single exploratory session. The responsibility lies with the supervisor and to a lesser extent with the supervisee to identify key issues and to prioritise those that need clarifying and agreeing either before *deciding* to work together, or before it is safe *to begin any 'work', or when the alliance is underway* and has become real to both parties.

Table 13.1 Contracting the working agreement: an aide-mémoire of contents and process

Negotiate	The working alliance	Information *re*: supervisor
Time:	Create trust by being	Theoretical orientation
length	empathic, respectful,	
frequency	authentic in respect of	Training
venue	supervisor working style,	Experience as
Cost:	supervisee learning style,	counsellor
how much	supervisee professional/	supervisor
method of	development needs,	Present work
payment		
(invoice, cheque,	values, passions,	Support for supervision
cash)		
when	strengths	
who pays	difficulties of both	Professional association
Missed sessions		Professional activities
Holidays – notice		
Discuss and	Using basic counselling	Information *re*:
negotiate	skills for	**supervisee**
Recording:	– relationship building	Experience, qualifications
of client	– exploring	as counsellor
of supervision	– negotiating	Theoretical model
of agreement	paraphrasing	Prof. association
Presentation of	reflecting	Code of Ethics
work:		
written	summarising	Free-lance/org'n/agency
tapes	focusing	Where working
verbal, other	questioning	Number of clients
Reviews	self-disclosure	Agency requirements
Evaluation,	immediacy	Legal implications
assessment		
Codes of ethics	purpose stating	Other supervision, etc.
	preference stating	In counselling/therapy

This table can be useful as an *aide-mémoire* for both supervisees and supervisors. If both carry responsibility for giving and getting basic information at the outset, the foundations of a healthy working alliance are already being forged.

The process – skills for clarifying and negotiating

Before moving on to take a look at how variables influence the making of an appropriate working agreement, it is worth pausing briefly to consider skills. It is to be hoped that even the newest supervisee will be continuously developing an aptitude for using clear and flexible language. Speaking to and fro in the service of shared intentions is, after all, both medium and message of counselling and psychotherapy. Familiarity with 'micro-skills' is one way of increasing and informing ability.

The supervisor, however, should have these micro-skills well in place as part of his developed working tool-kit. Some supervisors in training may not have had micro-skill training, or they may need to revise their use of language in a different context. For instance, they frequently need reminding to *clarify and paraphrase* as they negotiate; for instance 'It sounds as if you have some reservations about your agency's policies and practice. Is that right, or are you just raising the possibility?'. This process helps to hold at bay any urgency to 'frontload' – that is, to fit every-thing in at the outset, so that it has at least been said, if not understood. It also signals respect, and commitment to gaining understanding of this unique new acquaintanceship.

The distinction between *purpose* and *preference stating* (sometimes called *must* and *can* statements) is often new to them. Purpose stating (a *must* statement) might be, for example, 'I will expect you to work within the Code (or Ethical Framework) we both ascribe to, and to discuss with me any issues which you think may have ethical implications.' Such a statement may need clarifying and discussing, but if, for the supervisor, it is a non-negotiable demand this needs to be made very clear at the outset.

Preference stating – a *can* statement – might be 'As far as I am concerned, it is appropriate to talk in this group about feelings which arise in the course of the work, and in the supervision. What do you expect in this respect?' The supervisor needs to be genuinely prepared to negotiate around any preference statements.

Agreement variables

Context

Free-lance setting

Table 13.2   Contexts of supervision

Counsellor status	Type of supervision	Answerability of supervisor
Free-lance	Consultant/non-managerial	Informal collegial to profession
Employed/volunteer in counselling agency in organisation	Consultant/non-managerial and possibly some managerial functions	Informally to profession and possibly formally to agency/ organisation
In training	Training supervision and possibly managerial	Formally or informally to training body agency. Informally to profession

Table 13.2 underlines the degree to which the regular supervisor in a free-lance context is fully co-responsible with the counsellor for ensuring that good enough work is being done, including having monitoring responsibility for:

- work setting;
- working contracts;
- suitability of clients; and
- professional arrangements and backing, etc.

No one else, other than the client, may have right of access to the counsellor's practice. The supervisor may want to ascertain for herself that the counsellor is basically com-petent and working according to similar values before deciding to work with him.

Organisational setting

In organisational settings, attention must be given to negotiation with the organisation and agency as well as with the counsellor/psychotherapist. Not only has the supervisor the task of clarifying who holds responsibility for client work. She also needs to determine whether she is prepared to undertake any duties which belong with management. For instance, in *voluntary counselling services* the supervisor is often expected to be the channel of communication between management and counsellors. This might mean for instance explaining agency policies and assessing counsellor ability. In a *GP surgery,* however, the supervisor may not be acknowledged as having any significance at all. In a *student counselling service* in higher education where supervision is paid for by the organisation, it may need to be clarified whether the senior counsellor or other manager expects any report or feedback; and the supervisor may or may not be prepared to offer them. *Employee counselling services,* whether in-house or not, are commercial in culture – any supervisor working for them may want to decide if any duty they or their supervisee is expected to undertake contravenes any professional values, and to contract (such as about boundaries of confidentiality or practice expectations) either at the outset or when clashes become clear as the work proceeds.

A further contractual issue in such settings is the degree to which the supervisor is prepared to allow consultation about the myriad of issues which may arise in relation to the setting of the work, as well as about actual work with clients. There are no absolute rights and wrongs for the supervisor in organisations. What is crucial is that he is clear about the overall tasks of consultancy supervision for himself; that these have been clarified and agreed with the supervisee, and, where appropriate, the agency; that the supervisee has a chance to decide if these priorities best serve her needs and the needs of her clients; and that they both stay aware of the professional ethics within which they are working.

Supervising trainees

Creating a working agreement with trainees is complex. The supervisor will have some relationship with the training course and possibly also with an agency. Either of these may be well or badly organised in relation to supervisors. It is really the trainers' responsibility to the trainee and to clients of trainees to take the contract with supervisors seriously. However, this cannot be relied upon, and where it is not the case, supervisors may need to attempt to elicit a clear contract for themselves, or to encourage the trainee to elicit one, before deciding to supervise a particular trainee.

The lines of responsibility and communication between supervisor, supervisee, training course and placement agency may not be well established. If these are not clear, the establishment of a trusting alliance is particularly difficult – trainees need to know where they stand in relation to assessment in supervision, and supervisors need to be clear about the extent of their 'clinical responsibility' for their supervisees' clients.

Those issues come under the *normative* tasks of the supervision. In relation to the *formative* tasks, the supervisor needs to know enough about the training which the supervisee is undergoing to build a continuing learning agenda which meshes well with course work and client practice.

In respect to the *restorative* tasks, the supervisor may have to act on intuition and experience in contracting with each supervisee the appropriate boundary between work that pays attention to building confidence or allowing dis-stress, and work which challenges practice and pushes for competence.

Developmental stage

Trainees are likely to be at an early stage of their development as a counsellor. Stage of development is a further variable in the creation of a working agreement. It is obvious that a contract with an experienced counsellor will be collegial in nature – allowing a good deal of give and take. It may be less clear that, for instance, the right and responsibility to challenge may need to be more expressly built in. Contracting and reviewing mark and respect changing needs. With beginners, the agreement will probably be built up more gently – the whole enterprise is so new. Most issues need to be made explicit. With experience, more can probably be left implicit but at different points in the work it may become apparent that too much has been taken for granted, and the agreement has to be revisited and clarified. Each developmental stage calls for a different balance of freedom and containment. Michael Carroll, who undertook extensive research based on listening to tapes of experienced supervisors, concluded 'What supervisors often lack are interventions geared to meeting the changing ... needs that come with different levels of training and expertise' (Carroll 1996: 101).

Form of supervision

It is relatively straightforward to negotiate one-to-one supervision, so here I want to pay attention particularly to group supervision – led and peer. Other forms – paired, team, peer group with visiting consultant, etc. – can be viewed as variants of this.

Group supervision

In group supervision all three contracts – the overall working agreement, the session contract and the mini-contract – contribute to the building of group co-operation and a safe and facilitative climate. Good group negotiating builds not only a sense of shared ownership but also an awareness of the reality of the supervisory enterprise. Not many counsellors have experienced a range of supervision groups, so we mostly tend to think that group supervision not only *is* what we have experienced, but even that it *should be only* like that. Inskipp and Proctor (1995) suggest that there are four legitimate models for supervision (see Table 13.3).

Each model has strengths and drawbacks. Which is most appropriate will depend on supervisor style, orientation and experience; the context, including any course or agency expectations; and the developmental stage and expectations of members. Any can offer excellent supervision if the role and responsibilities of supervisor and group members have been clarified and are reviewed from time to time – especially as new members join, or as participants become more experienced and they and the supervisor become either more venturesome or more cosy.

Participants of Model 1 groups can suffer from having to discover by trial and error what it is safe to contribute; or they can feel delightfully free of responsibility. Model 2 groups can be very perplexing to someone reared in a Model 1 group – the purpose of active participation needs to be made explicit if they are to feel safe to take risks and be creative. A supervisor who automatically expects the group to be a Model 3

Table 13.3   Models of group supervision

1 *Supervision in a group*
   Supervisors supervise individuals; members as audience.

2 *Participative group supervision*
   Supervisor supervises; members taught and encouraged to participate.

3 *Co-operative group supervision*
   Supervisor facilitates group in learning to co-supervise each other.

4 *Peer group supervision*
   Peer group co-supervise: negotiating structure, leadership, roles, responsibilities.

group may discover that, without an agreement about ground rules, he has to maintain an uncomfortable balance of lying back and intervening.

Peer groups

Case Example

We went through several new members before it dawned on us that we needed to talk and agree about what were criteria for membership of our peer supervision. That discussion was very uncomfortable, and brought to light a number of stereotypes and prejudices which we felt a bit ashamed about – some issues we didn't even realise existed! But it was a good vehicle for speaking the unspoken, and as a result, we made not only more appropriate invitations to members, but also paradoxically, more creative ones. We also became aware that we must agree about responsibility for things like time and 'chairing'; and that establishing a kind of regular 'programme' would save a lot of aimless 'getting started' behaviour. Afterwards, we felt foolish that we had let things drift on so long, but it took someone to have the courage to assume leadership before we really addressed the difficulties. Luckily, that person was also adamant that he would not continue to 'take the chair' or be the unacknowledged supervisor – I expect in a lot of groups that is what actually happens without it being recognised or spoken about.

This statement probably does describe a number of failing peer groups, and also those which are only just 'good enough' for their purpose. It suggests the tricky balance between building respect and co-operation and wallowing in a leadership vacuum – a leaderless group rather than a leader-full group. One sneaky and acceptable way of assuming leadership in getting a group going on the right lines is to offer some suggested ground rules for discussion. This can avoid being experienced as overbearing or bossy. The agreement suggested here does not deal with the administrative contract, but with the roles, responsibilities and climate for good supervision work. (It, or something along the same lines, can be adapted for supervisor-led groups of the Model 2 or 3 variety.)

The group being described in the case example actually settled for a rotating 'chair'. A different member would lead negotiations and manage time each meeting;

and take responsibility for holding 10 minutes clear at the end to review the process of the session and identity any recurrent themes. Dates for six-monthly review sessions were booked a year ahead, and at the next review the group were going to discuss the possibility of inviting a consultant to visit once a year.

Mixed bag supervision

Many counsellors create a 'designer package' of supervision, e.g. one-to-one monthly; a led group with the same supervisor every two weeks; and supervision with a group of peers working in a similar setting to their own every six weeks. This allows for many disparate needs of supervision to be met creatively. However, as far as contracting is concerned, it means that accountability for the whole range of client work, clinical responsibility (if, for instance, the peer group is an agency team), boundaries of confidentiality, etc. have to be carefully contracted in each context. And each supervisory person – peer or 'expert' – needs to protect their responsibility to help the counsellor monitor whether the package helps contain her practice, or is allowing some problematic issues to fall between the cracks.

The session contract

In addition to this overall and general working agreement, each session of supervision can benefit from the intentionality of an agenda or menu. Canvassing an agenda allows both/all participants to focus on identifying their hopes and intentions for that session. It also encourages forethought on the part of the supervisee, and reflection by the supervisor on ongoing issues which she may want to raise and revisit.

The supervisee may well have two or more clients/issues which she wants to explore. Time for a review may be scheduled. The supervisor may wish to raise, for example, some thoughts she has had about the counsellor's professional development, or some query about course content or agency policy. This process, too, will be affected by the previously mentioned variables. What is legitimate 'fodder' for the session will have been previously determined in the overall working agreement. The priorities among these items may also be influenced by that agreement, but will depend too on the immediate needs of the counsellor. The session contract allows for negotiating priorities.

Box 13.1　Ground rules for a peer supervision group (adapted from Inskipp and Proctor 1995)

The main feature of peer supervision is that we are undertaking to be both supervisee and supervisor and, by inference, to develop our ability to exercise both roles effectively. Our 'rules and culture' will develop over time – we do not have to get everything right immediately. These ideas can be a starting point in setting up our working agreement.

(continued)

(continued)

As supervisor, we take shared responsibility for:

- ensuring safe enough space for each of us to lay out our practice issues in our own way
- helping each other explore and clarify thinking, feeling and fantasies underlying our practice
- giving clear feedback
- sharing information, experience and skill appropriately
- challenging practice we judge unethical, unwise or incompetent
- challenging personal and professional blind spots we may perceive in individuals or in the group
- being aware of the organisational contracts in which each of us operates

As supervisee, I take responsibility for:

- identifying practice issues with which I need help and asking for time to deal with these
- becoming increasingly able to share these issues freely
- identifying and letting you know the kind of response which is useful for me
- becoming more aware of my own organisational contracts and their implications
- being open to others' feedback
- developing the ability to discriminate what feedback is useful
- noticing when I explain, justify or defend before hearing and understanding feedback
- noticing and seeking feedback and reflecting on the way I compete or advise in the group.

The mini-contract

Even then, the contracting dimensions of supervision are not exhausted! A mini-contract for each agenda item allows the supervisor to focus on what the counsellor wants to explore or discover in that particular piece of work, and also, if the menu is lengthy, to set an estimated time limit. Any one item may otherwise overrun and squeeze out others.

These estimates may prove to be unrealistic. An answer to a casual enquiry may elicit some deeply felt response. As in counselling, the map of an agenda item – 'I want to update you on x but it will not take more than five minutes' – frequently fails to predict the nature of the territory which opens up. A mini-contract reminds both parties (or in group supervision, all parties) to decide what to do when that happens, rather than unwittingly drifting or being driven by the emotional energy of the moment. Such agreements are particularly important when there is more than one supervisee – a group or a pair, for instance. They alert all members to the necessity for fairness in the use of time and attention. They also help co-supervisees develop respect and discipline in their responses to each other.

In-the-moment and forethought

At this point, I want to declare that by temperament I am an in-the-moment supervisor rather than one who inclines to careful forethought – an 'intuiter' (see Chapter 8) more than a planner in my counselling and supervision work. As such, I have moved in the direction of purposiveness, waving to colleagues who pass by on their opposite journey to 'greater-trust-in-the-process'. So for me, contracts are not an end in themselves; nor a stick for beating myself or others with. A predominantly person-centred practitioner, I have come to see them as a friend to all – containers which allow two or more people to work as freely, enjoyably and intentionally as their chemistry and situation allow. They can do this if they are secure enough in the knowledge that both/all are committed to the proper welfare of the counsellor's clients and to the continuing development of this particular counsellor.

I have come to appreciate negotiated agreements because they assist me in focusing clearly, and choosing where to focus. To the extent that I am enabled, through contracting, to focus within a specified agreement, I do not need to be too concerned with boundary issues – like an elastic band hung around a fixed point, boundaries are flexible and inherently self-setting. The original working agreement determines the size of the elastic band. The minute-to-minute agenda – clarified by both parties – determines the fixed point at any one time (Figure 13.1).

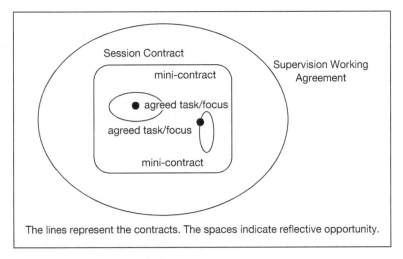

The lines represent the contracts. The spaces indicate reflective opportunity.

Figure 13.1   Task, focus, boundaries

Contracting task, focus and boundaries

The following description of a group supervision session may help to illustrate how stated and negotiated contracts can be used to steer task and process.

A counsellor in an agency brings to his supervision group an issue *about* how to work with a particular client using the new time-limited model which the agency has introduced. The group's *working agreement* has bearing on this situation – the supervisor has made clear to group members (purpose stating):

- that agency policy is to be respected; and
- that the supervision group is the major forum for learning how to put into practice with specific clients this model that was new to some group members.

It was also acknowledged at the outset, amongst other information, that some volunteers in the group are in training and have their own counselling/therapy as a resource. Others are more 'traditional' volunteers and do not have their own 'therapeutic space'.

The *session contract* elicited this member's 'menu item' for the session. It also allowed it to become apparent that the general issue was one which held a great deal of anxiety for most group members. It was agreed:

- that the issue of time-limited practice should occupy 20 minutes of shared time at the start of the session;
- that the member concerned would have half an hour to explore his issue; and
- that other members' concerns should be prioritised as agenda items for the remaining time.

The *mini-contract* for the *shared* item helped the supervisor decide to identify major anxieties and then to offer some straight teaching about time-limited work which would address the most common anxieties.

The *mini-contract* with the *counsellor* for his bit of work identified that he 'was feeling angry with the agency and that his lack of acceptance of the changed style of working' was contributing to his confusion. Since he was one of the counsellors who had his own therapy, the supervisor suggested:

- that the group take some time to acknowledge his feelings and confusion so that he would be clearer about what might belong in his *own* counselling; and
- that at least half his time was spent on focusing on the particular client and on how best to maximise the benefit of the counselling time together.

In this example, the 'elastic band' of the overall *working agreement* had determined:

- that in working with the agency, counsellors would accept agency policy on the understanding that it would be reviewed in six months' time. Time would not be spent in supervision on general argument about agency policy;
- that the supervision was, among other things, a 'formative' space – a place to learn about competent practice;
- that the personal reactions of individuals would be taken into account, and opportunities allowed for appropriate 'restorative' work within the overall task of promoting counsellor 'ethical competence, confidence, compassion and creativity'; and
- that the counsellors were accountable to the supervisor for best practice with individual clients.

The fixed point around which the elastic band hung – the *task* – shifted, both between each item, and within each item. In the first item, the first *task* was:

- exploring what the shared anxieties were;
  and the *second,*
- imparting the most useful information as succinctly and accessibly as possible.

In the second item, the first *task* was:

- facilitating self-understanding and, hopefully, self-acceptance in the counsellor ('this is what is happening for me and if I took it to my counselling I might discover more *about* myself and my choices');
and the *second*,
- enabling and ensuring good client practice.

The content of the working agreement was to a considerable degree influenced by the *context* – a voluntary agency – and the form of supervision – a group. The *developmental stage* of the supervisees – relatively new practitioners – further influenced what needed to be considered. The agreement *about* boundaries and focus – what could be worked on, what would have priority, the nature of group participation – would depend a great deal on the *theoretical orientation* of the supervisor and of the agency. The agreement above might be very different were it negotiated by a cognitive-behavioural supervisor, a TA supervisor, a psycho-dynamic supervisor or a person-centred supervisor. What the process needs to ensure, whatever the content, is that it offers sufficient purpose, freedom and containment for all participants to focus on the shared task of best practice.

In summary

Creating a customised working agreement for supervision ensures, as far as possible, that counsellor, agency, training course, professional association and, last but not least, the supervisor are engaged in an active, participative working alliance. The agreement and the alliance are forged in order that the clients of the supervisee can be offered the best possible service. The respect, empathic understanding and authenticity which the supervisor brings to the task will determine the nature of the relationship established with the supervisee, and will be an important model for the way a new trainee or counsellor creates rapport and establishes working agreements with her clients. It will also create the atmosphere which allows or disallows the disclosure of difficulty, fear or perceived failure and the sharing of delight or excitement.

The theoretical and personal style and orientation of the supervisor will affect the nature of the agreement made, and the style of the negotiation. The content of the agreement will depend on many variables, particularly on the working context, the developmental stage of the counsellor(s) and the form of supervision.

The session contract will be bounded and influenced by the overall working agreement. It is an opportunity for supervisor and supervisee to connect with each other and ascertain today's desired menu – which may comprise leftovers and recurring items as well as the dishes of the day.

The mini-contract ensures that the supervisee takes some responsibility for identifying what she needs from a piece of work. It also lays down sufficient parameters for both parties to notice if they are straying without consent or being prodigal with the time. The degree to which such contracts are 'hard' or 'soft' will largely depend on supervisor style and orientation.

Of course all sorts of agreements will be made at a 'psychological contract' (see Chapter 1) level between the parties to supervision work. Some of these – e.g. not to challenge today because of a death in the family – might not warrant being made explicit. Others act as inhibitors to truthful and authentic work: 'What on earth is she talking about?'; 'She obviously thinks she is doing well and does not want to be questioned ...' (a thought bubble which could be going on for either party). Such unspoken agreements can become intransigent covert contracts. Contracting to review the explicit agreement at regular intervals underlines the responsibility of each party to feed back information on what is going well, and also what is not working.

Negotiating can be powered by a variety of emotions – fear of uncertainty and unclarity; the need to 'get it right' – to be seen to be credible; curiosity and excitement of the new; determination to avoid previous mistakes; protective concern for someone who is new to 'all this'; protective concern – appropriate or unrealistic – for clients. To the extent that the supervisor can relax, identify priorities, and feel confident in paying them mind, she can be free to connect with the supervisee and engage in the minute-to-minute process of negotiating to support and help him work well with his clients and in his context.

References

BACP (British Association for Counselling) (1995) *Code of Ethics and Practice for Supervisors of Counsellors*. Rugby: BACP.

BACP (2000) *Ethical Framework for Good Practice in Counselling and Psychotherapy*. Rugby: BACP.

Carroll, M. (1996) *Counselling Supervision: Theory, Skills and Practice*. London: Cassell.

Inskipp, F. and Proctor, B. (1993, 1995) *The Art, Craft, and Tasks of Counselling Supervision*, Part 1: *Making the Most of Supervision*; Part 2: *Becoming a Supervisor*. Twickenham: Cascade.

Page, S. and Wosket, V. (1994) *Supervising the Counsellor: A Cyclical Model*. London: Routledge.

Appendix I:
Contract for Counselling Relationship

Joanna Purdie

This contract is between _____ CLIENT, and Joanna Purdie, COUNSELLOR.

Dated _____

The counsellor

I am a member of the British Association for Counselling and Psychotherapy and the British Association for the Person Centred Approach and as such subscribe to their Code of Ethics and Professional Practice (a copy of which is available from the BACP).

I work using the Person-centred Approach to counselling, which is rooted in the pioneering work of Dr Carl Rogers, an eminent psychologist and therapist, a theory which continues to develop. The Person-centred Approach is based on a belief that it is the client who knows what is painful and at the culmination of counselling it is the client who knows best how to move forward. I also extend counselling by offering Person-centred Expressive Therapy which involves using art materials such as paint and clay. This form of counselling may not be suitable for all individuals, as is the case with other theories.

I am committed to providing a safe, therapeutic environment for my clients. We are both making a commitment of time and energy to each other in deciding to work together. It is important for you to know what agreements we are making together and so what to expect.

Confidentiality and records

The content of the sessions are confidential to you and me. I will need to discuss our work with my supervisor. I will use your first name but will not use any other identifying details about you. It is important that you also respect the confidentiality of our sessions when outside the relationship, so as to protect the integrity of the work.

On very rare occasions if we discover there is a need to communicate with other professionals, this will only proceed after first seeking your permission and knowledge of what is to be discussed. I make brief notes after a session and also use audio tapes whilst I am working: this helps me to monitor my work. You will not be identified from these records and they are securely stored.

Sessions and fees

Sessions will be for _____ hour/s every week/month initially, I operate a sliding scale of £_____ to £_____ per hour, unless otherwise negotiated. Insert details here:

_____

_____

_____

_____

_____

The whole hour belongs to you. I will be there for you whether you decide to attend or not. If you come in five minutes from the end of our time together I will still be there, but it is important to end our session on time. No smoking is allowed inside the building and I will not see your if you are under the influence of alcohol, both for health and therapeutic reasons.

Depending on the length of time we contract to work together, I may require NOTICE from you to end counselling. In your case this will be _____ days/weeks/months (delete).

Cancellation

In any event of my not being able to give you your sessions because of illness, or because I may attend training sessions or meetings, I will give you as much notice as possible and offer you an alternative time. I require at least **48 hours** notice if you need to cancel a session. You will be charged for any missed sessions.

Our relationship

To be clear about our counselling relationship, there can be no other contact between us other than client/counsellor. I cannot be your friend outside of the relationship or be involved with you in any other relationship.

If we accidentally meet outside of this room I will acknowledge you in a brief and friendly manner, unless you express your wish not to be acknowledged.

Safety

It is important for you to be able to be yourself fully during counselling. This will involve showing different aspects of your personality and at times being able to express yourself by your behaviour, but please realise that it will not be acceptable if you damage this property, me, or yourself in any way.

Ending

We have contracted to work together for _____ sessions initially, continuation to be reviewed.

There may be times in the counselling when you feel very distressed and feel that counselling is not helping you. It is wise to come and discuss these difficulties and not to suddenly end the counselling. This will give you the opportunity to understand and perhaps resolve your distress.

Usually you will know when you are ready to cease counselling and together we will find the way that feels comfortable for you to do this.

PLEASE READ THIS DOCUMENT CAREFULLY

Check it is what we have agreed together today. Unless you have any queries, these are our boundaries and ground rules which will enable us to work together. If you wish to discuss or negotiate any changes I will be happy to do so before you sign.

This agreement is fully understood and agreed to and is signed as it stands, by:

Name:_____Client

Name:_____Counsellor

Date_____

Appendix II:
Contract for Gestalt Psychotherapy

Graham Colbourne

Your details:

Name(s)_____   _____   Date(s) of Birth_____

Address_____

_____

Home phone _____   Other phone _____

Your health details:

Name of GP _____   Phone _____

Address_____

_____

Any significant health problems   _____

Medication being used, and reason   _____

Mental illness and suicide, history of   _____

   yourself and birth family   _____

**Details of any other relevant professional you are seeing
(e.g. therapist, psychiatrist):**

Name _____

Profession _____

Address _____

Phone _____

I consent to my work with Graham Colbourne being respectfully, anonymously and confidentially presented to his supervisor and supervision group in order to monitor, maintain and enhance quality. I consent to personal information and work being recorded in writing or electronically solely for the purposes of record keeping, supervision and professional accreditation. I consent to my work being used/published anonymously for clinical dissemination, on the understanding that I will not be identified. I understand that I can request at any time that any electronically recorded information will be deleted, or that the conditions of its use be amended. I agree to Graham Colbourne breaking confidentiality if he believes this may reduce risk to me or another.

I agree to pay £   fee per session for sessions as agreed whether or not I attend. I agree not to enter into a contract with any other therapist/counsellor without prior consultation with Graham Colbourne.

Signed	date

I, Graham Colbourne, agree to work with you in accordance with the Gestalt Psychotherapy Training Institute code of ethics (copy available on request). I agree to protect your identity and to uphold our confidentiality agreement herein.

Signed	date

Appendix III:
Consent Form for Body-oriented Psychotherapy Treatment

James Kepner

Note: This form is reproduced with the permission of James Kepner (see Chapter 1). It is included in order to illustrate the sort of careful thinking and discussion that is involved when work with the body forms part of the therapy. It should NOT be copied as stated and used, since its tenets are based on a particular orientation to body psychotherapy, and particular intent for the use of touch. Other therapies may use touch for different purposes and in different ways.

What it is

Body-oriented psychotherapy is based on the understanding that the whole person cannot be artificially separated into parts, such as into body and mind. In this view, lack of attention to one's bodily nature would mean to ignore an essential aspect of the person, often left out in their own view of themselves. Body-oriented psychotherapy work can be used as a primary modality of treatment or as an adjunct to other forms of psychotherapy.

Body oriented techniques are used to:

- Support and increase awareness and insight.
- Develop the capacity for increased body sensation and emotional feeling.
- Work with psycho-physical stances and postures which influence our perceptions and interactions in ways in which we are otherwise unaware.
- Release tensions, emotions and postures which inhibit full functioning.

Body-oriented therapy may involve, but is not limited to, the following methods:

- Attention to body experience and process.
- Work with breathing to promote body sensation and awareness.
- Work with posture and body stance to explore their psychological meanings.
- Use of hands-on techniques to promote increased self-awareness.
- Use of hands-on techniques to promote release of tensions and emotions.
- Use of hands-on 'energy' techniques which promote a sense of flow, connection and wholeness.
- Use of exercises to promote self-care, increased energy and awareness.

Use of touch

- Touch is a commonly used modality in body-oriented psychotherapy. The use of touch is intended to support the development of self awareness.
- The intention of the use of touch is *never* to physically cause pain nor to sexually stimulate. If these or other problematic experiences occur, always inform your therapist.
- Some people find the use of touch to be detrimental or problematic no matter how clear the therapist is in his or her intent or usage of touch.
- *If you are concerned about the use of touch or experience any discomforts with the use of touch, it is essential that you discuss them with your therapist so that together you can decide if these things can be usefully worked with therapeutically, or whether touch is not a useful modality of treatment for you at this time.*

Client rights and responsibilities

Like all therapy, body-oriented work is a collaborative process.

- You have the right at all times to refuse *any* suggested ways of working.
- You have the right at all times to stop any therapeutic process for any reason.
- You have the right to ask questions about and discuss any techniques or procedures.
- Please let your therapist know of any problems, concerns or other issues that emerge during this, or any other kind of therapy work.

Cautions

Care must be taken in the use of physical exercises. Consult your physician if you have any health problems you are aware of before doing exercises. Let your therapist know about any problems, and try any proposed exercises slowly at first until you feel assured that they are safe. This, as with any psychotherapy, may inadvertently leave you feeling worse as uncomfortable emotions, sensations and situations are brought into your awareness. Although the intent is to work these through to some kind of resolution, this is not always possible within a particular session so these feelings may continue beyond session time. Please consult your therapist if this occurs.

References

You are encouraged to read the following for further information and understanding:

- Caldwell, C. (ed.) (1997) *Getting In Touch: the guide to new body-centered therapies*. Wheaton, IL: Quest Books.
- Hull, J.B. (1997) *Listening to the body*. Common Boundary, May/June.
- Kepner, James I. (1993) *Body Process: Working with the body in psychotherapy*. San Francisco: Jossey Bass Publishers.

Your consent or lack of consent to this form of treatment does not preclude other forms of treatment more suitable to you.

I have read and understood the contents of this document and give my consent to the use of the above procedures in my psychotherapy:

Signed:_____Date:_____

Print_____

This consent may be revoked at any time by informing: James I. Kepner, (therapist address and phone number).

Index